DREAMS, A PORTAL TO THE SOURCE

EDWARD C. WHITMONT

and

SYLVIA BRINTON PERERA

London and New York

First published 1989 by Routledge
11 New Fetter Lane, London EC4P 4EE
29 West 35th Street, New York, NY 10001
Reprinted 1990

Phototypeset in 11pt Baskerville by
Mews Photosetting, Beckenham, Kent
Printed in Great Britain by
Billing & Sons Ltd, Worcester

British Library Cataloguing in Publication Data

Whitmont, Edward C., *1912–*
Dreams: a portal to the source: a clinical guide for
therapists.
1. Medicine. Psychoanalysis. Use of dream analysis
I. Title   II. Perera, Sylvia Brinton
616.89'17

Library of Congress Cataloging in Publication Data

Whitmont, Edward C. 1912–
Dreams, a portal to the source: a clinical guide for therapists/
Edward C. Whitmont and Sylvia Brinton Perera.
p.   cm.
Bibliography: p.
Includes index.
1. Dreams. I. Perera, Sylvia Brinton, 1932–   . II. Title.
BF1078.H46   1989
154.6'3-dc19
88-36528
CIP

ISBN 0-415-01070-5

When we consider the infinite variety of dreams, it is difficult to conceive that there could ever be a method or a technical procedure which would lead to an infallible result. It is, indeed, a good thing that no valid method exists, for otherwise the meaning of the dream would be limited in advance and would lose precisely that virtue which makes dreams so valuable for therapeutic purposes — their ability to offer new points of view.

So difficult is it to understand a dream that for a long time I have made it a rule, when someone tells me a dream and asks for my opinion, to say first of all to myself: 'I have no idea what this dream means.' After that I can begin to examine the dream.

C.G. Jung, *Collected Works*

CONTENTS

Acknowledgements

1 INTRODUCTION TO CLINICAL DREAM
  INTERPRETATION   1

2 WORKING WITH THE DREAM IN CLINICAL
  PRACTICE   5

3 THE SITUATION AS IT IS   17
  The dream-ego   18
  Developmental possibilities through dream work   22

4 THE LANGUAGE OF DREAMS   26
  Image   26
  Allegory   28
  Symbols   29
  Rebus   30

5 ASSOCIATION, EXPLANATION,
  AMPLIFICATION: THE DREAM FIELD   34
  Associations   35
  Explanation   38
  Emotions and bodily reactions   42
  'Trivial' dreams   45
  Fantasy, imagination, and enactment   46
  Affect and feeling quality   49
  Amplification   52
  The therapist's responses   54

CONTENTS

6 COMPENSATION AND COMPLEMENTATION:
OBJECT AND SUBJECT LEVELS   56
   Compensation and complementation   56
   Object and subject levels in dreams   59
   Dramatization   61
   Application of the compensation and complementation
       principle in dreamers with undeveloped or fragmented egos   63

7 THE DRAMATIC STRUCTURE OF THE DREAM   67
   General overview of the dream drama   67
   Dramatic structure   69

8 MYTHOLOGICAL MOTIFS   79
   Recognizing mythological motifs   81
   The interplay of archetypal and personal material   83
   Dealing with mythological motifs   97
   Some special motifs   99
   The life play   100
   Birth   102
   Children   104
   Animals   107
   Interpreting mythological material   109

9 TECHNICAL POINTS   111
   Time sequence   111
   The re-evaluating function of the dream   112
   The day residue   117
   Dream series   119
   Variations on a theme   122
   Nightmares   125

10 PROGNOSIS FROM DREAMS   127
   Dreams of death or illness   132

11 BODY IMAGERY   137
   Sexuality   139
   Imagery of body orifices   144

CONTENTS

12 DREAMS OF THERAPY AND THE FIGURE OF
THE THERAPIST   149
    The actual reality of the therapist   151
    Transference reactions   153
    The inner therapist   153
    Countertransference dynamics   156
    Induction by the therapist   161
    Dreams of the process of therapy   163
    Variations on the theme of the therapy process 166
    Images of alternative therapists   169
    The archetypal transference in dreams   172
    Dreams of therapy for the therapist only   177
    Therapist's dreams about the client   178

13 CONCLUSION   180

    Notes   183

    Bibliography   191

    List of dreams   194

    Index   197

ACKNOWLEDGEMENTS

This book represents the accumulated fruit of many years of evolving analytical work and teaching. Our thanks are due to our patients and students for offering their materials and their interactive responses. From them we have learned as much as from the literature and our other teachers.

We owe thanks to Andrew Whitmont for his insistent encouragement to write this book and for his help in turning some of the early material, from which it grew, into workable form.

We are grateful to Patricia Finley for her thoughtful reading of the manuscript and to Gertrude Ujhely for her invaluable and careful critical revue of the final text.

Thanks are also due to Jerome Bernstein, Patricia Finley, Yoram Kaufmann, and Charles Taylor for their collegial discussions of the many aspects of clinical application.

Permission to publish their dream work has been generously given by friends, colleagues, students, and by analysands, who have ended the analytic processes in which the dreams appeared. To all of them we are grateful.

Chapter One

INTRODUCTION TO CLINICAL DREAM INTERPRETATION

Every interpretation is an hypothesis, an attempt to read an unknown text. (Jung, *Collected Works*, 16, para. 322, hereinafter referred to as *CW*.)

One would do well to treat every dream as though it were a totally unknown object. Look at it from all sides, take it in your hand, carry it about with you, let your imagination play around with it.

(*CW*, 10, para. 320)

This book is intended as an introductory guidebook for psychoanalysts and therapists who seek to integrate a basic approach to dream interpretation into their clinical practice. It is a practical primer for the analyst-in-training, growing out of a need for such a handbook, perceived as we endeavored to teach dream interpretation at the C. G. Jung Institute in New York. Its aims are modest. It barely touches on the rich philosophical issues raised by dreaming and fantasy.[1] It does not deal with material on comparative approaches to dream interpretation as this craft is practiced among the different schools of modern western psychotherapy.[2] Nor does it deal with the research coming from the laboratories on the necessity and patterns of REM sleep.[3]

This experimental material supports Jung's views that dreaming processes are undistorted and purposeful, having the goal of synthesizing experience[4] into images in meaningful and creative ways. They enhance learning and assist in the completion of individual development.

Our approach, indeed, owes most to the seminal work of Carl G. Jung. His insights have been personally clarified and extended through years of clinical work and teaching by subsequent practitioners. For the most part, regrettably, this work has not been summarized and published.[5] Many others, including writers of various 'schools' of

1

psychology, colleagues, analysands, students, and friends, have contributed to our understanding as well. The bibliography gives only some idea of our debt. To all of them we are grateful.

The dream itself is a natural and necessary expression of the life force[6] — one that manifests in sleeping consciousness and is sometimes remembered and recounted[7] across the threshold of waking.[8] Like a flower or a hurricane or a human gesture, its basic purpose is the manifestation and expression of this life force. It gives us images of energy, synthesizing past and present, personal and collective experiences.

With 'interpretation' we do not mean a mere translation of nightworld visions into dayworld consciousness. Not only is such tidy dualism an artifact in psychology as in physics, but we are coming increasingly to realize that it is not necessary. Just as REM processes serve to integrate complex information below the threshold of awareness, so dayworld consciousness is infused and structured by images which render it meaningful. Indeed, we are coming increasingly to realize that — although dreaming and the verbal telling of the dream are localized in different areas of the brain[9] — 'dreaming and waking partake of the same reality, which is both spiritual and physical.'[10] Both states can be understood from a variety of perspectives, and both can be read metaphorically or symbolically.

The dream as a whole may have many human 'uses.' Like the water in a stream dipped up in cups and used for cooking or for quenching thirst, channeled in sluices and pipes and used for turning water mills or filling swimming pools and flushing toilets. It can be left alone in its streambed and looked at quietly, thereby 'used' for rest or boating, for contemplation, or for stimulating the reflective streams of art. So energy flowing into dream images can have many uses. Among them the dream can be used for providing access into unconscious areas of life, for providing specific and appropriately timed messages of many kinds which can assist the dreamer with problem solving,[11] artistic inspiration, psychological development, and spiritual deepening. As one commentator put it, 'The superordinate function of dreams is the development, maintenance (regulation), and, when necessary, restoration of psychic processes, structures, and organization.'[12]

The dream can, thus, also be used for healing. As it holds up to consciousness metaphors and symbols of the unceasing energy flow, sustaining and shaping personal life, it shows the underlying patterns with which, for the sake of our health, we need to be in more conscious relationship. Equally, it shows also images of those mis-constellated patterns into which our personal lives are inevitably bent. The flowing interplay between these healing and 'dis-eased' patterns can provide inestimable guidance for the process of psychotherapy.

To the therapist, each dream reveals messages about psychic structures or complexes of the dreamer intrapsychically in past and present. It also conveys information about the dreamer's relations to others on whom those structures and complexes are projected. Each dream tells the clinician about psychological dynamics, developmental patterns and capacities. It also images the dreamer's relations to the spiritual dimension, to the Self and to archetypal patterns and energies. The dreamer and his or her therapist may seek to learn from all of these levels about hitherto unknown aspects of personal and transpersonal existence.

To approach dream interpretation adequately we need to find perspectives beyond those created by dualistic consciousness, which rests content with oppositions — exterior/interior, object/subject, day/night, life/death, functional-descriptive/imaginal, focused attention/openness, etc. While these opposites are valuable for defining rational awareness, we need also to develop an integrative consciousness[13] that can read both daily and nightly actions and events and nightly and daily visions from many perspectives and to integrate these perspectives for ourselves and the patient-dreamer before us in our consulting rooms. This capacity relies on an ability to shift between the many forms of magic–affective, body, mythological, allegoric, symbolic, and rational awareness. By developing these modes, or particular styles of consciousness, it becomes possible to shift between them just as we seek to shift from one situationally relevant typological function to another. Thus we may gain the fullest possible range of perspectives on the psychological significance of a given situation — be it an event or a dream or a dream event.

To use a comparable but simplified analogy of the possibilities of this multifaceted approach from daily life, we can consider a red spot on a tree: it can be viewed as a physical object with a specific physical purpose (a road marker), as a focus of action or attention or emotion, as a spot in a visual pattern, as a metaphoric or symbolic message, as an instigator of memory images, as a revelation of properties of energy bound into its molecules, as the expression of somebody's fantasy (a remnant of a picture somebody was trying to paint). It can even be perceived as a part of a color scheme among the forest greens. It can be functional in all these forms of awareness — and others. To investigate it properly, the investigator would need to be open to all of these possibilities and to discover which of them happen to be most applicable to the given situation.

To relate adequately to the dream, we need, then, the capacity to circumambulate it from many points of view. As Jung put it: 'In order to do anything like justice to dreams, we need an interpretive equipment that must be laboriously fitted together from all branches of the human sciences.'[14] And, we would add, from the arts and spiritual outlooks as well.

This book is an attempt to bring some of this rich diversity of approach — and the capacity to play back and forth among the approaches — to the attention of the therapist, who can then begin to use them for the sake of exploring the various levels and meanings of each dream.

We focus specifically on:

(1) the symbolic and metaphoric/allegoric language of dream images;
(2) dream imagery related to personal associative material, rational and collective explanatory material, and mythological amplificatory material;
(3) various relations between the dream and the dreamer's conscious positions;
(4) the dream's dramatic structure;
(5) the dream's depictions of the relations between healing archetypal image and personal experience;
(6) body imagery in dreams; and
(7) dream images of analyst and analysis as material revealing the transferential and countertransferential relationship.

All of these areas need to be held hovering in the therapist's consciousness as clinical dream interpretative work proceeds. Indeed, this book could be read as a circle, each chapter providing a way station from which to focus on the dream, which lies at its center.

Chapter Two

WORKING WITH THE DREAM IN CLINICAL PRACTICE

The art of interpreting dreams cannot be learnt from books. Methods and rules are good only when we can get along without them.

(CW, 10, para. 325)·

The clinical understanding of dreams requires both art and skill. The art consists of an ability to sense the dream as a multifaceted dramatic presentation, as if one were allowed to witness a scene from the play of life. The performance would require attendance with full respect, empathy, sensitive intelligence, intuition, and a sense of symbolic expression. These artistic/spiritual capacities a therapist either possesses or does not. But if such gifts are at all present, they can be further developed with disciplined apprenticeship. A clinician may learn, as he or she studies the art, to enhance perception of the many facets and levels of the dream's integrated dramatic structure, to determine its main theme and subtle variations, its perspective on the dreamer's psychological reality, and to work with its symbolism, its significant foci and energy patterns, its qualities of emotional expressiveness. Enjoying poetry, fairy tales, literature, music, and the images of the visual arts is good training for the art of dream appreciation.

For such an artistic approach to dream interpretation relies on awareness of factors that are similar to those functioning in the appreciation of literature, painting, or music. It requires — among other things — sensitivity to thematic content and the specific qualities of character, action, and the interrelations of figures, forms, and setting. It requires sensitivity to the rhythms of dream events (quick, slow, unfolding, fragmented, etc.); to emotional colors and tones; to qualities of coherence and incoherence, and to discrepancies in themes, images, actions, figures; to scale and space; to consonance and dissonance both within the dream and between it and consensual reality and the dreamer's consciously held positions; to qualities of relationships in the dream itself and between the dream images and the dreamer's conscious awareness.

On the other hand, to acquire skill in dream interpretation, certain directions for practice can also be given; but these should be regarded as no more than general orientations. Like scales and études, they serve to improve technique. They are, however, no substitute for the innate artistic capacity, which dream appreciation, as much as musical or dramatic performance, requires. Moreover, the skills acquired through the practice of techniques must always be subject to the *art* of interpretation. The first 'rule', then, is the paradox of all of the healing arts: the applicability of basic principles must be determined by feeling, sensitivity, and intuition.

As expressions of prerational, 'altered' states of consciousness, dreams are as variable as nature itself. Indeed they are a *lusus naturae*, a play of nature, that can never be fitted into rigid systems. Rather, our rational thought capacity has to learn to adapt itself to the Protean variability of the life processes which dreams represent. Rational or 'secondary' thought must learn to adapt itself to the feeling tones and images of the dream, to reflect in reverie and to play intuitively, as seriously as a musician does with a sonata, until meanings emerge.

While the Behaviorist viewpoint may dismiss dreams as 'the misfiring of neurons,' another, equally simplistic, popular view takes dream messages literally and concretely. The classical Freudian school generally reduces the multiplicity of manifest-content ages to signs pointing toward wish-fulfillment of repressed and trau c libidinous conflicts.[1]

It is noteworthy that the psychoanalytic community is currently in the process of reassessing the classical Freudian approach to dreams and dreaming.[2] Much of the new material 'rediscovers' Jung's basic ideas regarding the dream's function and some of his methodology of dream interpretation, without adequately, we feel, crediting that fact. It often seems as if Jung's seminal work has been generally defended against, first by denial of its existence or by derogation, then by claiming that it is obvious, or that it is a newly-made discovery of the psychoanalytic revisionists. More important than quibbling about precedence, however, is the sense that the various 'schools' of psychoanalysis — each one giving value to unconscious processes in the psyche — are moving closer together as they explore the evidence put before them with integrity and with respect for the individual patients in their care.

The Jungian approach has been, from the outset, based on viewing the dream as an allegoric and/or symbolic statement about the dreamer's psychological situation, precise and objective, tailored for the consciousness of the dreamer and/or his or her analyst. Like an X-ray, or perhaps more aptly, like a portrait by a great master, it reveals a multi-leveled message about the dreamer's current psychic situation seen from a hitherto unknown or unconscious perspective. Art, skill, and practice are required to read the subtle nuances; but invariably the clinician finds that the dream, with uncanny accuracy, depicts the psychological situation confronting the dreamer, exactly as it is. Indeed, when working through a dream carefully, one finds that both the overall dramatic structure and every image within that structure mirror aspects of the dreamer's psychological state and present a symbolic picture of currently relevant psychic energy patterns. No minor aspect of the dream is extraneous; all build together to convey a profound and thematic message.

Thus, in clinical practice each dream offers diagnosis, prognosis, and appropriate material and timing to address the dreamer's current psychological reality and to address and compensate the dreamer's — and/or analyst's — blind-spots of consciousness. Diagnostically, the dream's images and structure give evidence of ego strength and may reveal qualities of relationship between various forms of consciousness and the psychological and somatic unconscious. Prognostically, the dream calls attention to what confronts consciousness, as well as to likely clinical developments, and often, to how the present awareness and capacities of the dreamer and/or analyst tend to relate to those confrontations. Timing of interventions is made possible because each dream is part of a guiding process in an ongoing dialectic between conscious and unconscious positions.[3] Hence the therapist gets signals from the dream metaphors and symbols regarding which issues are to be addressed, and how and when they are to be addressed. The psychological reality and blind spots of consciousness are addressed because every dream points to an unconscious complex and to the archetypal dynamism behind the complex's emotionally charged layers.

Each dream may be seen as aiming toward a widening of awareness. It offers comment, correction, and contributions toward problem solving. Thereby it strengthens, coalesces, or balances the dreamer's (and/or analyst's) waking views, and, thus, it serves as an important vehicle to support psychological development. It can also be seen as giving evidence of a source within the dreamer that does see and present metaphor and symbol for the sake of potential psychological insight — a source which comments, corrects, and teaches.

Indeed, there is much evidence to suggest that dreams are manifestations of the guiding and ordering center of the personality, the Self, in Jungian terms. Both dreams and outer events can be fruitfully related to as symbolic messages coming from a source that sustains and directs the individuation process throughout the dreamer's life. The art and craft of dream interpretation, whether the interpreter is aware of it or not, is an act of reverence toward this transcendent guiding power. Working on dreams in therapy serves to provide access to this source.

The process of dream work over time can convey an extraordinary sense of containment within a constant, supportive, guiding matrix, which supplies the dreamer from an unceasing source. Thus, while dreams help to clarify and teach, they also help to bring about the creation of basic trust and of an ego secure enough to be able to be responsive to the changing messages from that Self. At varying times they support every aspect of psychological development — including those of object relations and ego-building as well as those of relating to unconscious dynamics and outer and inner figures and issues. In psychotherapy they even serve to assist in the resolution of the transference to the personal analyst, by pointing constantly toward the dynamics of the transference relationship as well as toward an inner authority — a sustaining and ordering center encompassing personal identity, or ego.[4]

Not only does the dream inevitably address the dreamer's and analyst's blind-spots, it also, to use Emerson's phrase, is 'an answer in hieroglyphics to the question we would pose.'[5] It presents its message in the language of metaphoric/allegoric and symbolic images. For both of these reasons, work on one's own dreams is fraught with difficulties. The dreamer is invariably unable to see those blind spots or to realize the nature of the 'questions' he or she needs 'to pose.' Too often the dreamer identifies only with the dream ego's perspective and its emotional responses to the images presented. At other times the dreamer fails to sort which aspects of the dream refer to objective 'outer' reality and which to projected or 'inner' subjective states and complexes.

Dream work, thus, requires a witness, someone to provide a perspective coming from other than the dreamer's context, with whom the dream can initially be encountered. Working with dreams, to be most effective, requires a dyadic or group setting. Further, a mirroring and challenging other can serve as a screen on which to project the dreamer's reactions. The witness or analyst or therapy group helps to elicit associations and explanations, and to ground the dream's message by drawing attention to relevant areas of the dreamer's psychology and behavior that are visible to others but fall into the dreamer's blind-spot.[6] Usually the images need simple translation into a statement about personal psychological material and/or relationships to persons and external events. At other times the images can silently reverberate into the unknowable depths of the psyche as dreamer and analyst receive them.

In addition to such shared interaction, the dreamer may find various imaginative techniques helpful. Meditation on the images of the dream, gestalt and psychodramatic enactments, dialogues with dream figures and objects, drawing the dream images, and other active imaginations are all modes of living with the dream to open toward its meanings.[7]

On the other hand for certain patients, already awash in unconscious material because of the level of their regression or the inadequate level of their initial development, such techniques may aggravate their sense of fragmentation and alienation. These patients may not be able to deal with figures in the dream as aspects of themselves. The only part they can relate to as an aspect of themselves is the dream-ego (if there is one), and sometimes not even that. Any confrontation with their negative part personalities (shadow) at such a stage is counter-productive unless that shadow energy can be seen as valuable — ego-enhancing and coalescing — when grounded in personal material and 'claimed' by the fragmented or weak conscious position. Thus they may get disoriented if asked to identify with a dream figure in role play. Often they cannot relate to the ambivalences within their own psychology imaged by the dream drama nor encompass the whole message of the dream. Dream work with such analysands usually requires the analyst him or herself to understand the message of the dream, and to use parts of it within the relevant clinical context.

But even at best, and even among experienced therapists themselves, dream work needs dialogue with another person. In spite of extensive experience with dreams, such collegial checking and confrontation usually reveals essential details and personal applications that were overlooked. The saying popular among doctors, 'the doctor who treats himself has a fool for a physician,' applies here, for the dream brings us unconscious dynamics, and we cannot, by definition, be aware of them easily.

An historical example[8] of the dreamer's fallacy of trusting his own perspective is provided in a dream of Hannibal, leader of the armies of Carthage against Rome. Before the Second Punic War Hannibal is reported to have dreamt that he was invited to the council of the gods. There Jupiter Capitolinus, the highest of the gods, challenged him to make war on Rome. Encouraged by the dream, Hannibal did exactly that. But he was soundly defeated. His own wishful interpretation of his dream had overlooked the fact that Jupiter Capitolinus was the name of Rome's guardian divinity. He took his advice from a god of Rome, not Carthage. Thus the dream did not portend victory, but confronted Hannibal with his own personal motivation for wanting to go to war. It showed him that he felt challenged by and envious of the power of Rome, represented in the image of the Roman god. So caught was he in his conscious position that he failed to read the dream's warning. Modern dreamers have the same propensity to bias when they are without a questioning and mirroring other who would focus on the compensatory quality of the message from the unconscious.

Although this book is written primarily for clinicians, the art of clinical judgement is not its subject. Our concern is the understanding of the dream as such; for only with such prior understanding, along with clinical assessment, empathy, and experience, can a therapist arrive at a clinical decision regarding what particular focus to take and how much to discuss, play with, or interpret to the dreamer according to his or her capacity to assimilate. Yet, equally true, the therapist's full understanding of any dream requires the dreamer's associations and emotional participation.

With every dream it is for the therapist to find the level and focus of interpretation which can be most meaningfully assimilated by the dreamer. When resistance occurs it often means that the approach is inappropriate or outrightly wrong. Then, either the interpretation does not apply or it has missed the point and is wrong in itself or in terms of how it is presented. In all probability the resistance itself is a component of the complex or problem area with which the dream concerns itself. When resistance occurs it is usually most helpful to back off and to start work on the dream again, staying carefully with the dream's image descriptions of psychic dynamics, and waiting until these metaphors can be assimilated. Sometimes work on the particular dream must be dropped for the time. In no case is pushing warranted. Competition and domination merely reflect a countertransference issue to be dealt with.

With some clients interpretive dream work may be neither desirable nor possible, or possible only in specially modified forms. On the one hand dreams, presented by the dozen each week or with an 'absurd melange of images,'[9] can be a defense against awareness of affects and the transference relationship. In such a case it is advisable to take only a fragment or short dream and to work exhaustively on grounding its images in current emotional reality and the life issues toward which the dream material points.

When working with individuals so severely wounded in development that they are split from their emotional associations or unable to process symbolic material, these inevitable lacks must be held in the therapist's awareness. Interpretations then offered to a severely regressed or undeveloped client may serve as forms of containment for fearful and split affects, and as forms of therapeutic mirroring. In such cases mutual work on the dream may be used less for eliciting its subtle emotional and symbolic meanings to the dreamer than for its messages to the therapist and its unsurpassed value as a focus of shared attention and creative, playful activity. Such mutual play with dream images is a special therapeutic activity analogous to art therapy. The dreamer, within the therapeutic container, may safely react to and explore dream images with the analyst. They may be 'played with:' picked up, described, summarized, rearranged, and discarded, and picked up again to gain a sense of mastery and stable identity in relation to them. Such safe creative activity in the company of the analyst builds the capacity for shared relationship — both with the outer person and with ever-fresh dream material arising from an interior ground of being and knowing. Musing on the contents of the person's 'own' dreams with an empathic other, associating to them, grounding specific dream images in analogous events and patterns of daily life, finding objective explanations, sharing reactions — all provide method and material to build the 'safe-enough'[10] therapeutic relationship in which, eventually, genuine affects and individuality can come forth. Repeatedly, such dream work brings about a sense of valuable individual contents and of awareness of capacity to deal with images.[11] Over time such mutual activity assists greatly in conveying and developing a sense of fluid and merged, yet constant and separate, identity — a felt individuality for which play and symbolic understanding is both possible and pleasurable.

Therapeutic considerations in each individual case need to determine how and when to use specific aspects of dream appreciation with each particular client. The material presented in this book leaves issues of case management to the therapist's own skills and orientation. While the tools of dream interpretation, as such, are always important, the therapist must seek to understand and to find healing use for all that the client presents. And while dreams are just one of many potential avenues to therapeutic life change, they are of inestimable value as an access avenue to the director and guide of the therapeutic process, the analysand's Self.

In clinical practice, while careful scrutiny of each dream is important and rewarding, there is often not enough time in sessions for every detail to be explored and interpreted. As Jung put it to his dream study seminar, one does not have to 'tell him [the dreamer] all that I have told you, only hints.'[12] The numinous force of the dream itself will aid and support the therapeutic process, working in the deep levels of the dreamer's psyche both before and after the analytic session. Indeed some dreams may be returned to at different times throughout the dreamer's life to be mined again for their rich and freshly relevant image patterns.

In no case, however, is it enough simply to gain insight about the meaning of a dream, nor to take the dreams' messages as indications that 'the unconscious always knows best . . . [thus] impair[ing] the power of conscious decision.'[13] Understanding the dream's messages as fully as possible on all levels of consciousness is only a preliminary step. Beyond 'insight' we need actively to ground the healing symbolic image patterns within the individual dreamer's personal experience, where she or he can practice or realise the insights. This implies choosing to live and test their meanings seriously and responsibly in daily tasks and relationships. Such realization helps to bind together various aspects of psychological functioning, coalescing the dreamer–actor–sleeper–waker into the whole individual she or he 'is meant to be.'

Since dream images are symbolic, not semiotic, the clinician must beware of premature 'understanding' of the dream 'meaning' as well as of reliance upon any kind of fixed equivalencies (i.e. a stick is a phallus; a cave is the Great Mother; an attic is the intellect or the future). Knowing immediately what a dream purports to mean rests usually on a projection of the therapist's own bias or countertransference, rather than on genuine, and often necessarily mutual, understanding.[14] Like all utterances from the 'other side,' the dream tends to be multi-leveled and oracular, hence ambivalent (even polyvalent) and resistant to a rational, black–white, simplistic approach.

A quick knowing, or a knowing without adequate associations from the dreamer, even if partially correct, tends to miss subtle implications. For example, a young woman, who described herself as 'frigid' and with little sexual experience, dreamed:

I am locked in a room with prostitutes, who keep the key in a small box.

Her associative explanation to prostitutes was 'sexual promiscuity.' One might speculate that her psychological state is 'locked in' with promiscuous desires, and that these hold the key to her 'frigidity' problem, which might be seen as a reaction formation. The analyst-in-training who put forth this interpretation to his client was met with a slightly depressive and passive acceptance.

Since the interpretation failed to elicit an emotional assent, and since it did not fit the analytic supervisor's impression of the client's psychodynamics, the supervisor reminded the analyst that it was important to consider confirmatory or refuting evidence — either in other dreams or in hitherto overlooked details of this one. The detail not considered here was the box in which the key was held — metaphorically an obvious clue. When asked about it at an appropriate moment in a session after the analyst's supervisory hour, the dreamer said that it reminded her of a little box belonging to her maiden aunt, Lydia. Asked now for further associations and explanatory memories of that aunt and her box, the client described her aunt as a very principled, stern woman, who tended to keep all her belongings neatly ordered, and who held strictly compartmentalized ideas about right and wrong. Sexuality for Aunt Lydia was very definitely in a black box. What was the color of the aunt's box? Brown wood. And what was the dream box? It was neither brown nor black; it was scarlet red. Since such variation from conscious memory is usually highly significant (see below), the color required inquiry. 'Scarlet red' released a highly emotional response. The young woman recalled that at age 13 that same aunt had given her a birthday present of Hawthorne's *The Scarlet Letter*, and at other times her aunt had treated her to sermons regarding the wickedness of both adultery and sex, making them seemingly identical. All of this had made a deep impression on the young adolescent. Even though consciously thinking otherwise, she felt emotionally charged and sexual feelings to be synonymous with adultery, prostitution, and sinfulness. Memories of previous home conditioning to foster sexual repression began to come up in therapy.

The detail of the scarlet box, indeed, unlocked the complex. Far from being a reaction formation against promiscuous wishes, the frigidity problem revealed itself as the direct result of the sadistic, repressive conditioning which locked her into thinking all sexual feelings were 'whorish.' On the other hand her identification with prostitution, in her

13

tendency to go along with authority and to sell out her own experience, was manifested in her passive acquiescence to the therapist's initially incorrect interpretation. An important transference and counter-transference dynamic was opened for the therapist's attention. He had neglected the detail which the dream posited as key, for an interpretation that might have locked the dreamer into as false and confining a psychological space as had her complex centéred on her aunt.

To begin to do adequately deep work with a dream, the therapist must revere the dream's image material carefully in its context and with open puzzlement until a corresponding associative affect–response emerges from the dreamer. Thus it is not enough, in associating to a particular dream figure, to find that she was 'a friend from high school.' Persistent questioning needs to find the current, emotionally charged, personal quality, event or memory ascribed to that person. Such an affectual dynamism of the symbolic image can then be used in building the 'rebus' pattern we shall describe below.

Since it is all too easy to get trapped prematurely in the apparently obvious interpretation, it is imperative to heed Jung's warning: 'The analyst who wishes to rule out conscious suggestion [must] consider every dream interpretation invalid until such time as a formula is found which wins the patient's assent.'[15] The only reliable criterion is the dreamer's assent — not necessarily conscious assent, for that may be colored by rational conviction, wishing, fear, or resistance. If assent is to be reliable, it must come from what might be called an embodied or 'gut' sense of 'Aha!' 'Yes!' '*Touché.*' This kinesthetic validation presents a deep confirmation from 'the Self in the body'[16] which knows even when the conscious 'I' cannot. Unless this response is forthcoming, the analyst's views of the meaning of a dream can only be considered hypothetical possibilities still awaiting confirmation or disavowal from the Self of the dreamer. Inevitably, too, following dreams will confirm, modify, or challenge an interpretation and the dreamer's understanding of a dream. Specifically, inadequate interpretation by the therapist or understanding by the dreamer is likely to call forth repetitions of the same dream theme, often in a more numerous, more drastic or more dramatic form.

Appreciation of the dramatic structure of the dream itself (see below) will also assist the clinician to avoid being impressed with particular details, which may have impressed the dreamer, or to lose sight of the images within the overall context. Since every dream tells a story or depicts a drama, no detail can be properly valued if it disregards this overall dramatic structure. A wisdom figure may appear in an impractical context or do mischief; a villain or intruder may be helpful; a dangerous interloper may carry an important message.

The total context and dream action convey the message. An example of this contextual corrective was provided by a young man who attended a psychological workshop and then dreamt that

> I meet an exotic guru who demonstrates to me the feats of a beautiful, magical peacock. The bird first displays its beautiful feathers, then performs a number of magic tricks, which culminates in its flying away with my wallet and dream notebook.

Much impressed by these 'wonderful' figures and flattered by the promise of magical powers, which he read into the dream, the young man talked of the alchemical and Hindu parallels he had discovered for the images. The therapist found himself thinking of the fact that the peacock is not only an image of wisdom, but also of vanity, and that a theft (albeit not so recognized by the dreamer) represents the crisis of the drama — an act of pickpocketing. He silently wondered about the transference implications of this, and inhibited his less than enthusiastic, initial interpretation of the dream, realizing its authority might entrap the therapeutic relationship in the dreamer's 'guru complex.' Cautiously he began to question elements of the dream and was met with intense, initial resistance. When asked, finally, how he would feel about losing his dream journal and wallet, the young man confided that he would hate to have the trouble of replacing his credit cards, but he would like to have someone to solve his problems magically. In the silence that followed, the dreamer heard his own response and took it in with a deep sigh. His body assented to the message that was so contrary to his initial feeling of enthusiasm. The dream's dramatic structure presented another message: the fact that the dreamer's fascination with what he idealized as great magical wisdom was, in fact, a robbery of his own personal possessions, his true identity and credit (the wallet with license and credit cards), and his (dream journal) work to make an individual connection to the unconscious.

The coherent logic of the dream images themselves is vitally important and must always be respected. However, one must also consider whether the dream context uses rational or magical logic. If a bridge ends in mid-air across the Hudson river, something is amiss; if the bridge is a rainbow that fades out in a mythic land, a different order may apply. If the dream image is of a smashed car motor, and the dream-ego has no mechanical skill, the implicit implication of the dream is that it might be more appropriate to find a garage than to try to mend the motor with amateurish attempts or by recourse to some hope of magical omnipotence. In other words, the dreamer needs to seek help because she or he is not qualified to deal with the problem. Likewise, if a dream presents the need for a hospital team, it could be a message to the dreamer's therapist, implying that the therapist needs backup or supervision (see below, Chapter 5, Explanation, also).

It is clearly important that every dream be worked through in respect to its specific dramatic intent, its images, and its affect and/or feeling implications. Only such careful work can assign the details their proper places and significance and, thereby, reveal the message of the dream.

Chapter Three

THE SITUATION AS IT IS

The dream is a spontaneous self-portrayal, in symbolic form, of
the actual situation in the unconscious.

(*CW*, 8, para. 505)

In each of us there is another whom we do not know. He speaks
to us in dreams and tells us how differently he sees us from the
way we see ourselves. When, therefore, we find ourselves in a
difficult situation to which there is no solution, he can sometimes
kindle a light that radically alters our attitude.

(*CW*, 10, para. 325)

Jung called the dream 'a highly objective, natural product of the psyche . . .
[a] self representation of the psychic life-process.'[1] It is an experience of
an involuntary psychic process not controlled by conscious will or outlook
which 'shows the inner truth and reality of the patient as it really is: not
as I conjecture it to be, and not as he would like it to be, but as it is.'[2]
Hence it 'rectifies the situation. It contributes the material which was
lacking and which properly belongs to it and thereby improves the attitude.
This is the reason why we need dream analysis for our therapy.'[3]

Every dream presents images that can convey information, informing
the dreamer and/or the dreamer's therapist of things unknown but of
vital importance about the dreamer, the dreamer's therapist or the process
of the therapy. The dream compensates or complements a deficiency
of the dreamer's conscious position; and/or of the therapist's position
in regard to the dreamer or the analysis.

Thus, every dream can be regarded as a message from a superior,
if archaic intelligence, bent upon offering meaningful new attitudes.[4]
This hypothetical entity Jung called Self. He defined it as 'an a priori
existent out of which the ego evolves . . . it is not I who create myself,
rather I happen to myself.'[5] Jung's Self is a symbolic postulate, an

17

'adequate' description of an, as such, undemonstrable (*Unanschaulich*) dynamic, analogous to the undemonstrable working models of nuclear physics.[6]

In order here to differentiate Jung's postulated Self from the self concept of psychoanalysis, which refers to the conditioned, empirical personality inclusive of psychological complexes, we shall capitalize it and refer to it as Guiding Self. This Guiding Self is to be viewed as source and director of the individuation drive, that archetypal urge to 'become what one is' (*Pindar*).[7] It is also to be viewed as the source and director of life events and of dream material, both providing invaluable metaphoric/allegoric and symbolic messages which aid the individuation process to those who learn to read them.

THE DREAM-EGO

Sometimes the dream-ego may represent *the dreamer's actual and felt sense of identity* as observing witness or actor. In the dream 'I see my children playing in the street and warn them to stay in the yard; instead they run into the street,' the dream-ego acts exactly as the dreamer tends to do, Here the dream points to the counter-productive effects of his usual behavior and good intentions.

In another example a man dreamt:

A carpenter brings me a boat to repair, assuring me I can do the work in my new shop.

Since the dreamer was unsure of his capabilities and skeptical about the outcome of such a task, the dream presents the Self's assurance to the dream-ego that it can do the work. If, on the other hand, the dreamer's associations to the carpenter were negative, and he was quite certain of his own capacity, the dream would more likely be a warning.[8] In either case the dream-ego is similar to the actual dreamer but receives assurance or warning from the unconscious.

More often and since the dream presents images from the perspective of the Guiding Self, when the person of the dreamer appears, this image may not correspond to the dreamer's empirical sense of identity, as she or he knows her or himself. Rather the dreamer — or what is often called the dream-ego — *appears as the Guiding Self sees her or him.* She or he may be depicted in terms of potentialities, tendencies, or debilities which are as yet unknown, unconscious. For example, a man, who consciously thought of himself as caring and helpful, dreamt that

18

> I am asked to rescue a hurt child. Instead of going to the scene of the pain, I send my handkerchief.

Protesting that he would never, in fact, do such a thing, for this was not the image he had of himself, the man was confronted with a view of his kind of helpfulness from the Guiding Self. With some difficulty, but with a strong 'aha' assent, he finally came to realize that the dream presented a true picture of his ego's refusal to take responsibility, replacing real caring of his own inner child with token, genteel gesturing. Further work on the dream allowed him to see that he also treated other people with such 'superficial gentlemanliness.'[9]

In general the qualities of the dream-ego can be assessed by the tone of the narrative, the kind and qualities of the attitudes and actions, and the modes of relating to other aspects and figures of the dream. These may be relevant as descriptions of the dreamer's ego as well. The dreamer's ego firmness or integrity is based upon awareness of moral and situational–emotional needs and upon the capacity as well as readiness to risk appropriate decisions and actions. The imagery of the dream expresses this capacity or failure in terms of executive ability: to administer, relate, drive (carriage, automobile, etc.), ride, sail, pilot, explore, support, care for, guard, etc.

At other times a dream may point up the Self's view of the dreamer's *identification (merger) with an ego-ideal or an inflated grandiosity.* For example, a woman dreamt

> I am a princess swimming in an idyllic resort pool, suddenly threatened by a dirty and angry street-kid.

Translating the dream images after enacting a dialogue between the princess and the pauper figures, she came to understand that when she sees herself as 'exalted and sensitive, someone taken care of by others, so she doesn't have to lift a finger' (her association to princess), in a wished-for 'resort pool' space of 'no-conflict, blissful, private ease,' her disregarded shadow[10] 'street-kid,' attacks. The 'street-kid' is an image for her 'dirty,' and despised — hence unacknowledged — aggression. The figure connects the dreamer with a 'tough, no-nonsense,' confrontational energy that she fears, for it threatens her self-image as sweet, helpless, cared-for princess — the darling of her father and husband.

Consciously, before the dream, this woman saw herself only as wounded by her mother's rejection and very virtuously hardworking to maintain her roles of good mother and professor. The dream challenged this view by presenting another, hitherto unconscious one. It provided, in one irrefutable and perfectly-timed image, a confrontation with an ego-ideal preventing development.

The dream's objective presentation of ego-ideal and aggressive shadow enabled the therapeutic alliance to support assimilation of the difficult material as both dreamer and therapist together worked to ground and personalize the confrontational images presented by the Guiding Self.

A man dreamt 'I am a lion.' This presented his Self's view of a potential lion force still negatively constellated. His dream-ego is shown as merged with the grandiose infantile self and ego-ideal in a manner that eliminates personal identity. When qualities of princess or lion are aspired to and able to be assimilated, the dream-ego would meet that entity as a separate figure and engage in some related action with it rather than being identified with it. Or the dream action might depict pursuit by the figure, or the dream-ego's need to feed it, etc.

Flying in the air without a plane, breathing underwater, or other such unusual capacities by the dream-ego may refer to possible out-of-body experiences such as those reported by near death survivors. These may be potentialities. But such representations of the dream-ego may also refer to escapist dissociations or to inflations with unrealistic powers depending on the associative context of the dream.

Sometimes the dream-ego is merely a passive observer. Events are watched as though from behind a glass screen, without active involvement. Such a distant, non-participatory stance implies a remote attitude to the issues described in the dream. An extreme degree may even indicate dissociational traits in the dreamer's personality.

At still other times the dream presents the dreamer with a diffusion or conflicting *fragments of identity* seemingly floating in some still uncertain relationship to the dreamer, and the process of dream work mirrors these facets of what is to become a relatively stable, limited, and constant sense of individuality. This is likely to occur when the borderline dreamer has little conscious coherence. In this case it is as if there were no consciousness of individual identity, action, affectivity, and intention to which the dreams present themselves.[11] The dream images then act as mirrors of pieces of the psyche, with which, in the facilitating environment of therapy, there can be created/discovered a coalesced sense of presence/being, to whom the dreams arrive as if from a constantly flowing, visioning, source. This source can be felt by the patient as analogous to the good or terrible breast — depending on the nourishing or persecutory quality of the images.

An example of such emergence work occurred with a borderline young woman, who complained that she 'could not tell day from night,' and who focused on dream images only when asked specifically for them by the therapist. At an early session she was barely able to remember and with flat affect:

Lying at the shore line, maybe asleep. The waves wash back and forth.

She did not have a sense of her personal presence in the scene, only of the motion of the waves. At the next session she recalled:

Someone standing at a file, putting sharp cards, like knives, in some order. Alphabetical? My fingers bleed.[12]

Months later she recalled a third dream spontaneously:

There is a dirty cockroach in a pot. Maybe there is food; maybe a spoon is stirring.

To none of these was the dreamer able to find associations, and in none of them is there even the word 'I'. A dream-ego is not present as a whole being, only intimated as an unconscious witness or as wounded, 'fingers' parts. There is an unknown or a dangerous 'someone' who made order (perhaps an image of the patient or the ordering part of the patient or of someone else, including the seeking-for-consciousness therapist). Whole identity emerges, finally, in the form of 'dirty cockroach' — an ego nucleus still identified with the furtive attitude of hiding in order to survive. But the dream images provided vivid, descriptive metaphors of the psychological situations of the patient, and conveyed material for the therapist's holding of her diffuse passivity until a much later stage in the work when 'the [dreams] which have no [dreamer] acquire or are acquired by a [dreamer].'[13]

Other dreamers discover themselves in dreams actually in pieces. For example:

There are dismembered fragments floating in a dark, watery cave, maybe they are parts of me.

or:

I am in pieces, all cut up beside a tree.

The process of fragmentation, as well as the whole issue of embodiment through the gathering of pieces of sensate identity in the therapy, are pointed to by such images of the inadequately or inappropriately embodied dream-ego.

These examples may come from severely disturbed and fragmented, borderline patients, but the images themselves might occur in the dreams of other patients, as a result of situational emotional upheavals or of analytic work that opened regressive wounds and felt like dismemberment of the ego identity. The stark image, 'A figure is flying, carrying my head. The rest of me is nowhere,' was dreamt by a woman as she was considering experimentation with LSD. It served as a warning of her fears and a possibly negative outcome of the event.

At still other times the dream-ego appears to image *the Self*. 'In dreams we put on the likeness of that more universal, truer, more eternal man dwelling in the darkness of primordial night. There he is still the whole, and the whole is in him, indistinguishable from nature and bare of all egohood.'[14]

In President Lincoln's dream the night before he was assassinated the dream-ego entered the East Room to discover the solemn pomp of his own state funeral. Upon inquiry, 'Who is dead in the White House?' he was told 'The President . . . he was killed by an assassin!'[15] Here the dream-ego seems to symbolize the transcendent, witnessing identity which stands apart from life events. Had the dream not foreshadowed his own death, we might read it that the dream-ego needs to disidentify from his presidential role, which is dying. But because the dreamer was killed, the presidential corpse images his existential persona, his life mission and identity, which is about to die. Here the witnessing dream-ego refers to 'that more universal, truer, more eternal man' we name as Self.

In the case of the dream-ego's hearing an imperative voice in a dream, it is important to find by association or imagination whose voice that may be and what are its qualities. The address may represent an auditory image of the Self, but it may also be the voice of a complex or a spoiling or deceiving shadow.

DEVELOPMENTAL POSSIBILITIES
THROUGH DREAM WORK

In general it is essential to compare the dream-ego's stance and action in the dream drama with attitudes and behavior consciously maintained by the dreamer to discover discrepancies and a focus for the next step in psychological development. In situations where the conscious

position is undeveloped or fragmented, the dream will support development and focus by presenting material that needs to be addressed at
the time (see Chapter 6: Compensation and complementation).

Receiving new insights can both help and/or challenge a coherent or
entrenched ego position. In either case it is necessary that the conscious
position be open and willing to assimilate the dream's metaphors and
symbols into conscious experience — feeling, thinking, acting upon, and
living with the insights. Only then can the dream effectively further the
development of the personality and offer help with interpersonal relationships. Thus, understanding must occur, not just abstractly, but also as
personalized emotional and feeling experience. It must eventually also
lead to appropriate reality testing and action — to effective, responsible,
behavioral modification. For what is seen or achieved in the dream needs
still to be made 'real' in waking life.

Solving a task or performing a particular deed, reaching a particular
level of understanding in a dream, does not necessarily imply, nor
substitute for its achievement in daily life. Equally, the rewards and
calamities that may befall us in a dream are only possibilities, not yet
facts in waking existence. The dream events point the way. They indicate
what is probable, or certain to develop, given the situation as it now
is. Thus, they encourage or warn. The dreamer may take a risk and
solve a difficult task, or may take a wrong step and fall off a cliff in a
dream. Such outcomes are metaphors, calling attention to something
that did happen or is in the process of happening outside of awareness.
Since the dreamer does not — before the dream's message — understand
the nature of this occurrence, the dream image is a call to examine the
psychological or external facts. But the outcome posited by the dream
may also be modified or averted as the dreamer's awareness and capacity
change.

The dream's dramatic outcome, then, is to be considered conditional:
given the situation as it is now (namely, the setting or exposition of the dream,
to be discussed below), *this or that is likely to develop*. As the present situation may change, by virtue of the dreamer's assimilating the message
of the dream and changing previously held attitudes, the ensuing effects
pointed to by the dream drama are also subject to change. And following dreams will occur in dialogue with the dreamer's changed attitudes.

Nothing in a dream outcome, therefore, is to be regarded as fixed
or unalterable; unless it is explicitly shown to be so by the terms of the
dramatic structure of the dream itself and by the symbolic or allegoric
tenor of the images. Developments depicted as images of spontaneous

and uncontrollable natural events (earthquakes, storms, floods, trees falling, etc.) are just-so, seemingly destined events, that will inevitably occur unless there are previous expositional factors that put them into a particular mitigating context. In what form — as external events or as psychological crises — and at what timing they will occur, given the nature of dreamtime, is another matter. But, as a general rule, the incarnated outcome of a dream drama depends upon the waking ego's response and attitude to the elements pointed to by the dream. Here the element of relative human freedom is encountered.

Moreover, some dreams with seemingly dire outcomes are pictures of the dreamer's fears, as seen from the Guiding Self, rather than consequences of action. It is important, therefore, to determine whether a given dream depicts the psychological situation from the perspective of the Self's view of an unfolding drama or whether it conveys the Self's view of the dreamer's expectations and assumptions of consequences, or both.

An example of the need for this distinction, and its subtleties, was a nightmare in which a man dreamt:

> I shake hands with a beggar and then fall down with a heart attack.

Work on the dream uncovered the dreamer's fear of his contemptible and hence unacknowledged, beggar-neediness. To welcome it into his life felt equivalent to enduring the pain of a heart attack; hence he had tried to keep emotions of dependency split from consciousness. When invited to re-enter the dream and to imagine the outcome of his heart attack, the dreamer discovered that it would be 'terribly painful, but not fatal; but it would require a new life-style.' The dream was symbolically prognostic; for, following the encounter that it enabled with his still raw, dependency needs, the dreamer underwent an agonizing regression to uncover emotions that, in the course of therapy, did radically change his life. It was analogous to a death and rebirth of his felt-identity. Looking back at this dream several years later, the dreamer recognized that the extent of his fear was comparable to the degree of change his individuation process required of him.

Rarely, if ever, will the dream tell the waking ego what to do. Even when a problem is solved in the dream this shows only a possibility that is available. The dream shows what psychological reality the dreamer is up against, what happens to work for or against his current attitude and position, and what the effects of that position or particular approach are likely to be. It leaves the matter to the dreamer to draw his or her own conclusions, to make decisions, and to act. In this way an ongoing dialectic occurs between conscious and unconscious dynamics. For better and/or worse, conscious freedom of response is respected and preserved.

The 'situation as it is,' seen from the perspective of the Guiding Self, includes both inner developmental potentials and trends, as well as the consequences inherent in the dreamer's current, 'just so' psychological situation. It also includes material relevant to the dreamer's outer life and relationships. It presents what needs to be consciously related to for the sake of possible transformation and integration on both 'subject' and 'object' levels. Thus dreams may startle us, forcing us to ask questions about our subjective attitudes or about the external situations in which we find ourselves — questions we did not realize needed asking, or ones we have been too loath or too unconscious to have considered. A startling dream or a dream that turns a familiar situation upside down may shock us into considering or reconsidering aspects of external reality or relationship issues we have ignored.

An example of such an instance was a dream Jung described from one of his patients.[16] This young man, betrothed to a girl of good and respectable background, sought advice for a neurotic symptom that had developed after his engagement. He brought a dream in which his fiancée appeared as a prostitute. Jung suggested simply that he inquire about the girl's reputation. What he discovered may have been what in his heart he perhaps had known, yet was unable to admit to himself — hence the somatization into stuttering. The discovery was enough for him to break his engagement. As he saw the situation as it was and remedied it, the symptom disappeared. We would perhaps like to take this dream more deeply today, and on a subject level as well, wondering whether the young man's own anima — and hence his own emotionality — was unwilling or unready to settle down. Did he give in to the marriage plans for some assumed gain, prostituting himself, and reacting to such self-betrayal with the affects bound into his somatic symptom? Apparently it was enough for him at the time only to project lack of integrity and commitment, both through his unconscious choice and rejection of his fiancée, and to blame and flee the betrothal. Deeper work on his psyche was apparently not then his aim, only symptom palliation.

Chapter Four

THE LANGUAGE OF DREAMS

It is characteristic that a dream never expresses itself in a logically abstract way, but always in the language of parable or simile. This peculiarity is also a characteristic feature of primitive languages. . . . Just as the body bears traces of its phylogenetic development, so also does the human mind. Hence there is nothing surprising about the possibility that the figurative language of dreams is a survival from an archaic mode of thought.

(*CW*, 8, paras 474, 475)

IMAGE

The experience of dreams operates in an altered state of consciousness 'below' the level of waking consciousness. It is 'primary process' or other-worldly, beyond our rational categories of space and time. It integrates affectively potent material from past, present, and future, using information that is familiar and unfamiliar, information that may even come from archetypal levels with which the dreamer is quite unfamiliar. However, our perception of the dream occurs in terms of our 'here and now' awareness, which is primarily imaginal. To connect to our capacities of consciousness dreams arrive translated, as it were, into a language of sensory images. The dream's 'logical' frame of reference, then, is that of the sense perceptions. These images can be visual, auditory, pro-prioceptive, or kinesthetic; although they tend predominantly in dreams to be visual. They occur in a spectrum ranging from bodily sensations to mythological images and abstract ideas. As in danced drama or painting, concepts and story are still embedded in the sensory image matrix, which expresses non-rational energy patterns.

This imaginal form of communication is 'primary'[1] in several connotations of the word. It is primary in that in it 'an unconscious a priori precipitates itself into plastic form,'[2] initially coming, thus, toward our capacities for perception. It is a foundational activity for other forms of awareness. Chronologically, it is primary in that it is similar to the mode of perception of the young child; as a prime mode of communication, it is similar to that of the artist.

As a form of communication, we also meet such images in ancient and sacred pictographic writings — for example, in those of the early Chinese and Native Americans and the hieroglyphs of ancient Egypt. Such hieroglyphic-sacred images have their own 'logic'[3] and often convey more subtleties of meaning than can readily be verbalized. In those other cultural contexts they provided a language for initiates; although the pictographic forms were often visible for all to see. Similarly, dream images are available to all, but their meanings open only to those initiated into the capacity to comprehend their metaphoric, allegoric or symbolic images.

We consider the image forms allegoric if their message can be translated into rational concepts and verbalizations. We consider them symbolic if they point to 'something suprahuman and only partly conceivable.'[4]

In order to gain access to this level of communication, a combination of artistic, emotional, and intuitive attunement and rational logic is necessary. When 'attuning' to the feel of the dream, the witness must feel and intuit significance rather than reason only logically. He or she must empathically enter the dream's own realm, its metaphoric, symbolic, and dramatic dimensions. As a second step the witness may return from this reverie to rational consciousness in order to integrate its products with those of our psychological understanding. And even then, we can apply our psychological understanding only to those aspects of the dream which are allegorical. Only feeling–intuition and a sense of the numinous can provide a possibility of orientation to those aspects which are genuinely symbolic.

Often it seems as if the dream uses whatever images are meaningful to the dreamer and to his or her therapist. To some extent the limitations of the therapist, therefore, limit the image range of his or her client's dreams. The same dreamer may dream different dreams for different therapists at the same time. It would appear as though the dream arose out of a shared relationship dimension or field — the same field which also induces the transference and countertransference. Hence, we find the seeming 'tact' of the dream source, which at times at least 'tries' to circumvent the therapist's blind spots and to speak in image languages accessible to the therapist. As a therapist silently and separately enlarges his or her capacity to deal with symbolic images and amplificatory repertoire, the analysand will be helped similarly to enlarge his or her own[5] — even though there need be no discussion of the symbolic levels of the material in session. At other times overt discussion of the symbolic material may be very pertinent.

Many dreams are remembered as no more than a single image, whether this be experienced visually, auditorily, or kinesthetically. This can be quite adequate for clinical work when the various vectors of approach within the dream field (see Chapter 5, Associations, Explanation, and Amplification) are applied carefully to it. The single image then becomes the center of a network of converging perspectives which can reveal its psychological–analogical and symbolic significances to the dreamer.

ALLEGORY

Dream images become metaphors — descriptions of one thing in terms of the image of another — as they are woven through the web of associations, explanations, and amplifications which they have evoked.[6] This web, in turn, provides psychological context and meaning for the images.

When such metaphorical images point to contexts that can be rationally understood and expressed, we consider them allegorical. When their context or meaning is beyond the possibility of rational understanding, we speak of symbols.

Allegorical aspects of a dream describe objective, 'outer' or subjective, 'inner' situations that are to be brought to the dreamer's psychological attention. When worked through in every detail (which may not always be clinically necessary or even advisable in a given situation), these allegorical aspects function like X-ray pictures of both those external events and relationships, which have current psychological meaning, as well as those inner psychological structures and situations, which the Guiding Self holds up for examination at this particular time. They reveal through analogy what the naked eye of day consciousness cannot see directly, but can still grasp psychologically and rationally — once it has become alerted to the 'vocabulary' of the metaphorical language.

The dream image of the dream-ego's finding 'a muddy penny' evoked associative memories in the dreamer of finding a penny at camp where he remembered that 'it rained a lot and [he] was homesick and depressed.' A penny, by explanation, is the lowest denomination of value, often considered expendable and cheap. The dreamer was in the process of reconnecting to some of his old buddies, full of hopes that he would find support and fellowship. The dream image corrects in allegorical terms his high estimation of the potential reunion by reminding him of lonely depressiveness and low value.

Allegorical descriptions refer to rationally understandable facts or psychological dynamics, which have been overlooked or have been out of reach of awareness. Even though the message may use metaphor, poetic license, and dramatic exaggeration, its imagery refers to a situation which can be verbalized in terms of rational consciousness. It can and needs to be clearly interpreted, comprehended, and grounded in application to the dreamer's current life situation. We can — and need to — find what the allegorical image implies psychologically.

Its subject matter refers to 'object level' — external — events, or 'subject level' — inner — complexes, events, and the psychological dynamics of the dreamer. Which level happens to apply in a given instance is a matter of clinical judgement. But this can often be clarified by reference to the theory of compensation: the analyst and dreamer can determine on which level of the understanding the dream's message better fulfills a compensatory or complementary function (see Chapter 6: Compensation and complementation).

SYMBOLS

Symbols, by contrast to allegory, point to what can be seen only 'through a glass darkly.' A symbol, in Jung's definition, is 'the best description, or formula of a relatively unknown fact; a fact, however, which is none the less recognized or postulated as existing.'[7] It is 'an admittedly anthropomorphic — hence limited and only partly valid — expression for something suprahuman and only partly conceivable. It may be the best possible expression, yet it ranks below the level of the mystery it seeks to describe.'[8] An example would be a burning bush — an image pointing beyond itself to the mystery of self-consuming fire and renewal as aspects of 'the dimly discerned nature of the spirit.'[9]

Symbols point to existential or even suprapersonal significance, to the realm of the spirit. The inclusion of this transcendent dimension as a basic concern of psychic life expresses the need for meaning in life, through and beyond the experience of sensory–instinctual needs. Any approach to the symbolic dimension, hence, remains in the realm of felt intuition and calls for an artistic and spiritual sensitivity from dreamer and interpreter alike. Symbolic images point to contents which we can only partly know, at best. We attempt to circumambulate their possible or likely significance with reverential and meditative attention in order to attune ourselves to their inherent archetypal energy and meaning patterns. The sensitivity which this requires can be pointed at, but neither described nor taught in technical terms.

At times Jung's dictum regarding symbolic images may apply. He wrote:

> Image and meaning are identical; and as the first takes shape, so the latter becomes clear. Actually, the pattern needs no interpretation: it portrays as a therapeutic requirement.[10] [For the archetypal images] . . . have, when they appear, a distinctly numinous character which can only be described as 'spiritual,' if 'magical' is too strong a word.[11]

Then the potent force of the transpersonal works directly on the psyche of the dreamer, and silent contemplation of the numinous images may be the best therapeutic reception for them, at least initially. At another point finding their spiritual and psychological meanings and how they are to be incarnated is essential.

REBUS

Dealing with allegory, on the other hand, is part of the craft of dream interpretation. It can be compared to working on the understanding of a rebus.

A rebus is a representation of a phrase by pictures. These pictures might more or less clearly suggest syllables, words, or ideas. For instance, a picture of a cat on a piece of uncut wood (log) may be a rebus for 'catalogue.' A picture of a deer and the letters 'p U' next to a picture of a pill might mean 'dear pupil.' In the rebus, the image is translated into words by the 'logic' of sounding, regardless of the illogic of the picture order itself. On the face of it, therefore, the rebus may appear to be a hodge-podge of senseless sequences, while, translated in terms of its sounds, it conveys intelligible meaning.

Similarly, a dream usually does not produce neat conceptual messages; the sequence of images it shows us often appears confused or at least devoid of conceptual logic, for dreams 'obey' their own laws. When a story line appears, for example, the sequence of the images, seemingly temporal within the dream itself, points to what often turns out to be a causal relationship between them. And each image needs to be understood in terms of its psychological meaning for the dreamer.

Consider, for instance, the following dream:

> I am sitting at my desk. I find a pill with a deer image
> imprinted on it. Then my father puts a highway STOP sign on
> the desk. It turns into a flower and I discover a shining diamond
> in its center.

All this makes little, if any, overt sense. However, as in the rebus, a psychological meaning can be found through a form of translating the individual images by means of the dreamer's associations and through the general meaning of the images in terms of collective conventions (see Chapter 5, Association, Explanation, and Amplification).

To take part of this example: the deer is an animal, hence a collectively valid expression of life energy, operating largely on an unreflective, instinctual level. Its image *symbolizes* a quality of primordial energy. This dreamer *explained* the deer as shy and flighty. (Another dreamer may give a different reaction regarding the particular emotional qualities the deer represents to him or her — such as devourers of shrubbery, victims of the hunt, etc.). The dreamer may also remember a particular encounter with a deer. Such *personal associations* would modify or support the explanation.

The pill may remind our dreamer of aspirin which he is using for relief of pain. So far, then, the sequence suggests something on the line of unreflective or instinctual shyness and flightiness imprinted upon (or is the emblem of) a pain-reliever. Understood and translated as psychological concepts, this could mean that shyness and flightiness are functioning in this person as a source or means of relief from pain.

The desk reminded the dreamer, who endeavors to be a writer, of his own writing desk; father was said to have been an authoritarian, literal-minded, dry business man who dismissed the dreamer's reverie and writing ambitions as impractical. The dreamer is shown, then, by this image that there is an authoritarian, perhaps too practically-minded narrowness in his own psychology, an aspect of his father complex, that puts a STOP to his writing endeavors. Sequentially, this stop follows upon his withdrawal to avoid pain. We may conclude that when he withdraws to his writing to avoid the pain of confrontation, then his private, creative expression is stopped. This may be positive or negative,

31

depending on the rest of the dream. The fact that the stop comes from the father complex, opens the larger issues of pain and withdrawal in relation to dismissing paternal authority. Writing itself may have served defensive purposes. All of these issues need to be explored further with the dreamer.

Since the meanings of the images are determined in large part by the meanings offered by the dreamer, the interpretations must vary accordingly. Suppose, to another dreamer, the stop sign does not imply simply halt, but 'Stop, look, and listen, and then go on,' as it does, in fact, on the street. This meaning would change the implication of the dream. Father's skepticism, and its introject in the dreamer, may then be seen as a factor of caution rather than of obstruction. Even if the dreamer should happen to regard his actual father or the paternal value system as unreasonably authoritarian or restrictive, the dream may still suggest that these restraining influences and introjected habits, the effects of which hitherto have been primarily in the direction of avoidance and evasion (deer on the pill), can perhaps now consciously and deliberately be used as restraining cautions for the sake of more effective and safe proceeding.

The image of the flower is traditionally and collectively associated with growth and flourishing. The fact that the stop sign turns into a flower suggests that such a stopping and looking around is to be viewed as a part of and perhaps essential to this person's growth and unfoldment, to a personal flourishing process. The development of voluntary restraint and circumspection may be seen as a desirable discipline for this otherwise impulsive and impatient (in need of a stop sign) dreamer, as an alternative to oversensitive, withdrawing shyness. This would be similar to reminding a motorist to pay attention to traffic signals instead of either expecting unhindered progress or shying away from driving entirely.

The diamond is an image of indestructible substance, hardness, and great value (explanation). Traditionally, it has come to represent an aspect of the central core of the personality, the immortal Self. For instance, the image of the 'jewel in the lotus' in Eastern tradition points to the transcendent value encountered via the disciplining effect of meditation and devotion. Amplification of archetypal context points to a symbolic, no longer merely allegoric, dynamic. In our sequence the appearance of the diamond from the flower might then suggest that, rather than only being pathological or neurotic, an awareness of the urge to flight and the conscious development of its transformation as 'stop, look, and listen' may constitute central creative life tasks of personality maturation — ways, by means of which this particular individual is to find and develop his or her true nature: the individuation task.

Conversely, if the dreamer happens to be overidentified with Eastern philosophical systems and quietistically to misinterpret them in the service of his escapism, the above implications might be reversed. This is because the compensating function of the dream (see below) has to be taken into account. Then the jewel in the lotus may be only an allegorical image to represent his Buddhist theories. The stony rigidity of diamond in the flourishing life of the flower would be equated with Stopping, the message from father. The dream, then, would have to be seen as confronting the dreamer with the reason for the stalemate: namely, that his religious or philosophical views serve as rationalizations for not moving on. By implication, the message would be: bestir yourself and risk. Or, if it turns out that aspirin happens to be anathema and/or poisonous to an advocate of natural healing methods, the interpretation becomes more negative again. The deer on the aspirin and the stop sign on the desk may suggest that both, shyness and avoidance of pain, are 'poisonous' for him; both collude in putting a hard stop to his creative expressions.

The enumeration of so many possible variations of interpretation of the same motifs in a dream, often diametrically opposed to one another, and depending upon the dreamer's personal reactions and emotional responses to them, goes to show why a quick interpretation without the dreamer's participation is always to be avoided. To do adequate work with any dream, it is always necessary, first, to evaluate carefully the dreamer's associations, value standards and, foremost, the dreamer's conscious position and outlook, since these are likely to be opposed, complemented, and/or compensated by the dream. Only after these variables have been taken into account is it possible to do justice to both dream and dreamer.

Chapter Five

ASSOCIATION, EXPLANATION, AMPLIFICATION: THE DREAM FIELD

A dream is too slender a hint to be understood until it is enriched by the stuff of associations and analogy and thus amplified to the point of intelligibility.

(*CW*, 12, para. 403)

The psychological context of dream-contents consists in the web of associations in which the dream is naturally embedded. It should therefore be an absolute rule to assume that every dream, and every part of a dream, is unknown at the outset, and to attempt an interpretation only after carefully taking up the context. We can then apply the meaning we have thus discovered to the text of the dream itself and see whether this yields a fluent reading, or rather whether a satisfying meaning emerges.

(*CW*, 12, para. 48)

The meanings and implications of the various dream motifs are never fixed.[1] They vary in accordance with the individual dreamer's reactions to them, as expressed by personal associations and explanations, as well as with their possible allusions to cultural or collectively-held explanations and mythologems, with which the dreamer may or may not be familiar. All of these — associations, explanations, and amplifications — form a unitary field with the dream itself, and with all the events, including the bodily and emotional reactions of both dreamer and therapist-witness, which happen to occur as the dream is being told and discussed. In addition, dream meaning often varies in accordance with yet another criterion: complementation or compensation. This we will consider in a following chapter.

ASSOCIATIONS

The first factors, always to be considered before any interpretation may be attempted, are the individual dreamer's associations. Associations are any ideas, notions, memories, reactions, or whatever else, that may jump into the dreamer's mind as the dream and its particular image are considered. Associations are, thus, connected to or evoked by the images. But they are not necessarily rational evaluations of, nor judgements about, the images. Associations are utterly subjective, whether rational or irrational. They may, in fact, seem arbitrary or random elements, and they need not be logically justified.

For instance, a desk may remind the dreamer of father's desk, or of the desk of his or her high school days, or of one that was seen in a furniture shop, or of some old broken down one in the attic that he bumped his nose on as a toddler, or of a particular piece of cloth used by mother to clean a desk top, or of Mr so and so who used to talk about a desk he wanted to buy but never did and who made a nuisance of himself by always dropping in at the wrong times.

To ground adequately the dream's meaning it is essential that any associations which occur be explored until they reveal their emotional core and psychological significance. This means finding the emotional charge related to the association, and grounding that in the dreamer's current psychological reality. The affect–response may be forthcoming spontaneously, or it may have to be elicited by further exploration, questioning, imaging, word repeat technique or other working through method.

Evoking associations and explanations may be done through questions to the auditory sense — as when the therapist below asked the dreamer 'where does that ring a bell?' Visual or body and feeling responses are more readily forthcoming with queries about 'how do you see that?' or 'how does that feel?' or 'take you?', etc. It is important to use for questioning the same sensory mode used by the dreamer for describing. This permits the therapist as participant–witness 'to enter through the dreamer's door.'

To ground the image in personal psychological reality the therapist needs to inquire what events, emotions, or feelings — painful, joyful, or seemingly indifferent — happen to come to mind in connection with it. In the dream of the desk the analyst may gently probe, 'what about that desk, what comes to you?' The dreamer may recall that it looks like father's, and go on to re-evoke the emotional, embodied experience connected with father's desk at the present moment of telling the dream in analysis. There may be many possible reactions: the feeling of getting hurt from being unstable on one's feet, for instance, and bumping against it; the feeling of being reprimanded by father for some commission or omission; the memory of father's work attitude and the dreamer's emotional reaction to it, leading to exploration of what was the work attitude and what was this reaction. The one or ones which have emotional intensity are, thus, singled out for focus.

The synchronicity of the emotional charge with the image, thus, points to the pertinent, psychological issue to be explored analytically. In other words, whichever association has emotionally charged significance needs to be grounded with respect to the dreamer's present and past psychological situation. It has current psychological meaning. Associations to the images (visual, auditory, and kinesthetic) and feeling reactions in the dream reveal then how they are to be connected with the present contexts in the dreamer's life as well as in past and childhood memories and in specific experiences of the client–therapist relationship — the transference dynamics.

An example of two dreams, which were manifestly similar, points up the necessity for such careful attention to associations. In both the dreamer awoke to find the therapist sitting on the sleeper's bed. The first dreamer's association was already emotional, 'Oh, no, that would never happen.' He exhibited a tight fear. Upon inquiry, he associated 'intimacy' with such a setting, and began to smoke in the session. He was clearly afraid of the emotional, potentially erotic, intimacy which he was waking up to confront in the transference. The second dreamer associated to the same image 'sitting on the bed like when you visit a sick person.' The therapist asked, 'Where does that ring a bell?' — an open-ended type of questioning most effective for eliciting associations. The dreamer paused, then remembered, 'I did that when I visited my cousin in the hospital. She was dying.' After a long silence, she went on, 'Oh, you are going on vacation, and that feels like forever, dying.' She awoke to her own separation fears, which felt like her death.

When two or more elements, such as associations, explanations, or amplifications of seemingly different implications are charged with affect for the dreamer, a point of intersection needs to be found. As an example from the dream above, the dreamer's fear of intimacy was behaviorally connected with smoking as he focused on the dream image. It functioned, thus, as an embodied association. To smoking he further associated 'holding down anger.' Fear of intimacy and need to repress

36

anger intersected. Consequently, he avoided intimacy because it stirred his rage, which, he felt, would destroy relationships. Thus, he tried to manage intimacy with ritualized distance. He, thus, feared the positive transference as much as feared the negative one, and maintained 'in and out' relationships.

Associating to dream images is 'free' at first but soon becomes focused around the pertinent issue or complex, as an affect is touched. It is, thus, insufficient for the dreamer to leave an image with the association, for instance, that Mr X, in a dream 'reminds me of a friend from high school with whom I went out.' There is no embodied, emotional experience alive in the dreamer's psyche yet. The image cannot, therefore, be grounded experientially for the dreamer in terms of its psychological relevance to current emotional reality. Further inquiry is required. It needs to be open-ended, rather than suggestive of any particular answer. Yet it needs to seek for specific, affective experience: what was that friend like as a personality — what qualities do you associate to him? How did he make you feel? What emotional experiences were connected with that relationship? What affects did he, or did any events connected with him, evoke (fascination, admiration, shyness, disgust, pain, or whatever . . .)? While these questions are not necessarily specific ones for any clinical situation, they indicate the nature of the necessary approach. Only when an affect is touched may we assume that the essential core of psychological reality, including whatever complex happens to be touched, has been reached experientially. Intellectual understanding is not enough.

An example of such inquiring occurred during discussion of the following simple dream:

I am carrying some old bags into my son's bedroom.

While the dramatic structure indicates that some old issue is being put into the dreamer's relationship to his son (object level, see below) or to his inner son (subject level), extensive questioning was needed to ground the image of the bags meaningfully in emotion. At first, the dreamer could identify the bags only as blue. They were unknown to him. And blue? The color reminded him of a backpack he had used when he was 17. He had gone on a trip to the Rockies with friends. Neither the Rockies, the trip, nor the friends elicited any affect. 'What about when you were 17?' The dreamer suddenly blushed and got angry, remembering that he had been caught then in a sexual act by his parents. The sexual shame and insecurity before the superego, then, was being

37

carried or projected into his relationship to his son. This was the current, personal issue the dream was raising for consideration.

Occasionally in working on a dream the dreamer may block, and be unable to come up with any associations. The material may be too psychologically potent for the dreamer to approach, or there may be too little free imagination available for associating. Sometimes the block needs to be interpreted. Alternatively it can sometimes be circumvented by asking for explanations. These permit more distance from the dreamer's complexed relation to the images or to the unconscious matrix itself. Thus questions that allow for distance can often provide the safety needed to enable further work on the dream. Examples might be 'If that were an objective situation, what might be your reaction? or 'If that were happening to someone else, how might you feel?' Such questions move from association to explanation.

EXPLANATION

Whereas associations are subjective responses, regardless of their inherent rationality, explanation is the term used for the expression of generally accepted and agreed upon facts. In this sense explanation conveys rational meanings. Explanation expresses what the image typically stands for, in terms of its objective function or meaning, either for the dreamer and/or for the collective. Here the therapist must beware of his or her own personal bias in determining the objective explanation of an image, an explanation which may not be consensual. As with association, any explanation may point to a meaning that is allegoric or symbolic, or both (see above).

Explanations are of two kinds: objective–collective and subjective–individual. In terms of objective–collective explanation, a pen is a tool for writing or drawing, no matter whether the dreamer's association may evoke a memory of having used it as a weapon to stab his or her brother or whether he or she happens to think of a phallic implication.

The subjective–individual explanation of the pen as writing tool is likely to vary from individual to individual. Writing or drawing may be a means of self-expression: communicative, imitative, and/or creative for some people. For others it may be a writing tool for tasks he/she would rather avoid, such as keeping daily accounts. Hence, writing tool stands as explanation for pen. But the therapist would still have to find the intersection of objective and subjective explanations with the personal associations: writing as communicative self-expression or avoidance of tasks, intersecting with brother-stabbing, to find the psychological relevance of competitive aggression to self-expression or avoidance. It may turn out that the aggression is conveyed by sarcastic remarks or by avoidance, that the self-expression is motivated by competitive striving, or that there is some other meaningful correlation of the two.

In another example the pen (explanation: writing tool) may remind the dreamer of an occasion when her aunt gave her such a pen. Now, we need associations to and/or explanations of the aunt. She was an important voice in the family, frequently present (explanation). The dreamer felt her to be highly imaginative (association). We may surmise from this that the dreamer's imagination was inspired by the contact with or example of the aunt. However, so far no feeling reactions or affects have been evoked. We may have to ask further questions to elicit those. What was the aunt herself like as a person? And, equally important, what were the dreamer's feeling reactions to her?

The dreamer may describe her burst out with 'she was a cutting, critical bitch,' or 'she was warm and supportive,' whatever the association. From criticalness or supportive warmth (the aunt's qualities), then, would seem to originate (the aunt gave the pen to the dreamer), the expressions or forms of communication.

In order to establish an adequate range of individual explanations, the therapist must avoid taking meanings for granted but instead ask the dreamer such questions as: 'What does it represent to you?' 'How come?', 'Why?', 'How would it be if it were a real situation?', etc. In short, the therapist needs to assume a stance of curiosity and ignorance. Only thus, can he or she avoid premature jumping to conclusions.

Sometimes the crux of the dream's drama involves behavior that ignores obvious collective explanation. In a dream in which the dreamer reports:

> I stand backwards to the river current on an empty raft and spend huge energy trying to turn the craft around in order to steer it,

we can see that the explanation holds an important clue to the dream message. A poled, empty raft has no bow or stern. To steer in the other direction the dream-ego needs simply to turn himself, not the raft, around. That he does not know to do this is the unusual point to be explored psychologically in therapy.

In a similar example, a woman dreamt that

> I am given some jewels by the owner of a jewelry store. As I handle them, I become anxious that my fingerprints are all over the counter and I flee from the store and down the street to hide from the police.

As she told the 'nightmare,' she was unaware that her assumption of guilt for stealing followed her receiving the valuable jewels as a free gift. This was, therefore, the primary subject of the analytic discussion about the dream. Both of these examples rely on the therapist's pointing to the discrepancy between private and collective/objective explanations of the images.

Work with any dream image requires finding this intersection of consensual explanation and personal association or explanation, as well as with analogic or symbolic meanings, as we will see later. A desk is explained as a piece of furniture, usually used for writing or paper work, and/or for the storage of documents relating to communication. This is regardless of the dreamer's associations. If the association to the particular desk happens to be 'a table for beer parties,' the implication might be that a work or writing situation or propensity to work or write, led to, or, perhaps, was replaced by, or associated with, merrymaking, play, drunkenness, or whatever the further associations and explanations to the beer party happen to be. Explanations and associations always have to be combined by finding the meaningful psychological intersection of the two.

On the other hand, there may be incongruities between individual and collective explanations. Then these must be separately considered and balanced against or interlaced with each other. What an object is, or functions for, may be seen by the dreamer as fairly congruent with the general collective view, or the two views may be different. The dreamer's idiosyncratic perspective may point clearly to an underlying complex, and/or it may be so extreme it may show a radical diversity, providing evidence of the dreamer's isolation from collectively shared reality, as well as providing descriptive access for the therapist into that isolation. In a dream image of 'a live but bloody lamb spinning, skewered on a door handle,' which the dreamer explained as a 'carousel,' the therapist discovered excruciating pain denied — by likening it associatively to a carousel in an amusement park — and a lamb-like masochistic complex of mangled instinctual expression, which prevented opening the door to therapeutic work. The therapist could then take some initiative to address the dreamer's severe problem in shared language.

Not only may the dreamer have a personal explanation at variance from that of the collective, the therapist may have a still different explanation, at variance with that of either dreamer or collective. While it may be relevant to the material, it needs to be shelved until all material from the dreamer is first explored. And when there are discrepancies between dreamer's and other explanations, or between the dreamer's associations and reality explanation, clinical skill is required to bridge the discrepancies with understanding. In an example of mishandling such explanatory material, a therapist dismissed the dreamer's image as 'unrealistic,' when the dream was:

I powder my feet with bathroom cleaning powder to go to work.

Without inquiring to find out that the bathroom powder was named 'Bon Ami' and that the phrase was, by association, his wife's term of endearment, the therapist assumed it referred only to the name of an abrasive cleaner. The therapist, therefore, wrongly decided that the dream suggested a cleaning obsession, dangerous for a human foot or standpoint. In fact, by explanation, 'Bon Ami' is a powder claiming 'it hasn't scratched yet' and depicting a chicken emerging from an egg on each box.

Failure to elicit associations and explanations, as well as to consider the amplificatory symbolism of the hatching chick, missed the potential significance of the dream. The dream points to an intersection between his wife's mirroring support and the seemingly unrealistic dream image. Incongruence must be explored rather than used to dismiss the validity of the given dream image. It will then discover the deeper psychological context.[2] In this instance, the image can be seen to reveal both that to be loved felt unrealistic unless he was 'clean enough,' and that the dreamer's stance in the world depended on the protection of his wife's affection and on harmlessness — being like a little chick. Thus powdering his feet with 'Bon Ami' points to the basic significance of this problem in the context of renewal and individuation. Needless to add, clinical skill and experience will be required in each case to sort the various vectors appropriately. Then, the dreamer's embodied 'aha' experience will confirm the apt meaningfulness of the result.

An attic, for instance, is a store room and the highest floor of the house. This is a general, collectively valid explanation. It is a fact. But one person may use an attic as a store room, another as an additional bedroom, still another as empty space to be finished in the future. For one person it may be a store room for things of past use, currently in discard, for another the explanatory stress lies on the possibility of potential use of some of the objects in the future. In general, the individual explanation must get first consideration.

If this explanation should happen to deviate to a considerable extent from the general explanation — for instance, a pen being explained as a means to stab little brother, or attic 'as a pun on the word ''tic'' and as a place used for masturbation' — then that sort of explanation would be handled like an association. It would then modify, occasionally even overrule, the generally accepted meaning in discussion of the dream. One might inquire, in the instance of the masturbation explanation, about its compulsive ('tic') nature. One might explore why just the attic was chosen. Was there something erotic among all those old things, was it the attraction of the view from on high, or was it the only private place available? Affirmation of the first might point to a self arousal (masturbation) by withdrawing into the past. The second would place it onto the 'head' — top storey of the body — or onto an attempt at self elevation. The third one stresses the search and need for privacy to get in 'touch' with self (see below for further discussion of sexuality in dreams).

In another example, that of the rebus dream above, the aspirin pill is a pain reliever; hence it refers to the motive of avoiding or relieving pain (explanation). The association may link it with mother. Mother again may be described or associated to in terms of over-solicitousness and her tendency to overtreat any childhood malady with aspirin. Or, she may not have been able to stand any painful discomfort herself. Relief of pain is here linked to over-solicitousness and intolerance of discomfort. The timidity and shyness associated with the deer stands midway between association and explanation, inasmuch as it is factually recognized that deer readily take flight. Thus, shyness is shown to have been engendered by mother's attitude of avoiding pain or difficulty whenever possible. Or, since to the child, mother is a source of comfort and emotional protection (subject level interpretation), emotional comfort or protection are shown to be linked to shyness and avoidance of pain. The psychological point of intersection has been found.

EMOTIONS AND BODILY REACTIONS

Affects or bodily reactions occurring within a dream, as well as affects or body reactions occurring while talking about the dream are to be treated like an image. They are to be considered as, potentially, part of the dream, and they require the dreamer's associations to them. Such reactions in the therapist may be relevant to the client's dream, as well, but they require the therapist's associations and private working through before they can be added to the dream field (see below, p. 54). Along with the dream setting (see Chapter 7, Dramatic structure), these affective reactions are often the most direct route bridging dream and current emotional reality. They often lead to vivid memories surrounding the dream presentation of the dreamer's currently relevant complex. In the above example the guilty fear resulting from the gift of jewels led directly to discovery of the dreamer's panic at the exposure of her excellent professional work, with which she was personally over-identified, and to memories of parental envy and other injuries to her capacity and sense of selfhood in childhood.

Particular body positions in a dream, as well as while working on the dream and even though they arouse no verbal or verbalizable associations, are significant. When re-enacted in session, they often lead directly to the emotion underlying the dream message. For example, a woman who dreamed that her hands were twisted and tied was asked to assume that posture. She began to struggle and perspire. She discovered herself in panic, which she soon was able to identify as the emotion she felt at needing to ask for a raise at work. It further reminded her of childhood fears of her alcoholic father's return home. Still feeling twisted in that terror, she could not assert her legitimate value before authority.

Another example of strong emotion connected with a body image:

> I dream that something has happened to my index finger. I can't feel it from inside or with my other fingers. I am afraid I may have lost my finger. I am very scared. Then I see my grandfather's face and suddenly I realize that now my finger is full of sensation and I know it is all right.

Here fear, the dreamer's emotion, is associated to loss of her index finger. Her association to the dream fear brought her to the emotion of helpless terror she felt when confronting her immanent appearance in divorce court. The index finger she associated to 'pointing the finger at, allocating blame.' She remembered it being shaken to scold her. There is an amplification (see below) from chirology wherein this finger symbolizes the capacity for executive power.[3] The dreamer felt she had lost her capacity to allocate responsibility; in fact, she was feeling abjectly guilty and valueless, in danger of losing her children in the divorce battle. By contrast, her grandfather, she said, was 'strong, stood his ground as a powerful labor leader even when his position was unpopular.' In contact with the image of his sense of power and justice, her own faltering and fear-ridden executive authority is restored. The dream led to a series of active imaginations with her grandfather, through which she contacted the authoritative force necessary to stand her ground in the divorce case and elsewhere in her life.

In one instance while an analysand recounted a dream of flying and soaring, to which she associated freedom from constraint, the analyst noted an oppressive sensation in his own chest. Since it occurred with the dream description and was not a usual sensation, he asked the dreamer where she might be feeling any constraints from which she needed to free herself. She was unable to relate the sensation to any current situation. The therapist then asked her to concentrate on her chest and to try to be aware of constriction there. Almost immediately the client remembered childhood asthmatic states, which she verbalized as 'a spider enmeshing [her], constricting breath.' From the sensation, first induced in the analyst, then grounded by the dreamer in poignant memory, it was but a short step to touch her feeling of tyrannical control by her mother and her habitual escape, 'flying and soaring' into fantasy and an altered state of consciousness (induced in some measure physiologically by lack of oxygen). This realization then elicited her current, hitherto unconscious, feelings about the regularity and limiting controls of analysis, where the same pattern of stymied constriction and flight had again become relevant. As she was able to begin to voice her reactions, the breath constriction eased.

In another example a business-man had repeated dreams of being condemned to jail for smuggling. No relevant associations or explanations were to be found, but the analyst's attention was caught by a gentle rocking movement of the dreamer's trunk, while the dream was discussed. To this movement the dreamer's attention was drawn, and he was asked to intensify the movement and to feel what images or memories it conveyed. He soon discovered that it felt like *davening* (a Yiddish word for praying attended by similar back and forth rocking motions), and he recalled his father's pride in his accomplishments at Hebrew studies. He found himself reliving his Bar Mitzvah, an occasion for his father's receiving much praise and taking credit for his accomplished son, while hardly any attention was paid to the son. He remembered that to feel significant to his father he tried to excel in those areas his father valued even though they had no personal significance for himself, for which he even had some contempt since they kept him from his peers. At the same time he regarded himself as a cheat for dissimulating and pretending to something he did not want — 'like a smuggler conveying contraband.' From this awareness, he became conscious of his current need to please the therapist and other authority figures, by attempting to win affection with what he felt they would like. He pretended to feelings and convictions he did not even know if he held, and he hated himself for both his neediness and his pretense. He was 'locked in jail' by the hidden pretense and the need for what he felt was illicit, contemptible gain.

It is important also to watch the dreamer's emotional and bodily responses when telling a dream, for gestures, tensions, sensations are relevant associations. The therapist needs to note her/his own reactions also, and to sift them for countertransference factors (see below).

Anything that happens coincidental in timing with the dream or in the immediate environment while a dream is being told is also important. For such synchronistic[4] events are manifestations of the encompassing 'field' of which the dream is a particular and partial expression. They may point to basic archetypal dynamics involved and relevant to the dream. Thus dreaming of having an accident and also having an accident about the same time would emphasize the breakdown danger inherent in the dreamer's psychological–spiritual situation.

'TRIVIAL' DREAMS

No dream or dream fragment, as simple or irrelevant as it may seem, need be dismissed as insignificant or 'trivial'. The dream, particularly when only a fragment is remembered, may appear so to the dreamer. But, when investigated in terms of associations, explanations, amplifications, and, possibly, gestalt enactments and fantasy improvisations, every dream will be found to shed light onto some blind spot. It may point to important insights on the object, but more frequently on the subject, level.

With snatches and fragmentary dreams, in particular, it falls upon the therapist to elicit additional information and associative material by encouraging the use of imagination, even if this imaginative activity may initially appear like 'plain inventing' to the dreamer. In fantasizing or 'inventing,' the unconscious myth-making function is active, no less than in the act of dreaming. Even the most deliberately 'invented' story bears the involuntary imprints of the inventor's or author's unconscious psyche.

Often to stimulate such activity, the therapist may inquire into the *whys* and *hows* of the various occurrences and/or encourage additional associations and explanations.

An example of a dream felt to be 'trivial' by the dreamer:

> I am the leader at an adolescent dance. It is my job to get the girls and boys to mix and have a good time dancing.

The dreamer's only reaction was that she did that often when her daughters were teenagers. Otherwise, the dream did not seem to touch on any more than a sentimental memory. It appeared to be quite irrelevant and, indeed, trivial to the dreamer. In the face of such easy dismissal, the therapist continued to ask questions to find the psychological relevance of the actions and images. The questions 'why' and 'what for' are often helpful here, probing for deeper levels. When asked why the dreamer felt she had to do the mixing, her response was, 'to help and encourage them.' Again 'why' is needed to push the association toward its psychologically relevant core. The dreamer responded, 'to overcome their shyness.' Overcoming shyness, then, is the motivation, to which the dream's 'trivial' imagery refers. Since the dreamer could find no association to actual shy teenagers, the issue of shyness had to be looked at on the subject level. Memories of the dreamer's adolescence were elicited. They revealed issues which made it clear that the 'adolescent' within the dreamer's psyche was still shy and in need of encouragement through a deliberate, conscious effort of 'mixing' to get into the dance of life. The dreamer's sense of the dream's irrelevance might even be discovered — after the dream is worked through — to be part of her own self-dismissive and shy style.

FANTASY, IMAGINATION, AND ENACTMENT

> In sleep, fantasy takes the form of dreams. But in waking life, too, we continue to dream beneath the threshold of consciousness, especially when under the influence of repressed or other unconscious complexes.
>
> (*CW*, 16, para. 125)

Since the complex underlying the dream synchronistically also affects outer events and waking 'altered-conscious' states, any dream may also be amplified by the dreamer's spinning it out and enlarging it through the use of imaginative techniques. These operate by allowing images to arise before the inner eye, or even by simply 'inventing' to fill in missing pieces of the dream story. The methods of 'active' and 'guided imagination' have been described repeatedly by other authors,[5] and to them the reader is referred.

Any part of a dream can be made a starting point for expanding the dream, with newly-added imagery — either to carry the action further, in order to see which way it might develop, or to extend it backwards from the beginning of a dream, in order to find out how the opening situation itself came into existence. As long as the dreamer is open to the dream and returns in consciousness into the dream's space/time, there is no need to fear that the dream's message may, thus, be distorted. Any image or images that arise in this way are productions of the unconscious and will, regardless of the dreamer's conscious ideas, manage to sneak in their messages.

One frequently quite useful method is to invite the dreamer to imagine looking at a movie or television screen on which the dream situation to be explored is projected, and then watching to see how the action develops further. The dreamer can equally imagine reversing the film to see how the action developed initially. In one example a dreamer brought in repeated reports of flying and spoke of his unshakeable joy in being able to fly in his dreams. When the analyst asked him to look down and see if he could see what he was flying over, the analysand saw crowds of beggars and street people. These were aspects of his own psychology from which he flew high to maintain an illusion of joy. Encountering them brought on a depressive descent into reality.

These personal enlargements of the dream are particularly helpful when in doubt about the intended thrust of a dream action or implication. For instance, in the case of the dream of the picnic at the volcano's edge (see below) we might ask the dreamer to 'finish' the dream imaginally. The image arising might be anything from a destructive eruption to an unexpected rainstorm that breaks up the party, forcing them to leave before anything terrible has a chance to happen. In that latter instance we may assume that some comparatively minor disturbance is likely to stir the dreamer out of conscious denial and complacency and, thereby, help to avoid catastrophe. Or the dreamer may realize, by virtue of the fantasy, what the implications of such complacency are. No further interpretation may be necessary, provided the dreamer understands to which particular psychological attitude or situation, in actual life, the volcano-picnic happens to correspond.

Another technique involves asking the dreamer to 'put the dream on stage' either with the dreamer acting or pantomiming the various parts, or, in a group therapy setting, assigning roles to various members to play part personalities.

The dreamer may role play figures or objects — or in a group setting the dreamer may assign roles, participate, and/or act as stage director. Generally it is preferable to do this first non-verbally, as a pantomime, in order to avoid intellectualizing or premature rational interpretations and explanations, and in order to let the unconscious express itself as fully as possible through muscular movement, rhythm, gesture, facial expression. Often it is useful to employ the Gestalt techniques of speaking in the first person, even if the dreamer is representing or enacting a non-human figure, and to let various dream figures or objects have inner dialogues with one another to state their differing positions and even to discover possibilities of synthesis.

Eventually, the dreamer's attention is then focused on how the enactment 'feels' in the body, whether acted or pantomimed alone or while watching the others. All these reactions are then subject to further associations and explanations, as may be the case.

An example of such imaginal and psychodramatic working through occurred with a seemingly innocuous, little dream image:

A tomato was thrown away.

When the dreamer, an earnest, accommodating minister, took the role of tomato, he expressed it: 'I am slow to ripen in cold weather, but with a little bit of sunshine I become red and soft and juicy. Then I am delicious.' The description given, when taken metaphorically, is a self-description. The dreamer expresses a distaste for coldness and a need for warmth and slow ripening nurture from his environment. The dream states, however, that 'the tomato is thrown away' — his need and capacity for slow, sensuous development are inwardly scorned and rejected; thus he requires outward support. Asked where this might be currently relevant, the dreamer had no response. Thus, to pursue the dream image further to find how such rejection occurs, the dreamer was asked to describe, feel, or attempt to enact the person who threw away the tomato. Since that person was absent from the dream, there was no immediate response, and the dreamer's need for some warm support from the analyst became apparent, in order for him to risk a creative task. The analyst suggested that the image of such a person be invented or imagined, for whatever is so created or imagined when working on a dream 'belongs' and can express relevant, though still unconscious, dynamics. The form of a dark, mustached man emerged from the dreamer's imagination. Since he reminded the dreamer of no one in personal life or memory, the analyst inquired if he might be sketched. Readily, the client drew a thin face with a sneer emphasized by the mustache. Then he spoke for the figure, expressing its feelings. 'I am a real man, smart, cool. I scorn stupidity and feeling. Emotions are like rotten tomatoes. They only make for weakness and vulnerability. All that matters is getting ahead.' Thus spoke an hitherto totally unconscious aspect of the dreamer's personality, one that professed 'real' masculinity to be smart, coldly unfeeling, full of cynical practicality and ambition, a shadow figure that scorned and even 'threw away' processes of inner and relationship ripening and capacities to enjoy softness and warmth. From previous material it was clear that this coldness and ambition was acted out and projected onto partners, but not seen as an aspect of the dreamer's own psychology. Unspoken in the dream enactment, but apparent to the witnessing therapist, was the dreamer's sense of vulnerability to being devoured if he was soft, ripe, warm, and delicious like a 'love apple.' And indeed, the sneering, cold, masculine shadow was a defensive energy pattern that opened in subsequent months to reveal primitive fears of engulfment by a seductive-devoted maternal figure.

This client enjoyed the positive exhibitionism of role play, and had a relatively stable sense of himself as performing persona, which enabled him to undertake and even initiate such enactments. For others more deeply wounded by early shaming or caught in fragmentation and denial or splitting defenses, such methods of dream enactment can be counter-productive and disorienting. Those clients need first to find a center of stable identity. They feel threatened and/or resistant when asked to take any role, certainly any other than that of the dream-ego. Instead, they may be asked to describe or to 'feel into' a dream figure, to associate to it, or to ask it questions. Again such considerations are part of the management of individual cases.

AFFECT AND FEELING QUALITY

Feeling tones in a dream range from highly subjective affect reactions, arising from complexes, to seemingly objective judgements evaluating the dream situation. On the one hand, the dreamer's judgement of a dream or dream motif, as well as the reaction it induces in the person who listens to the dream, may reveal a complex-toned, inappropriate or distorted reaction to the objective situation depicted. On the other hand, it may express a complex-toned value judgement that is appropriate and concordant with the 'intention' of the dream dramatist, the Guiding Self. In initially assessing a dream the fact that a dream situation feels 'good' or 'bad' (either while dreamed or upon recall) indicates no more than that: it *feels* good or bad to the dreamer. Such subjective evaluation does not necessarily imply that it *is* good or bad objectively. Particularly, when the witnessing listener's reaction happens to be at variance with the dreamer's, the discrepancy must be noted. It may need to be taken as a warning that the way the situation is 'staged' in the dream needs to be carefully and objectively evaluated in terms of the implications of the dramatic intent.

Take the following example:

> We were sitting at the edge of a depression like a big crater and having a merry picnic. From the center of the crater there arose smoke and fire, and we realized we were on top of a volcano. But we were amused by the eruption. We thought the color patterns were interesting.

This dream depicts an extremely dangerous situation, relative to which the dreamer's feeling reaction — amusement and esthetic abstraction — is highly inappropriate and unrealistic. At the edge of some dangerous life situation a good dose of fear or, at least caution, would be called for. Here there is depicted instead foolhardy denial and frivolous amusement. The dream's intent, evidently, is to shock and to induce a sense of fear, thereby compensating the dreamer's unrealistic detachment and curiously compensatory collectivity — he sees himself merged with a group of undiscriminated 'we.'

To vary the example, suppose the dream setting was the same, showing the party sitting at the edge of a smoking depression. Suppose the dramatic development was changed, and the dream imaged one of the party, a Mr X, claiming the mountain was Vesuvius. In associating to Mr X, the dreamer then said he was 'a person who tends to cry wolf.' Even though the dreamer's reaction might be to be scared, the implication of this dream would be the opposite of the preceding one: here, even though he or she is at the edge of a potentially eruptive depression, yet she/he tends to get unduly alarmed. Perhaps there is more smoke than fire in this depression.

To picnic on the edge of an active volcano is to be accounted reckless or crazy behavior by ordinary everyday standards. It might express irresponsibility or a high degree of unconsciousness and/or denial of emotional eruption. The archetypal motif of volcano, however, *symbolizes* an active cleft giving access to and from the otherworld, one connecting to the awesome powers of death, of hell, of changed and often prophetic consciousness. Knowing this symbolism increases our understanding of the dream: the potential connection to the transpersonal dimension and a capacity for otherworld awareness that comes through eruptive emotion might be treated with casual frivolity, perhaps denied out of fear of the transpersonal. Beyond explanation, such an understanding of the archetypal dimension provides a deeper view into both the dream and the dreamer's psychology (see below, Amplification, and Chapter 8: Mythological motifs).

Another example:

I am in my car on top of a high cliff. The front wheels are dangling over the edge; yet I am quite calm.

In the situation depicted here, the dreamer's dream identity feels a calm which somewhat surprises her in the dream, as indicated by the little word 'yet.' This calm may or may not be appropriate. The questions in this instance would be: what is the dreamer going to do about the situation? Is she going to get out and seek help? Or will she remain in the car and 'unconcernedly' allow it to slip forward and fall? We may have to resort to fantasy (active or guided imagination) to get this additional information, as well as the additional: where are we? Near or far from help? Can the car be pulled back to safety without slipping? etc.

In some instances only by filling in, or rather, extending the dream by imagination, can we decide whether the feeling tone is appropriate or unrealistic. Knowing what conscious state the dream compensates would also be important (see below).

A novice group therapist had the following dream:

There were two strangers in my group. I told them to leave, but the group felt that I was too formal and rigid. I was not sure whether they were not right and I should be less insistent.

The dreamer was an extroverted feeling type, who found it difficult to hold his own position and to set limits. He was easily swayed by his needs to please and to be in agreement with others, in an attempt to offset his strong abandonment fears. As in this dream, his feelings usually were ambivalent and his ego position unsure. In exploring the dream he was asked to consider the reality issue, which the image raised: what would he advise a therapist in training, under his supervision, to do in such a situation? What might be the appropriate way of handling it? When, given this permission to find an objective center of appropriate work authority, his answer was definite, 'Clearly, you have to ask them to leave; you cannot permit total strangers to intrude into the group process, it definitely would be a disruption.'

This dream, then, confronted him with his own ambivalence due to his unsureness of his inner authority. It showed him how he tended to feel when he had to make unpopular decisions. It did not tell him in so many words whether his feeling reaction was appropriate or not, but held up a mirror to him for his own conscious judgement. This way of staging the dream seemed intended to alert him to the necessity of achieving an objective, firm ego position.

The above question, 'How would you feel if the situation depicted in the dream were real?', is one of the simplest ways of dealing with uncertainties about the implications of the 'dramatic intent' in such situations. The dreamer with the car over the precipice answered, 'terrified.'

AMPLIFICATION

Amplification is the enlarging of the dream's personal context with parallel and corresponding motifs from myth, fairy tale, art, literature — the cultural storehouse of archetypal images. It is explanation in mythological terms. In focusing upon such traditional and collective motifs, amplification elucidates archtypal significance, regardless of the dreamer's familiarity with the mythological context. Myths point beyond themselves to the symbolic transpersonal or suprapersonal dimension. Our unconscious 'knowing', apparently, draws freely from this stratum, regardless of personal beliefs or familiarity (see Chapter 8: Mythological motifs).

The dream of the diamond in the flower is one such example. In Eastern lore the corresponding image of the Jewel in the Lotus, the *om mani padme hum*, points to the union of Yang and Yin, the unfathomable union beyond the worldly opposites, which is the path and goal of spiritual development. Since the dreamer was unaware of both that parallel motif to his dream, and of its significance, neither his associations nor his explanations could respond to it. In such a case it falls to the therapist to supply the relevant explanation of the collective mythological or religious significance, guided by his or her own knowledge of the similar themes, when and if required by the therapeutic process.

It is important, however, to bear in mind that such amplifications, coming as they do from another source than the dreamer, can be applied only tentatively and sometimes not at all. Not only must the analyst beware of intruding his or her own notions and be ready to withdraw or to try a different tack, unless and until the contribution 'clicks;' but also in many instances it is, clinically, a mistake to intrude any archetypal amplification. It may feel to the analysand like deflection by the therapist of personal relatedness; it may confuse the level on which the analysand is working, or lead to preoccupation with mythological elements and 'symbol-hunting' rather than thorough analytic work. The dreamer may feel envious of or idealize the knowing analyst or otherwise use archetypal amplification as a defense against personal feeling or affect.

In turn, at other times, the client may need to hear a story of mythological experience which matches or orders her or his own confusion and pain, in order to be better able to bear it. These are matters for the clinician's judgement. But it is always important for the therapist to know that the archetypal image is present and to feel its presence and the transpersonal depths from which it reverberates (see Chapter 8: Mythological motifs).

In each case the analyst must seek to discover in which specific and particular ways the general mythological motif fits with the particular dreamer's life problems and patterns. To do this the analyst must be guided by the context and perspective on the motif, provided by the dreamer's personal associations and explanations. They determine and sometimes even overrule the therapist's ideas about the way the mythological amplification is to be understood.

The mythological motif in a patient's initial dream refocused the therapist's awareness of the case from the presenting problems of 'an absent father and some difficulties with [his] girl friend' to an underlying deep-seated fear of devouring aspects of the mother complex. In the dream the dreamer finds that

> My right hand is held in the jaws of a downpointing, abstractly triangular wolf head, and I cannot get it out.

There were no personal associations forthcoming from the dreamer; no affect. Yet the therapist's knowledge of mythological material permitted an approach to the image, which allowed her to make silent hypotheses, and to explore them with the patient. The dream image is a parallel, but distorted, version of the myth of the Norse god Tyr, whose hand was given as hostage into the mouth of Fenris Wolf, because the god wanted to trick the monster into allowing itself to be shackled. In the dream the monster wolf with its aggressive-devouring potentials is distorted and reduced to an abstract, downpointing triangle, emblematic of the feminine. The dreamer, in the position of Tyr, is imaged as endeavoring to shackle the instinctive energies of the wolf, which in childhood he experienced coming towards him from a psychotic mother, by reducing them with intellectual defenses that decapitate and abstract. He wards off — in projection — his own embodied expression of rage and dependency energies as he seeks to shackle them. The dream places him as the heroic god in the process of sacrificing his own right hand — his outgoing, 'sword-wielding,' assertive capacity. But, unlike Tyr, who was willing to have his hand bitten off, the dream-ego cannot get his hand out by releasing the 'monstrous' energy from its bonds, nor can he bear to lose his hand — give up as sacrifice his defensive–trickery position. He is stalemated trying to tie up his own problem. Denying the strength of the negative mother complex's hold on his life, he is equally in danger of losing his own capacity for assertion by remaining caught in ineffectual trickery. Because the female analyst soon realized that his work with a woman kept him in his stalemate, she referred him to a male colleague, who could more effectively support ego development without arousing old fears and paralyzing defenses.

THE THERAPIST'S RESPONSES

The fact that the therapist is asked always to subordinate his or her own associations, explanations, and amplifications to the dreamer's does not mean that they are to be dismissed out of hand as irrelevant. Quite to the contrary, the encounter between two people never occurs without unconscious mutual psychic participation and the activation of corresponding, interlocking complexes. The analyst's reactions while a dream is being told or worked on may sometimes be regarded as 'induced' by dream and dreamer. They provide material revealing affect patterns constellated by the dream 'field.' Hence, the therapist's countertransferential material and associations[6] may, indeed, point to hidden dynamics, and even sometimes may provide the substitute for an association of the dreamer's that happens not to be forthcoming.

It is, however, in dream work as in all therapeutic interactions, of utmost importance that the therapist carefully monitor his or her own countertransference reactions to sort out what belongs to his or her personal complexes and might contaminate any interpretation offered to the dreamer. For the therapist's reactions may 'belong' to the therapist alone. Hence, it is important that he or she wait until the dreamer's context can first be established. Only after its careful evaluation, in terms of associations and affect responses, is it safe to decide whether the therapist's associational and amplificatory contributions, which now are emerging by psychic induction (projective identification) as elements of the countertransference, do indeed belong to the dreamer's material. Otherwise they need to be worked through by the therapist him or herself as his or her own problems aroused through resonance with the dreamer-analysand's complexes.

Thus, if, in listening to our above pill-with-deer dream, the therapist notices an anger reaction arising in him or herself at the discussion of the STOP sign, the therapist needs silently to ask: whose anger is this — mine or the dreamer's? Only when the therapist has adequately worked through his or her own problems with 'stop' may he or she decide which measure to ascribe to the dreamer, who may have remained completely calm, either because there is no affect forthcoming, or because, perhaps, he is still out of touch with his own anger reaction. Only with the precautions of such careful sorting can we avoid the opposite pitfalls of either missing important contributions from our own unconscious reactions, or the ever-present danger of foisting our own problems and biases upon our client under the guise of objective dream interpretation.

Chapter Six

COMPENSATION AND COMPLEMENTATION: OBJECT AND SUBJECT LEVELS

COMPENSATION AND COMPLEMENTATION

Working with dreams over time establishes and maintains equilibrium among patterns of constantly changing psychic energies. It permits a kind of ecological balance both within the psyche and between an individual striving for awareness and the experience of the outer (objective or projected) environment.

This is not because dreams release tension and serve as wish-fulfillments — which is the classical Freudian position. Nor is it easy to maintain the classical Jungian position that every dream is compensatory to the conscious ego position, for we are increasingly aware that there are many levels to the sense of self, as well as many aspects of identity. 'Ego' is not easy to define — much less to experience. And often our severely wounded or regressed clients have only a grandiose, diffuse, or fragmented sense of identity and cannot find a consistent ego position (due to splitting or lack of development).

Jung himself spoke not only of dreams which *compensate* or *complement* the conscious situation, of dreams which add a perspective so at variance from the conscious position that the two are in conflict, of dreams which challenge and aim at changing the conscious orientation, but also of dreams that are more or less unrelated to the conscious position. These are *prospective* dreams,[1] ones which anticipate in the unconscious, future conscious achievements, and, thus, for example, provide solutions to conflict in allegoric or symbolic form.[2] Sometimes these are seemingly *oracular* and are considered to bring enlightenment. Alternatively, they may occur as a prelude to psychosis. Jung also spoke of *parallel* dreams, 'dreams whose meaning coincides with or supports the conscious attitude.'[3]

All and any of these various possibilities can be seen as ways of presenting the *'situation as it is.'* The dream source, whatever that may be assumed to be, operates as if our conscious views were incomplete and in need of being supplemented. In this sense, dreams may be said to *complete* the situation. The most frequent, even though by no means the only, ways of completing are compensation and complementation.

Compensation and complementation are overlapping concepts. They refer to a balancing correction of the one sidedness of the conscious position and viewpoints. In compensation this occurs by bringing forth, often in exaggerated ways, the polar opposites of our conscious views. A situation of which we happen to take too optimistic a view may, for instance, be presented as quite dismal. Thereby, the dream may imply that the situation *is* dismal; or it may simply show the 'other' side, namely that such a potentially dismal aspect is being overlooked or not sufficiently taken into consideration.

Complementation adds any missing pieces, not necessarily the polar opposite ones. It tends to complete or at least widen our views. It says: look also at this and this and also that. The functions both of complementation and compensation serve to correct our blind spots. Both work for a widening of awareness and for the overcoming of fixed positions in favor of change and growth of the personality.

It may appear as though the Guiding Self ever and again were bent upon challenging our existential positions and, particularly, our unawareness of our ways of being and of the implications of our behavior. Challenge is offered when the ego is confronted with unexpected views that threaten to overthrow a false or counter-productive sense of stability. Or sometimes a dream presents complexes of the dreamer which are threatening and need to be stood against by an increasingly coalesced and stronger ego position (see below).

In trying to improve and extend our awareness, a dream may confront and challenge us with images of present situations, personal affects, and character tendencies which we happen to overlook because we are not able or do not care to see. It may expand our views by bringing up past feeling experiences which were repressed, and developments likely to arise in the future from our present stance. All of these, however, are to be considered in their effects and significance upon the here and now.

A dream may complement our views of ourselves by bringing up painful experiences of recent or childhood past. Such experiences may be either directly referred to by the dream or reached by means of the associations or explanations which the dream elicits. Thus the dream reconnects us with feeling qualities that, currently, are repressed or denied.

A young man, ostensibly quite self-sufficient and without many personal relationships, the need of which he persistently denied, dreamed:

> My next door neighbor tells me of his intention to give his little son a puppy for Christmas.

The associations led the dreamer to memories of loneliness at an age corresponding to the neighbor's child and of his own, then unfulfilled, wish to have a pet animal to play with, as well as of his shyness and sense of inability to find friends. These feelings of loneliness, longing for relationships, shyness, the sense of inability to connect with others and depressive sadness in response, had been inaccessible in the present — overlaid as they were by the defensive sense of self-sufficiency. But as of the past, they could easily be remembered. By reconnecting with these past feelings the dream complemented or completed the view of the 'situation as it is' now, at the time of the dream, and offered an avenue of approach for the dreamer to discover these feelings under the cloak of his defensive self-sufficiency.

Often dreams point to neglected aspects that are of positive value when the ego is hated or devalued and the shadow is generally positive. These images reveal aspects of the dreamer's psychology currently available to be integrated within conscious comprehension to support areas that need shoring up. Examples of hungry or neglected dream figures are not then uncommon. Or the dream may present an image far from consciousness, but complementing the dreamer's sense of identity. In one example:

> An Indian woman walks alone on a huge prairie.

This dream image appeared to complement despair and 'lostness' in a self-hating woman, who had begun to realize that her grandiose ideals of her intellectual capacities were unworkable. It suggested to her a mode of 'being with nature' which could orient 'in ways [she] didn't know how,' but which would transform her felt aloneness into a 'being with,' as she put it. The scene was presented as distant from the observing dreamer with no dream-ego related to it. Relationship to the Indian occurred in the following months as the dreamer began to study Native American culture, employing her good thinking capacity toward new goals, and as she found new ways to relate in the transference.

Sometimes the dream offers support through 'parallel dreams,'[4] where the dreamer's insecurely held, conscious views are supported. For example, a dreamer ambivalent about a certain course of action dreams that she is carrying the task through successfully. The dream in this case supports a still uncoalesced ego position or intention.

OBJECT AND SUBJECT LEVELS IN DREAMS

By bearing in mind the likely complementary function, we might be helped at times in deciding whether a dream is to be looked upon as pertaining to subject or object level. We might decide in favour of that level on which it would most likely fulfill a compensatory or complementary function, on which it would provide any information or insight hitherto unavailable and at variance or contrary to the conscious outlook. The above dream (referring to the neighbor and his son) would appear quite trivial when looked at on the object level. The associations clearly point to the dreamer's own feeling problem.

But it is not always that simple or obvious. The following dream:

I am being threatened by a friend's aggression

would have first to be examined on the object level, namely, as a potential warning about that friend's real feelings and intents. But this would be relevant only if the dreamer has always fully trusted that friend. If the possibility or reality of such a threat were already a conscious suspicion, this interpretation would not account for any complementary function of the dream because nothing new would then have been added to the conscious view. Only if the dreamer considered the situation to be safe, harmless, or irrelevant would the object level warning be likely to apply. However, should the dream's message seem to repeat, or even confirm, a conviction already held, only a subject level interpretation would be truly complementary or compensatory. Only thus would previously unavailable information be found. In this case it would confront the dreamer with his or her own unrealized or relatively minimized aggression, which is represented as posing a threat to his or her overall functioning rather than being a 'friend,' namely a supportive function, at least in the current state of unconsciousness. This threatening aggression is shown by the dream as being projected upon the suspected friend.

A projection is the expression of an as yet unrealized unconscious tendency, seen in the image of an external object or person that most adequately represents it to the dreamer. Hence, hate may be represented in a dream by, for example, a poisonous snake or by a person that actually is full of hate. In waking life the projection is marked by intense affect and overreaction to the object or person. To the extent that the projection is not assimilated the reality factor to which it attaches itself cannot be correctly or adequately assessed by the dreamer.

A dream of seeing oneself or another person cutting recklessly into traffic and being knocked down may point to a tendency of which the dreamer may be unaware, that he or she does in fact behave this way in traffic, or metaphorically in the traffic of life. On the object level the dreamer should become aware that such a habit might lead to an actual accident. But the dream may also be valid on the subject level, given the fact that she or he is unaware of the tendency toward impetuous 'cutting in.' It may point to the relationship of the ego attitude to the 'psychic traffic,' that is, to the current of life within his or her own psyche. The dreamer may have an overbearing manipulative or recklessly controlling power attitude toward the unconscious. In terms of practical psychology, however, as this example shows, these two interpretations are frequently synonymous. It is precisely such a reckless ego attitude that will lead to this particular behavior in actual traffic. This dreamer may be an accident-prone person who is being warned of the likelihood of an accident, and she or he may also be a person who will actually meet with an accident upon the stage of life.

Often it is quite obvious that on the object level an interpretation would be not only devoid of new information but, indeed, quite trivial. If the dream is

> My long deceased grandfather converses with the candystore
> owner from my childhood,

this will hardly make much sense on the object level. In such a case the dream can be taken directly to refer to a possible subject level complex. There, it is likely to be complementary by expressing a personification of unconscious partial aspects, partial personalities, drives, affects, etc., as represented by the images of those objects and persons in the dream action.

Invariably, when a dream repeats the day events, it is to be understood on the subject level.[5] Taken 'objectively,' it would constitute merely a meaningless repetition of something known and remembered. An exception, of course, would be a dream that brings up day residues which were forgotten or minimized, or were associated with feelings, subsequently denied but important for an adequate evaluation of a situation in question. A dream may recall to awareness a gesture, remark, or affect, one's own or another person's, that, carefully considered, may change the dreamer's view of the situation. In emphasizing such a disregarded detail, the dream would complement the situation. Such bringing up of day residues is really the same process as pointing up a current feeling by reactivating relevant past memories, as described above in the dream with the puppy (see also Chapter 9: Technical points).

DRAMATIZATION

In their compensating challenge dreams often appear to exaggerate and overdramatize. In depicting the tendency to repress a certain quality a dream may show the dreamer murdering a person who carries the projection of that quality for him or her. Or, someone of whom the dreamer happens to hold a rather low opinion may appear in the dream as a saint, or intellectual giant.[6] The dream's compensation is roughly proportionate to the dreamer's own deviation from the truth of the situation. Our too little is responded to by a proportionate too much and vice versa. We may compare this to having a green object that I happen to see as blue, represented in the dream not as green but as yellow. For, blue and yellow together make green. Similarly when the dream following in a series shows a repeated image increasing in number or size or archetypal context, it is a call for the analyst and dreamer to pay attention to that element, which may have been overlooked or incorrectly assessed as insignificant. Thus in a dream series the ignored motif of a beggar, who looked like the dreamer's brother, as a figure leaning against a doorway reappeared in a following dream as a toll-booth operator on the road to 'Lone Mountain.' When this was still not adequately assimilated, a nightmare provided the image of colliding stars that made the dreamer feel the lonely terror of human existence.

The dream compensates and complements by overrating as one sidedly as the dreamer's conscious view underrates, and/or vice versa. Failure to take this into account may make us miss meaning and proportion. In particular, we may become unduly alarmed by overdramatizations, dreams depicting catastrophes, murder, mayhem or what not. Such dreams, usually, are trying to 'rub it in,' in the face of relatively insensitive consciousness. When we are not aware of this compensatory tendency, we may wrongly assume a finality of dramatic outcomes where there is no more than a temporary compensation of a particular attitude held by the dreamer at the present moment. Reflecting back over the series of dreams leading to the current one is invariably helpful in such cases.

An example of such a complementary tendency is expressed in the dream of a man who dreamt of his wife as a violent shrew. This corrected his conscious assumption that both she — outwardly — and his own inner feeling approach were 'unperturbable and benevolent.'

Viewing the dream as 'completing' and complementing, if not compensating, is at variance with the traditional, classical concept of psychoanalysis which regards the dream as a manifest and censored version of a hidden wish or fear. At times, a dream may indeed quite obviously, even brutally, depict a fear or wish — and in quite an 'uncensored' fashion. But this is most likely to occur when the bringing up of the fact of that wish or fear would complement the dreamer's view because such wishes or fears are not in consciousness. On the other hand, seeming wish or fear dreams that to all practical purposes restate a consciously held position will reveal more significant meanings when looked upon as subject level compensations or complementations. For instance, dreaming of being in bed with a much desired woman may make one aware of this desire, on the object level, when this desire has been repressed or not yet reached consciousness. But suppose that the woman happens to be the Mona Lisa or a version of the dreamer's dead grandmother. Or she may even be an actually desired woman and the dreamer happens to be aware of the desire. In all of these instances an interpretation as wish-fulfillment makes little if any sense. Nor does it offer much, if any, new information.

Such dreams will reveal a deeper and more significant meaning when investigated from the angle of complementation or compensation on the subject level. The woman in question would then be taken allegorically or symbolically as an inner figure or part-personality representative of the particular qualities and life attitude ascribed to her by association, explanation, and amplification. Dreaming of being in bed with her would, thus, signify a state of unconscious intimacy or merger with those qualities, whatever they may be — vainness, gentleness, assertiveness or whatever happens to be ascribed or associated to her. Whether such unconscious connection is desired, or already actual, may be revealed by the dramatic details of the overall action or by imaginal work to further the dream (see Chapter 7, Dramatic structure). Looked upon as having psychological significance on the subject level, even the seemingly most trifling or commonplace dreams or fragments can reveal important insights.

It is always helpful to consider a dream inadequately understood unless and until it has revealed information casting light onto a blind spot, and/or it has challenged a one-sidedly fixed position of the dreamer's (or analyst's) consciousness.

Equally important is the differential diagnostic contribution of the compensatory view. Whenever conflicting/different possibilities of interpretation present themselves, the one likely to be most appropriate for consideration is the one that is most clearly at variance — or opposed — to the dreamer's position and perspective. This makes it clear why no adequate dream interpretation is possible without equally adequate knowledge of the dreamer and his or her problems and psychological functioning. Conversely, by asking what this dream might compensate, light may be shed on aspects of the dreamer's psychology that were hitherto unknown or overlooked.

Take the previous rebus dream example with its STOP sign on the desk. If the dreamer happens to be identified with an impulsive, impatient attitude, the dream confronts him with the existence of inner or outer limits to his approach. If he happens to be unaware of possible outer obstacles, we would first look for those. If he happens to be in fear of or knows about outer obstacles or even has been in the habit of blaming difficulties always only upon outer limitations, then his attention is drawn now to something that opposes or paralyzes his drives from within; perhaps he is forcing himself beyond his capacities, or does not really care to do what he has been planning. Should the dreamer be rather timid or shy and repressed, the message might read: 'You feel stopped whenever you approach the activity represented by the desk, hence, stop, look, and listen into yourself; perhaps then you can get going.'

In such diametrically opposed interpretative options, serious errors can be avoided when one proceeds on the premise of the compensation hypothesis. But, as always, the dreamer's 'aha' assent provides confirmation of the validity of the perspective taken.

APPLICATION OF THE COMPENSATION AND COMPLEMENTATION PRINCIPLE IN DREAMERS WITH UNDEVELOPED OR FRAGMENTED EGOS

In clinical practice we often encounter dreamers who have an undeveloped or fragmented conscious identity. They have been prevented or safely hidden from developing a focused and subjectively valued identity when their early environment was too threatening. Often they

63

are buffeted by unmanageable affects which have split their consciousness into fragments. The principles of dream compensation and complementarity still apply, but, clinically, dream interpretation and dream work with such analysands must avoid challenging the inadequate ego position, which cannot integrate negative projections because the self-image is already so negative. Often the dream is for the therapist — to point out complexes and dynamics in the dreamer's psychology and the therapist's own countertransferential elements that are interfering with the creation of an environment in which the pre-ego can incarnate (see Chapter 12, Transference reactions).

It is important to remember with such dreamers that there are two aspects of subject level dynamics. The emotion induced *by* a figure or situation in the dream-ego needs *to* be discriminated and dealt with separately from the emotion ascribed to or projected onto that figure. In situations in which the dreamer is inexperienced in psychological work, or has a split or fragile ego position, it is usually safer and more effective for the therapist to deal exclusively with the former until there is a minimal capacity for integrating psychological contents that are foreign and negative to the self-image and ego-ideal.

For example, in the dream of the dream-ego being scolded by the dreamer's mother, it is important to deal first with the sense of unworthiness and helpless rage that may be ascribed to the dream-ego and remembered by the dreamer in situations with the actual mother. Projection is a subjective experience, regardless of the nature of the person on whom the qualities are projected. That person must, however, have provided some hook — small or large — on which to hang the projection. Dealing with those ego-alien qualities as 'other' than the dreamer, and with the dreamer's emotional reactions to those qualities, helps both to coalesce an adequate sense of identity and to correct the dreamer's inadequate perception of objective reality (if the mother was not recognized as a scold). Only later can the corresponding critical and tyrannical tendencies of the mother complex within the dreamer be dealt with to make conscious how these qualities get projected onto the figure of the actual mother and others in authoritative, nurturant and/or therapeutic roles in relation to the dreamer.

The dreams of dreamers with undeveloped or fragmented egos usually depict energies unable to be integrated by the dreamer except in the transferential and countertransferential work, but they show the analyst what needs to be worked on, thus compensating or complementing the therapist's conscious position about the analysis. And they may convey images to help the dreamer's consciousness begin to grasp both potential development and the forces preventing it. In the above example it would be important to explore how the dreamer may have felt scolded by the therapist; or felt unworthy and helpless in relation to powers and idealizations projected onto the figure of the therapist from the mother complex.

The dreams may depict in allegory or symbol the spoilers that attack the bonds between the parts of the dreamer or between dreamer and analyst. They may provide images of sadistic parental complexes, envying destroyers, personifications of unconscious rage, etc. that operate through projective identification in the analytic field as well as in intrapsychic dynamics. For example, a borderline man dreamed:

Outside the therapist's office I am met by a shadowy woman
who laughs as she grabs my parcel of fruit and scratches for my
eyes.

With this image the dreamer began to be able to identify the sensed quality of fear in his experience of his mother, which made his analytic work terrifying and extremely difficult, since the meager fruits of every session were attacked by the savage and mocking thief. Even the fact of this fear had been hitherto unconscious to the dreamer for, as the dream shows, the fear prevented him from seeing both himself and even his fear.

Sometimes the dreams present hitherto unknown fragments of the various split conscious positions, pointing out the facets of what is to become eventually a relatively coherent and constant sense of identity. An example is from the dream of a woman who dreamt of herself under a tree in separated parts. She could not describe the scene verbally, but drew a picture of her limbs, torso, organs, and head, etc. lying disjointed on the ground under the simply-drawn, thriving tree. While the dream-ego identity is dismembered, the strong, archetypal image of the tree of life shelters it and suggests a potential for integration, far from the dreamer, but seeded by the Guiding Self in the therapy process. The image of dismemberment served for several years as a metaphoric representation of capacities to see (eyes), assimilate (stomach and bowels), think (head), act (hands), find her own position (feet), create (womb), etc. All of these were gradually connected together over the years of therapy.

A dream series over many months or years serves a similar function.

Like a set of mirrors around the fragmented aspects, it shows each part to be worked on in turn. The timing of work on the various aspects is indicated by the timing of the dreams themselves.

Chapter Seven

THE DRAMATIC STRUCTURE OF THE DREAM

There are a great many 'average' dreams in which a definite structure can be perceived, not unlike that of a drama.

(CW, 8, para. 561)

A dream is a theater in which the dreamer is himself the scene, the player, the prompter, the producer, the author, the public, and the critic.

(CW, 8, para. 509)

The motif of theater is an archetypal representation of the psyche's mythopoetic activity, which equates existence and dramatic performance. The dramatic unfoldment of energy is a process inherent in life activity. It is not surprising, therefore, that dreams are often structured like dramas,[1] having a theme enacted in a particular setting with dramatic action that starts, reaches an impasse, and resolves into a solution or catastrophe; and the next dream continues the process in a new staging. Crucial for the art of dream work, therefore, is the ability to get a sense of the dream as a dramatic presentation, to understand it in terms of its dramatic structure.

GENERAL OVERVIEW OF THE DREAM DRAMA

In order to begin to discover the psychological meaning of the dream's message, it is invariably helpful to seek a general overview of a dream or a dream series. This perspective on the whole provides a grasp of the theme(s), or particular complex(es) in the dreamer's psychology, which the dreams seek to illuminate. It also shows, in image form, the dramatic interplay of energies as they are constellated. Such a view is furthered by clarifying the main lines of the dream action in the interpreter's mind, noting the 'cast' of dream figures or images, and the quality and thrust of the action.

What *is* happening, what is *not* happening that might be required by the context, and what might be the unusual features of the figures, setting, events, or action — all of these require attention. It may be important to note qualities of change, direction of dramatic development, and kinds of placement, relationships, such as containment, polarization, etc. Often the order of sequence implies a causational chain to be discovered. Invariably it is helpful to group the images mentally according to qualities of similarity or difference. For instance, when there are several different dream figures, it is important to see what they have in common or in what ways they express, polarize, differentiate, and/or vary a common theme.

An example of such variations on a theme occurred in a simple dream image in which the dreamer found her dream-ego lying between her husband and her dog. Her association to the dog was 'affection' and to her husband, 'remoteness.' Thus the dream quickly dramatized the polarization of her psychological attitudes to intimacy.

There is often complementarity and compensation within the drama as the dream images of energy interact. The interpreter needs to approach the drama in terms of these relationships. A shadow figure may complement or compensate the dream-ego, adding hitherto unconscious elements, rounding out, or supporting and furthering.

Often, the major content of the dream drama may include images posed as protagonist and antagonist — juxtapositions of alternative tendencies, emotions, styles, motives, and perspectives. These portray oppositional factors within the dreamer's psychology that need to be seen, consciously related to and, perhaps, brought into balance. Such polarizations are often the basic determinants of the dream meaning. They may appear as separate from the dream-ego, or the dream-ego may identify with one side and need to become conscious of the other. Or the oppositions may be posited as problems to be met appropriately. This may be by combat, yielding, befriending, avoiding, etc., whatever the overall dream story implies for the purpose of establishing or ending a relationship between the dream-ego and those factors or figures. The opposites may be in open conflict, or they may be in any of a number of kinds of relationship, including that of union or 'marriage.'

An example of the common structure of complementarity within one dream, here polarized as opposition:

On the main street of town I find a cage. In it a black goat stands with pieces of raw meat around him. My boss keeps the goat there.

The dreamer's association to raw meat was the frenzy with which the maenads of Dionysus rended live animal flesh. Her association to her boss was rigid, judgemental behavior. This dream links the boss and the goat; one as jailor, the other as prisoner. Thereby it dramatizes that it is this narrow-minded attitude in her which keeps its opposite — a Dionysian (goat), dismembering impulsivity — penned up. But the exposition puts this drama on the main street, suggesting that the dream is about the main or central problem of her psychological functioning.[2]

DRAMATIC STRUCTURE

The dream's overall structure may usually be contemplated in terms of the unfolding sequence of its basic dramatic elements, most succinctly expressed in the form of classical Greek drama: exposition, peripeteia, crisis, and lysis.[3] These can be roughly translated as setting, 'walking about' or development, crisis, and outcome.

Even while we use this conceptual mode of structuring, however, we must bear in mind that, in contradistinction to the dream, drama is an art form that has been consciously crafted and structured in many cultures. And while both drama and dream present unconscious dynamics — at least in respect to their psychological allegories and symbolism — the dream is, in itself, the product of unconscious and non-rational processes in the individual. However, as we make mental notes and dialogue with the dream to grasp it into waking consciousness, we often tend to remember it in the terms of its dramatic structure. As the mind encounters the prerational, it dramatizes.[4]

The fact that we tend to remember dreams in terms of their drama, as stated above, is an expression of the dramatizing function of the mythopoetic stratum of our psyche. It may suggest that the archetypes or 'deep structures' of mental organization, those which help waking consciousness to remember and order dream states, have an affinity for such dramatic patterning. On the other hand, in decompensated and drug states and in severe pathology, such cognitive structuring potentials do not seem to exist, and the dreams reported by dreamers in such states often do not have much or any dramatic structure. At other times, dreams may occur or be remembered as mere, albeit intense, flashes of just one picture or event. Such dreams are as though reduced to merely an exposition or crisis. Such structural matters, themselves, can be diagnostic and are worth further research.

Even when only a single image or sense impression is recalled, that can be explored through its associations, explanations, and amplifications to flesh out and ground the fragment as a dramatic clue or message that must be relevantly grounded in the dreamer's life.[5] This process itself has the drama of great detective work.

Usually for the sake of clarity and deliberate impact in a drama, the exposition (setting of the theme), peripeteia (development), crisis (impasse), and lysis (resolution) or catastrophe, are sequentially ordered. In a dream, however, parts of the sequence may overlap or condense. In a dream some elements may be extended; others, contracted, or presented in rudimentary and/or fragmented form. The exposition may be brief or merely intimated by some detail. The development may be skipped or merged with the crisis. The crisis may occupy most of the activity or be merely intimated. The resolution may be absent or replaced by a catastrophe or impasse. However, for the purpose of understanding the dream, it is extremely useful to separate out and distinguish these four structural elements.

Every drama opens with some problematic situation that is brought to the viewer's attention by the exposition, a *setting* in a particular time and space with particular characters. This states the theme of the play and orients the viewers to the author's perspective on that theme. The problematic situation often refers to some issue that is stuck or fixated, and which presents the starting point for the ensuing development. In a dream we usually find what the problematic issue is by examining the opening setting of the dream. This means exploring the psychological meaning of the affect-laden associations and the explanations that are connected with the dream's particular location in time and space as well as with the qualities of the particular people present, and their relationship to the dreamer. All of this conveys the psychological/symbolic context or focus of the dream. Stating the theme or the problem with which the dream deals is, then, the task of the dream's exposition. *The exposition states the theme.* We may compare it with a business bulletin's or form letter's superscription, 'Re:' which means 'referring to' and which states the basic subject matter of the communication — i.e. appointment, personnel, scheduling, or whatever.

If we take Shakespeare's King Lear as an example, we find that the exposition acquaints the audience with the king's problem: how to distribute his realm among his three daughters by finding which loves him the most. In simplest terms he seeks to relieve himself of the burdens of responsibility while maintaining control.

To repeat a too often neglected fact, in a dream the psychological *setting* is primarily conveyed by means of geographic location in which the dream opens and/or by the initial situation of the dramatis personae in the opening scene. Understanding the psychological meaning of the setting will tell us what the dream is all about.

The setting also puts everything that follows into a specific context. For example:

I am going to a formal reception dressed in sport clothes.

The dream depicts the given psychological situation as 'formal reception' — a stylized meeting of an important personal element. The dreamer's approach, response, and/or adaptation to this setting are shown as problematic in that the clothing is inappropriate and unfitting to the situation. Likewise in the setting of the army, if the dream-ego asks for a special dessert at lunch, there is an implication that the dreamer seeks or expects special sweetness in a setting oriented toward collective duty and discipline, where individualized preferences are not forthcoming.

I am with a group of people. A poem is being read and I carefully keep track of the frequency of occurrence of nouns, verbs, and adjectives.

If the setting were to place this dream into a group of linguists it would depict appropriate behavior. If the dreamer's association or explanation points to a poetry reading in a group of artists, the implication would be of too dryly an intellectual attitude toward the world of imagination and, perhaps, the magical dimension of consciousness.

Without the comprehension of context granted through the exposition, we may interpret bits and pieces but miss the overall issue to which they refer. It is always important, therefore, to give adequate time and effort to the clarifying of as many details and their associations as possible of the opening scene, no matter how trivial it may sometimes appear. For example, although a dream opened in a specific friend's bedroom, the therapist asked only about bedroom, and found that the dreamer associated bedrooms to sexual intimacy. The dream that followed did not make much sense until the analyst thought to inquire about the friend. Then the strong feeling–association regarding her dismissive coldness made it clear that the issue was the impossibility of intimacy due to the dreamer's shadow qualities of dismissive coldness. The full specifics of the setting were necessary to clarify both the theme of the dream and the rest of its development.

Associations, explanations, feeling reactions, and amplifications (if it happens to be a mythological setting) must always, then, be elicited in reference to the opening scene.

A dream opened:

> I am in a grocery store in China. Then I go out, but it is only into mother's bedroom. A strange man is trying to open a closet.

The dreamer was asked to give her associations, memories, and feeling reactions about grocery stores, and/or this particular store. She said, 'Father never was at home. When he did not work he used to hang out at the grocery store.' To China, she associated, 'I wanted to go there once. I guess I felt all alone and desperate. They have strong family ties in China.' To mother's bedroom, the setting of the development, she associated, 'There were always things going on there that I was not supposed to know about; they were always fighting.'

Her explanation — in addition to associations — of grocery store was the place to get any food you need, namely, in modern life, a potential cornucopia.

The setting immediately tells us that the dream refers to the subject of seeking (psychological) food in a distant, and possibly idealized, family context. Subsequently, we can see from the associations that the dreamer's need resulted from an absent father, maternal secrecy, rejection, and conflict — all of which caused her tentatively admitted feelings of loneliness and desperation.

The following dream illustrates how, without considering the locational aspect of the setting, a dream may frequently be misunderstood.

A young man with ambitions to write, yet feeling unable to get on with it, dreamed:

> I am talking to a blonde girl and tell her that my typewriter is inadequate.

His typewriter — by association and explanation — represented his writing tool, hence his writing capacity. To 'blonde' he associated superficiality, lightness, and joyfulness. His equivocation of these qualities is in itself revealing: joyfulness, in effect, is equated with superficiality. We may assume at this point that he tells his light, joyful side (his anima) which he considers to be or which is also superficial, that his writing means are inadequate. But, since this is a view which he is holding consciously anyway, this understanding of the dream would seem inadequate and not take us anywhere. Moreover, what does it mean that he tells this to his joyful or superficial side?

The therapist assumed at this point that, perhaps, a more careful working on the setting might help and asked him where, in what locale the scene was taking place. It was on a field to which he associated the baseball field of high school days. What memories or associations attach to the baseball field? The dreamer stated that he felt extremely competitive and always had to excel and to try to be special.

Now, the dream makes sense. It says that in the locale or frame of reference of always having to be tops and special, the dreamer feels his means of writing to be inadequate and this he tells to his potentially joyful side: that is, he cannot enjoy his work, because, unless he can feel from the very outset that what he is about to produce is going to be spectacular (and obviously, that is impossible), he cannot take pleasure and satisfaction from what he is doing. As a result he feels too inadequate to work.

The expositional detail, often not even mentioned by the dreamer, nor indeed remembered from the dream (and then in need of being imaged afresh), can provide a missing key to the whole dream.

The *peripeteia* or development depicts the beginning of the movement out of the fixation: the trends, dynamics, and possibilities inherent in and likely to make themselves felt out of the issue to which the exposition/setting has pointed. In King Lear it would be the king's unexpected and irrational disinheritance of the beloved daughter because she does not verbalize her feelings and subsequent discovery that the favored daughters cast him out. In the dream of mother's bedroom some action may now develop or some object be discerned to which the dreamer happens to react. In this, as in all other phases, the significance of the developing action is to be comprehended by 'translating' it by means of associations, explanations, and amplification.

The *crisis* is the high point of the drama where the tension of opposing or threatening dynamics reaches the point of culmination. Lear is at the height of despair and madly rages over the heath. The crisis indicates the maximum possibilities, positive or negative or even nightmarish, that are potentially inherent in the development the dream happens to be pointing to.

Finally, the *lysis* — or its opposite, *catastrophe* — indicates the ways in which the crisis could be resolved. At some times instead of resolution a catastrophe is shown to occur. In such a case it shows the unlikeliness, given the present position of the dreamer (as described in the exposition), of a favorable resolution. The lysis shows the possible way out; the catastrophe may attempt to shake up the dreamer's consciousness by an urgent warning or (less frequently) acquaint him or her with an unalterable situation. In a positive sense the lysis shows the direction or goal of the new possibilities to be created/discovered.

A more detailed example enables the application of all those categories:

> I am in a shack, playing with some old toys. The place is dusty and run down but I seem not to care either. I just while away the time. I watch the ants crawling on the floor, over there on the window flies are walking. Then I look in an old trunk for something to read. I want a drink of water but cannot find a glass and do not know where the faucet is. My sister is there too. I ask her what she wants to do to spend the time. I am not sure whether we are bored or not. We talk about this and that; then we seem to be arguing about something. She says something that I don't agree with, it is nothing important but I contradict her anyway and she has to show that she has her own opinions, so we are in quite a fight. Then we hear a noise outside. She says, 'Listen do you hear something?' No I did not hear anything. But somebody is trying to open the door. We don't know who it can be. I look through a crack in the ramshackle door and I can see a guy like a bum. We tell him to go away but he still tries to get in. We put a chair and a table in front of the door but it's no use. Somehow, slowly the door seems to push open, regardless. Then we tell him that it is not the place he belongs to but he does not listen. Now I am really scared and run to the phone and dial the police. No answer. I dial again. Now somebody answers. I ask is this the police? The voice says: 'Whom do you want?' I scream, 'Is this the police?' But instead it is my sister, whose voice comes through on the line. I hang up and try again. Now I am in an office and all desks and wires are all tangled up. I ask them to fix it but they do not seem to listen. They say, 'The police have other business, they cannot bother with you and your problems.' I scream that I am paying taxes, but it is to no avail. Then I see my sister talking to my mother at home; she is talking on an extension line. I tell her to get off because I need to call the police quite urgently. But she tells me she has as much of a right to use the telephone as I, she won't get off. It looks a though she almost

74

wants to sabotage me. Then I see that she exchanges knowing looks with the guy who is trying to come in. Apparently, they are in cahoots and want to get me. She tells me that I never talk to her, even though we just had an argument. Apparently she wants me to talk to her in a different way. I realize that this may be the thing I have to do in order to have her help me, and I wake up.

With such lengthy and chaotic dreams, it is often initially helpful to summarize and, thereby, to discover the main outline of the story. The therapist may do this in his or her own mind or preferably ask the dreamer to do so. For once the main elements are clear, the relevant details can find their fit and proportions within the overall dramatic pattern. Not only does this give a coherent set of images on which to work, it also trains the dreamer to focus. Later specific details can be dealt with as time permits. Simplified down to the skeleton action this dream might read as follows: 'I am in a shack with my sister, playing and arguing. We feel threatened by an invader. I try to call the police but my sister blocks the line by talking with home. I realise that she is secretly allied to the intruder and I will have to talk to her in a way that satisifies her.'

Here the setting is given by the locale and the presence of a person: 'I am in a shack with my sister.'

Being in the shack with her sister states the problem or issue the dream is trying to deal with. What is that problem? We need associations and explanations.

The dreamer's explanation of the shack was a ramshackle, decrepit, neglected, and messy outbuilding. It was the place she tended 'to withdraw to as a child in order to be left alone' when she felt 'misunderstood, unappreciated or unwanted and out of touch' with her family, particularly her mother. There she felt 'safe' but also lonely and somewhat bored, not knowing 'what to do with herself.'

The sister reminded her of playful companionship and petty fighting. These were her associations. By way of explanation, she described the sister as a sullen and rebellious person who, however, in contrast to herself, had managed to find an independent place for herself in life.

This exposition takes us back to a past 'place' of her childhood. However, since the dream always describes the situation as it is, that is, as it happens to be now, in the present, we must assume that psychologically speaking the dreamer still is in that shack, namely (applying the explanations we were given), feeling withdrawn, misunderstood, unappreciated, unwanted, and out of touch. We may further assume that those feelings give her a sense of security but also make her feel bored with life and herself. All of this seems confirmed by her initial behavior in the shack. She is in an existential 'place' of neglect, discord, and messiness.

But she is not alone: in that isolated stance her sister is with her. Trying this on the object level did not lead to anything. The sister lives far away and there is no particular feeling of connection, one way or another. The sister will have to be seen as an inner figure, a part personality or an unconscious 'shadow' attitude, namely an unrealized, sullen, resentful, and rebellious side of herself. (Later we are shown that that sullen rebellious sister shadow communicates with mother: in other words, it is somehow connected with her relationship to, or identification with, a similar set of attitudes in mother.)

In an abbreviated form, the exposition can be read as referring to: loneliness, outcast feelings, and rebellious resentment. The subsequent tone of the narrative itself and its vocabulary ('seems,' 'while away,' 'not sure,' 'no use,' 'somehow,' 'cannot bother,' 'all tangled up,' etc.) reinforce the qualities of tentative vagueness in the dream-ego and her helplessness punctuated by inconclusive outbursts.

This expositional statement of the dream fitted quite well with the facts. The dreamer came from a broken home where she had lived with mother and sister. The mother had had relationships with various men and was harshly neglectful of her children. The dreamer saw herself as a victim of circumstances, beset by failures and frustrations beyond her control. In showing her where she is 'fixated,' the exposition both affirms and challenges her view: she is idling in the place that was a refuge for her child-self. For the adult to continue thus is an anachronism, it is no longer appropriate to spend time and life in bored isolation, feeling herself a rejected and helpless, always misunderstood, victim. Moreover she is shown to be out of touch with what might be of help: her rebellious, but also potentially independent, side.

The setting of the dream provides both a view of the diagnostic situation and an orientation regarding what the following developments pertain to.

The development is the attempted intrusion. The dreamer's associations to the would-be intruder connected him with a mental patient in a half way house in which she once had been a social worker. This man she described as 'a sociopathic, alcoholic delinquent'. He had committed a number of petty thefts; once he attempted to steal her purse. These associations show her as being threatened by being invaded by sociopathic behavior and addictive tendencies, either overtly to substance abuse or, allegorically understood, to day dreaming and escapism. All or any of that may deprive her of her 'purse', the container of her identity papers and money — metaphorically her identity and energy.

We have not yet explored the affect motivation of that figure of the intruder. Why, in her judgement or association, does he behave like that? What is the motive for his sociopathic behavior? As she sees it in him, it is a deeply felt sense of deprivation and emotional neediness. This neediness is trying to reach her; negatively, as sociopathic behavior, positively, through awareness of her dissatisfaction as a spur to willed action on her own behalf.

The latter positive implication arises from amplification of the intruder figure as such. The intruder is an archetypal image. It is a frequently recurring, mythological motif in dreams (e.g. 'The Shoemaker and the Elves' in Grimm's tales). When confronted, accepted, and properly related to, the threatening intruder frequently turns out to be a helpful friend and benefactor.

Whereas the setting pointed to the past roots of the present problem, the development shows the current movement or tendencies arising from the problem and leading to a stalemate or threatening impasse. The crisis is the high point at which the conflicting forces are most tensely opposed and at which a decision or turn of events, one way or another, must occur. The crisis may be said to show present or future. It shows what the development is aiming at or is already in the process of establishing.

In this dream the crisis occurs when she cannot get help from the police, the collective guardian principle of law and order. The police's function is to enforce a generally valid, not an individual, principle of order. They are not psychologically available to her, nor can such an attitude deal with that intruder problem. Attempting to do what generally is considered 'right' is represented here as an inadequate answer to the problem of unsatisfied neediness and passive-aggressive escapism. Another more individual way of dealing with the intruder must be found if the threat is to be neutralized.

In this dream the possibility of such a lysis is hinted at in the dreamer's awareness that she will have to talk to her sister in order to enlist her help and, thereupon, 'wake up.' The sister, representing her rebelliousness, is not only allied with the intruder but also connected with 'home,' with the core of selfness. She is also in contact with mother in response to whose promiscuous behavior our dreamer adopted an oppositional stance of inertia, 'lest she be like mother.' To relate consciously and acceptingly to her rebellious side would lead to a psychological 'waking up.' (At the end of the dream she, indeed, did wake up.) This we would consider a favorable development, hence, a lysis. In connecting with her shadow problem, and giving responsible expression to her rebellious, potentially delinquent, needy side, even at the cost of the risk of being like mother, she would be connecting with 'home.' She would discover her true identity which, while she relies on a 'false ego,' is denied and can express itself only negatively and destructively. Instead of day dreaming she might learn to become assertive and work and fight realistically for what she individually wants and needs. This would be the positive value of the sociopathic energy.

Within the dramatic structure of one dream the energic opposites of the dreamer's psychology are represented: police and sociopathic tendencies, inertia and promiscuity or rebelliousness. Because the opposites are hitherto unmediated, both sides have been polarized negatively. The dream focuses upon this fact and serves to begin to build the dreamer's awareness of their places in her life drama.

The lysis (or catastrophe) always points to the future, to what, while not yet in actual existence, is in the making, is possible or even likely. Crisis and lysis (or catastrophe) hence may also be prophetic, not only subjectively but also on the object level. However, only by hindsight can one be sure that a particular message was to foretell outer, object level events. Except for hints that could be read as possible warnings about overlooked objective factors, it is best to deal with apparent prophecies as subject level, psychological possibilities. These may show what is potentially available as an answer to the challenge or as a way out of the difficulty; but they still need to be acted upon in real life. Taking the dream message seriously and into life will help to make the favorable aspects of the prospective function become conscious reality and, equally, it will help to avoid what the dream has been warning about.

Solving a problem only in dream is not sufficient. An equivalent activity in waking life must still follow. Relating to a dream merely with abstract understanding or even emotional insight is not enough. It requires our living with the images and messages and attempting to work with them responsibly and realistically in daily life. The dream shows us where we are, how we may be amiss, and what possibilities and ways are open to us; but unless we also attempt to test those ways by going with them and wrestling with their difficulties, the dream message is in vain.

Chapter Eight

MYTHOLOGICAL MOTIFS

It may easily happen that a collective idea . . . is represented in a dream only by a subsidiary attribute, as when a god is represented by his theriomorphic attribute . . . [or] the 'goddess' appears as a black cat, and the Deity as the *lapis exilis* (stone of no worth). Interpretation then demands a knowledge of certain things which have less to do with zoology and mineralogy than with the existence of an historical *consensus omnium* in regard to the object in question. These 'mythological aspects' are always present, even though in a given case they may be unconscious.

(CW, 9ii, paras 55, 57)

Archetypes intervene in the shaping of conscious contents by regulating, modifying and motivating them.

(CW, 8, para. 404)

Dreams may present and even be structured by specific motifs from the mythological storehouse of mankind. All such images are archetypal, expressive of basic form and ordering patterns, and symbolic, describing 'in the best possible way the dimly discerned nature of the spirit . . . point[ing] beyond [themselves] to a meaning that is darkly divined yet still beyond our grasp.'[1] They convey the nuclear, collective energy patterns, around which any individual dreamer's complexes[2] are constellated.

Such mythological motifs in dreams represent to human consciousness fundamental principles of form and meaning, ordering patterns of transpersonal and, probably, even suprapersonal, creative power which have been discovered, expressed, and celebrated across the ages in rituals, art, legends, tales, or historical presentations. They represent the ways in which mankind's collective unconscious in its different cultural expressions has responded spiritually, philosophically, socially, ethically, and esthetically to the grand themes of existence. The mythic images emerging into dream consciousness are patterned by the as-such, unrepresentable basic form principles that we call archetypal. They present one way in which these patterns reach our perceptions and underlie our religious rites, emotions, and behavior. Through their appearance in dreams, they enable direct confrontation with the numinous, transpersonal, and ultimately unrepresentable general elements that structure human activity and consciousness — patterns of life, death, rebirth, childhood, development, sacrifice, conflict, suffering, achievement, order, relationships, separation, connection, to name but a few.

Such mythological structures are thematic field configurations. They describe and offer orientation, meaning, and guidance both within the subjective psychic realm as well as in respect to interpersonal relationships and events. As with all dream symbols, these mythological structures can be most helpful, however, only when assimilated in terms of their relevance to the specific psychological and life situation of the dreamer. They need to be experienced in terms of personal, psychological dynamics. Archetypal image and personal complex and adaptation need to be seen and worked on together as mutually interwoven aspects of the individual dreamer's life situation.

Such motifs, arising as they do spontaneously into dream from the vast storehouse of the collective unconscious, are more often than not hitherto unknown to the dreamer.

But while they often resemble parts of extant (ancient or modern) myths or folk tales, they may also be novel products individually created/discovered to resonate with the underlying life themes played out in the dreamer's psychology. For as Jung has aptly written, we all 'dream the myth onward and give it a modern dress.'[3]

In fact, it would appear as though the myth-making or story-telling capacity of the psyche were a powerful organizing and healing factor. By weaving events, hurts, and experiences into a meaningful dramatic story or play they integrate them into an organismic whole of overall functioning.

Archetypal images arise from a layer of the psyche that is beyond both personal consciousness and rational–intellectual functioning. They are transpersonal, indeed often suprapersonal, in that they are representational expressions of patterns of powers that are beyond personal volition, control, and even understanding, operating as they do in a dimension of field awareness, seemingly independent of the limitations of time and space as we know them. Therein they show a close analogy to what we loosely call instinctual functioning in animals.[4]

On the other hand, they also connect us with the dimension of spirit and of spiritual experience. Archetypal motifs, therefore, point to potentials of development, as yet unrealized. Even in the face of the most overtly apparent mis-constellations or frightening imagery, the therapist should remember that the archetypal energies, which currently may form the cores of destructive complexes, are destined to become factors of healing. Rather than being suffered or acted-out in compulsive or obsessional ways, their energies can become available in a constructive fashion, once the conscious, personal adaptation changes to one of careful acceptance and responsible expression of the archetypal 'intentionality.'

RECOGNIZING MYTHOLOGICAL MOTIFS

We may relatively easily recognize such magical–mythological motifs when a dream confronts us with elements which are rationally impossible, in terms of our everyday reality. Sometimes the characters appear or act strangely. Sometimes, as in the examples below, someone is shot in the heart and stays alive, or a cat changes into a raging lioness, which can be appeased by giving her a rattle. Such sorts of behavior occur only magically in myth or fairy tale. We know that we are in the realms of myth and magic in the dream, when the underlying psychic energy manifests via shapeshifting, when flowers can speak and behave like human beings, when animals can turn into princes and princesses, when gods and goddesses appear in animal shape, and cats can grow into lionesses.

While the appearance of such irrational elements clues the interpreter into a need to seek for mythological motifs in the dream, it is also important to be on the lookout for the presence of potent psychic material so disconnected from ego consciousness that it suggests a vast psychological distance and/or severe difficulties in relating the material imaged to the dreamer's daily life.

Such weird irrationality and chaos must not be confused with mythological themes and fairy tales. Mythical and fairy-tale motifs may seem irrational, but they show an overall, inner, formal coherence, an esthetic and motivational consistency, and even a logic of their own. Often, the difference between them and chaotic disorder is akin to the felt difference between a musical composition, even an atonal one, and a wild banging on the piano, or between a Picasso or Klee and a spattering of disparate form or color fragments. Trained sensitivity and experience are required by the therapist, to sense these differences.

When there is a lack of coherence in the dream images themselves or a representation of seemingly unrelated and chaotic elements, this may point to the activity of borderline or psychotic levels in the dreamer. The appearance of stark, grossly impersonal, and/or weird or destructive archetypal imagery in dreams is often indicative of the dreamer's or the therapist's distance or even dissociation from the energy in question. In such a situation, relation to the potential healing factor is unlikely, for as long as such dissociation persists, the energy cannot be channeled constructively.

While myth and fairy-tale motifs, when they happen to be genuine, must not be reduced to mere psychopathology,[5] the appearance of certain mythic themes of destruction (such as scenes of hell, of decay or dismemberment, or of the chaos of the last battle) may signify critical transition phases in the analytic process with uncertain outcome.[6]

Apart from fairy-tale like action, mythological motifs can also be recognized by their quality of seemingly destined, dramatic, encompassing power. They are the images of structures whose basic patterning underlies whole aspects of the dreamer's life. Often their appearance in dreams has a peculiar, slightly otherworldly tonal quality, a 'numinosity,' which creates a sense of awe in the dreamer and/or analyst.

Sometimes, but not necessarily, the mythic dream action takes place in historical or cultural environments other than the present one, or in overtly fantastic time/space. These settings apprise us of the presence of a complex, as far from the dreamer's conscious awareness as the time and place is from his or her current reality. They suggest the presence of a dynamic which is still expressive of, or even fixated within, the frame of reference of that past cultural or historic period. Associations, explanations, and amplifications relevant to that period will be needed.

A dream setting in an early Roman period may, for instance, have to do with the motivational problems and value orientations of fortitude, self-control, responsibility and service to state and community, or negatively, with ruthless conquest urges elevated to the rank of virtue. A rococo atmosphere may bespeak lightness and grace of style or superficial playfulness, but also, possibly, a beginning of enlightenment and rational order, depending upon the kinds of associations and explanations offered by the dreamer.

When confronted with mythological/archetypal dynamics, our judgements of right or wrong, of valid or invalid behavior must be guided by fairy-tale and mythological modalities, rather than by ordinary, every-day rationality. The material thus imaged comes from a deep source far from the dreamer's daily awareness, where the laws of the magic levels of consciousness apply.[7] Sitting on the edge of an active volcano demonstrates irresponsibility by ordinary everyday standards, and psychologically it reveals a high degree of unconsciousness and/or denial of emotional eruption. On the other hand, as pointed out above,[8] in archetypal terms, the motif of volcanic cleft symbolizes an access to the transpersonal Yin/Great Goddess dimension with its death and rebirth connotations. It may point to the capacity for otherworld awareness which comes in terms of volcanic, eruptive emotionality.

Should there be a direct allusion in the dream to a 'supernatural,' mythical or fairy-tale element — say, for instance, a faun-like creature playing near the crater — suggesting Dionysus' companions — or a tripod stool — suggesting the Sibyl who received the oracles — or a mysterious voice issuing from out of the smoke, or even a sense of numinosity and awe, the interpreter's focus would be called equally directly to the archetypal level of the dream's message. The message would then stress the sexual aspect (faun) or the potential prophetic wisdom (sibyl) of the depth source. The image of the inappropriate stance relative to that locale (volcano) warns the interpreter that the dreamer is playing carelessly with the potencies of the symbolic dimension, perhaps with mental games, 'head-tripping,' or 'symbol-gathering.'

While every dream contains allegory and symbols, which require attention and understanding, archetypal elements in dreams require the therapist's sensitive comprehension of the many motifs in the vast mythological storehouse of humankind. It is, thus, generally important for any psychotherapist to increase his or her familiarity with this material, not to rest content with one mythology, which too often is closest to the analyst's own. Such wide study provides material adequate for amplification of a wide range of analysands' dreams.

THE INTERPLAY OF ARCHETYPAL AND PERSONAL MATERIAL

Amplification, as explained above, is a method of coming to an understanding of the dream through linking its motifs with general mythological meaning by comparing these motifs with extant mythological material. Rather than only reducing the dream *ad primam causam*, in terms of childhood events or current problem, it utilizes the

83

dreamer's or therapist's familiarity and associations with the body of traditional myths and stories for the purpose of establishing the likely thrust of the given tale. This serves to integrate the personally-constellated complex with its archetypal core.

Without such sensitive and wide-reaching mythological awareness, crucial elements in a dream may be lost or reduced in interpretation and/or misunderstood or seen only as rational or personal distortions. Equally, aspects of the dream which depart from the mythologically given pattern will not be noted. These are particularly important since the variations invariably call attention to crucial elements in the dreamer's individual psychology that need exploration.

A nightmare repeated with variations over twenty years was brought to therapy by a 38–year–old woman with some borderline features. She was either vague and indefinite, or given to rebellious negativity, often panicky, and prone to self-destructive acts. She dreamed:

> I go downstairs to the cellar. It's dark and terrifying. A man is hiding there. He comes out and stands in front of me. I feel so scared I cannot move. He smiles and shoots me calmly straight into the heart. I don't die. I wake up.

The work began by getting associations to the dream. The dark figure reminded the dreamer of 'a janitor-type.' She described him only as 'terribly silent and threatening.' Janitors, by explanation, 'take care of the building and the garbage, and live in the basement.' Being shot in the heart 'would certainly kill, but here I didn't die at all.'

Dreams usually repeat their messages until they are understood and dealt with in life. This dream had been worked on in previous therapies as a revelation of the dreamer's hidden wish for masochistic gratification and as Oedipally-based fear of penetration by the father-analyst. There is a partial and oblique truth in both of these interpretations, but they failed to touch the essential core of her problem, and what is more, they were therapeutically ineffective. The archetypal themes here are not Oedipus but Hades–Dionysus, the god of the underworld (underground, dark cellar), and ecstasy, and Eros, the heart wounder who does not kill. The nightmare was clearly repeating itself in order to be accurately attended. As a repeated and archetypal dream, it pointed to a basic life problem.

The therapist's amplifications were held silently, according to the basic precept that personal elements need first to be worked through.[9] But by providing orientation to some of the archetypal dynamics behind the case, they served their purpose.

Hades is god of the dead and the rich underworld, where seed and garbage are stored. He is abductor of Demeter's daughter, Kore, and sometimes he is equated with Dionysus, silent lord of ecstasy.[10] In this dream, however, the theme is varied. Rather than being abducted, the dreamer herself descends into the basement underworld, and there meets the threatening male element in her psychology. This descent motif, reminiscent of Ishtar's search for her beloved in the underworld, is mixed with that of Eros–Cupid, whose arrows cause the sweet agony of love. The interlace of themes suggests that there is a drive-impulse in the dream-ego, perhaps connected with a search for passionate love, which takes her out of everyday life, and confronts her with fear of rape and death and with a connection to fated, ecstatic passion.

The therapist wrote down the dream after the session and reflected on it:

> There is a dark and terrifying 'underworld' space, a space filled with what has been related to the level of 'garbage.' This realm is in the charge of Hades–Eros–Dionysus, a power called 'Lord' of ecstasy and love and creativity who is bent upon penetrating her heart. Scared as she is of this power, she can only feel a threat of death in the encounter. However, in keeping with the mythologem and the lysis of the dream ('I don't die, I wake up'), it may be assumed that, in her case, a favorable return to the 'upper world,' namely an integration of the unconscious material into her personal life, will be possible.

The therapist also posed some tentative interpretative questions, but did not, of course, share them with the dreamer. The therapist noted in the case notes:

> In the dream she goes down. Why? And in the unconscious, she is confronted with what is split off in her psychology and feared — a silent threat of death that is also an awakening to what she loves. What is that beloved Mother? an old love? some unconscious passion? . . . The caretaker–ruler, who dwells below, like Hades–Dionysus, shoots her in the heart, penetrating her feeling center — not a 'displaced vagina,' as someone told her — with his own phallic love/power, and yet she does not die, but wakes up. There is, here, the motif of Eros, so the dream message is clearer. . . Was she told that it's unfeeling and selfish to claim what she loves for herself? — The dream puts it that

she needs to wake up to the potential for love, joyous self-affirmation, self-expression, and even love relationship that would become available if she faced her fear and claimed her heart's desire. But she is also afraid of that 'garbage.' What ecstasy was discarded? A lot to wait and see.

The dream setting was unknown, but since it involves a descent to another level, an unconscious or previous awareness, the dreamer was asked to associate to a previous time in her life when she had felt the fear that she experienced in the dream. The dreamer remembered being punished with 'the silent treatment' for defying her mother, and nights of sobbing alone, until she was restored to grace. The therapist silently noted the analogy between the silent treatment and the silent, threatening janitor, and recognized that the fear of abandonment and a punitive animus in the mother complex had intruded into the client's early experience of lovingly accepted self-expression. Nothing of this was said, as yet, however, since the dreamer was involved in emotional remembering. The rest of the session and the following sessions for several months dealt with working through painful memories of her relationship to her needy and controlling mother, guided in part by other dreams that came up.

When the dreamer began many months later to sense the irretrievable loss she had suffered at age 18 in abandoning her potential career as a concert violinist, which she had then rationalized and dismissed as 'selfish and impractical,' the therapist recalled that the nightmare had first appeared when she was 18. Since the dream was, thus, again relevant, it was brought back for the dreamer's attention. Another level of understanding then opened for both dreamer and analyst. This time the dreamer saw that she had defended against claiming what she loved by shooting herself in the heart, rebelliously spiting her own passion for music to avoid feeling it was stolen from her by the narcissistic mother. She began to mourn. The therapist silently noted a further insight derived from the discussion of the dream and the remembered historical material:

With good reason she fears to receive the dark god's ecstatic energy, for she was cut off from maternal holding and then cut herself off from the vessel of art which would enable her to contain and mediate it into life creatively. Because she had no maternal nor creative grounding for transpersonal energies, they, thus, threatened to overwhelm her ego vessel. Repressing artistic expression to spite and deprive her mother (or as a love offering also to the bond with her mother, as suggested by the shooting in the heart), she can only experience the terror of death before the transpersonal. Equally she cannot receive sexual passion within the security of a maternal or body vessel, which could support/contain ecstatic pleasure.

After many weeks of despair and rage the dreamer mentioned the dream indirectly, wishing that she had, indeed, died rather than killed off her gift. In working through the dream again in analysis, she realized that reclaiming the passion that she had felt for music would redirect her life. Along with its repression, she had put away a capacity for intensity that now seemed both frightening and desirable. She realized that she was terrified even of the memories of pleasure that playing the violin brought her. This fear of the unmediated awe and ecstasy, she began to see, was the underlying reason she had had to turn from her own musical gift and had remained in bland relationships. Over the next years she began to take responsibility for opening her heart to the pains and joys of Eros–Dionysus as the archetypal energy manifested through her personal desires and passions. Thus, she was able to realize the message of the repetitive dream in the enrichment (Hades–Plutus is also god of riches) in her life.

The above is an example of the sometimes slow work necessary with one archetypal dream over several years, each time deepening and getting closer to being touched by the archetypal, healing core of the complex.[11] However, in clinical practice the personal and archetypal are often manifest simultaneously, side-by-side in dreams of the same night, and, as always, both 'big' and 'little' themes and dreams need to be attended carefully.

A highly successful business-man who suffered from intermittent spells of depression, feelings of alienation and emptiness, alternating with manic periods of excited fury and destructive hostility, brought the following dreams from the same night:

My business partner long ago left his wife and children, so now he has to declare bankruptcy.

The family cat has gone on a wild rampage, biting and clawing at whatever got in her way. I feel that this was because I had failed to pay attention to the animal. As I try to restrain the cat, she grows bigger and bigger to lion size and shape. I fear there might now be a threat to life and limb unless I can propitiate her by giving back her rattle.

The first dream's action is within the sphere of the relatively common-place, at least as far as dreams go. Certainly, abandonment and bankruptcy, while they are archetypal events, are conceivable as personal, everyday life occurrences. Since, however, no part of this dream's action applied to actual events, nor to the actual person of his business partner, it was clear that the dream is an allegorical description of subject level dynamics. It was necessary to discover the qualities of the business partner — as they applied to the psyche of the dreamer — in order to see what qualities had cut him off from feminine relationship (wife) and the fruitfulness of future development (children), and had made him psychologically bankrupt, without possible energy to further the dreamer's business of life.

The second dream is more complicated. Here we are confronted with events which are rationally impossible, in terms of our everyday reality, but are consistent with mythic and fairy-tale dynamics. We are, thus, alerted to a mythological–magical motif, and our everyday, rational standards of evaluation must change.

A cat that can change into a lioness is not an ordinary cat. In the dream drama, this change follows the dream-ego's attempt to restrain the cat. Hence, on a personal level, such restraint, attempted discipline, or repression may be seen as the psychological cause of the shapeshift: the rampaging cat, restrained, becomes more powerful. But that such change occurs at all suggests a fairy-tale or mythical realm where magical order obtains, hence the need for a symbolic, not only metaphoric/allegoric approach.

What is absurd in ordinary reality may be possible, make sense, or even be helpful or required behavior in a particular myth or fairy tale, even though not in another one. In each dream instance, then, we have to discern what particular ways of reacting and behaving are likely to be called for by the mythological situation confronting us. That means, we must always must first identify the action, thrust, or goal of the particular story referred to by the dream structure and events. This we can accomplish in two ways: by mythological amplification and by fantasy: active or guided imagination.[12]

In any dream the significance of an image will be determined by what it 'is' and by what associations happen to occur to the dreamer.

Metaphorically or allegorically, in terms of associations, the image of a cat in a dream may refer to personal experiences with cats, to a specific pet, on which the dreamer's projections fell, or to the memory of a particular situation that occurred with a cat. It may be sharp-clawed or playful or erotic. It may remind the dreamer of grandmother's parlor or of Tom Sawyer's cure for warts.

Explanatorily, 'cat' is a domesticated animal, hence it represents an instinctive energy and a sense of being fully one with the body, but an energy that is relatively 'domesticated' and in close relation to consciousness. Furthermore, by contrast to dog or horse, the cat behaves independently, moves sinuously, sees at night, plays with its prey, etc.

Symbolically, the cat images a theriomorphic 'divine' power of spontaneous autonomy, devouring and playful, generative and reactive in nature, a particular quality or aspect of embodied, instinctual, transpersonal energy.

In this dream the image of the pet cat changing into a roaring lioness can be amplified with the ancient Egyptian myths of Bast and Sekhmet. Both were considered aspects of the same archetypal feminine power. Bast, the cat goddess, was a goddess of joy, dance, music, and playfulness; she represented the fertilizing power of the sun. Sekhmet, the lion goddess, the 'Mighty One,' as she was called, symbolized the scorching, destructive power of the sun. In the myth, her fury at the hybris of false priests became uncontrollable blood-lust. Had not Ra, the supreme solar power, given her an intoxicating drink, which led her to 'making love, not war,' her rage would have led to the destruction of all humankind.

The probable allusion to Bast and Sekhmet is also borne out by the dreamer's association to the rattle which he was to restore to the cat. He described it as 'something like an upside down horse shoe with a handle.' It made him think of a rattle he used to play with as a little child. The noise of this rattle, he remembered, disturbed his mother, and she had told him that she had had to take it away from him. In ancient statuary we find such a 'rattle' in the hand of Bast. It was called her 'sistrum' and was used in festival processions involving music and dancing, which honored the goddess.

Thus, in this instance, the dreamer's associations coincide with the therapist's amplification; they seem to fit the same mythologem, which, therefore, may be used for interpretation. When this is not the case, the therapist has to search further. It would be highly inappropriate for the therapist simply to use what she/he considers the fitting mythologem, regardless of whether or not the dreamer's associations happen to be congruent with it. Such a way of proceeding would constitute the foisting of a foreign element upon the dreamer's material.

When the thrust of the story cannot be established by amplification through linking it with an extant story or motif, the dramatic context may equally well be found by 'active' or guided imagination. With either technique, the dreamer is encouraged to complete the dream's story by fantasy or outright inventiveness. Any form of story-making rests upon unconscious activity, regardless of the storyteller's conscious intentions; hence it serves to complete the dream story and establishes its dramatic intent.

In our case the dreamer's fantasy imagined the lioness turning back into a cat and playfully nestling in his lap, purring and playful, once the rattle was restored to her.

We can now attempt a preliminary interpretation of the mythological motif which this material has presented us with, so far: cat and lioness are 'divine,' that is, transpersonal powers. (Here they coincide with motifs in Egyptian religion.) Gods are represented in theriomorphic, animal forms because each animal species was held to represent a typical, transpersonal essence. It is relatively 'pure' in that particular species, and, therefore, god-like. This essence was presumed to be only partially present, diluted by other factors, in humans. The cat power or cat nature is presented here as disregarded or neglected. (The dreamer failed to pay attention to the cat.) In terms of the dreamer's associations this had to do with playfulness and bodily closeness to others and taking pleasure in one's own body. In terms of the historical Bast figure this also would refer to joy and enjoyment. Disregarded, these instinctual needs become vengeful destructive forces which threaten — in the myth — to destroy humankind, namely the dreamer's humanity as well as his relations to other human beings. Repression and denial, as well as ego 'inflation,' invariably invite psychopathology within, and potential catastrophe without. In turn, respectfully related to and given its due — in this dream the rattle/sistrum that is the goddess's property — threatening power can be appeased and even transformed into life supporting energy.

This dream gives us a symbolic overview of a leading 'leitmotif' in the dreamer's present situation, if not of his whole life. But dealt with only archetypally, the interpretation is not specific enough. At best it leaves us with the question of how and where the ego hybris is to be sought. (Hybris is implied by the mythological amplification: Sekhmet's task was to punish the false priest's disregard of the gods.) At worst, it may be heard by the dreamer as sermonizing about abstract philosophical or religious principles. In order to 'ground' the symbolic overview we must connect it with personal material that would show us in what particular concrete actions or attitudes the 'neglect of the cat' has been taking place.

Such *personal grounding* we can accomplish by means of those 'ordinary,' personal, non-archetypal, allegorical dreams, which happen to coincide with the archetypal ones, and/or, as in the first example, by personal associations to the archetypal one. Usually, such 'ordinary' dreams are not difficult to come by. For every one archetypal 'big' dream there are usually a number of 'little,' that is personal, dreams. If the therapist falls for the temptation to neglect and disregard those in favor of the archetypal material, she or he risks losing the personal anchoring. Frequently, in fact, it may not even be possible to understand the relevance of the archetypal drama as such (an example will be given later) without simultaneous or prior working through of the personal material.

Here the personal dream was brought *with* the archetypal one, and we may *look for structural and thematic similarities*. The business partner's bankruptcy may be taken to be the equivalent of the destruction wrought by the lioness. The associations and explanations given about the business partner made him appear as a person overwhelmingly bent upon achieving success in business and finance, upon acquiring prestige and power, but he was described as emotionally withdrawn, personally inaccessible, and regarding playfulness as frivolous. Looking at himself in the light of this mirror image, the dreamer brought up memories of his childhood struggles of having to close himself off emotionally for protection from being flooded by the depressions and hysterical violence of his mother. Not literally, like the business partner in the dream, but metaphorically, he had 'left wife and children,' in that he emotionally continued to withdraw from feeling connections. He felt lonely and alienated. In terms of feeling and self authenticity he was 'bankrupt:' his affects denied, he was carried away by his manic outbursts like a raging lioness. Expressed in these concrete personal terms, he could now see and, indeed, experience the threat of the lioness and the need of appeasing her with a 'drought' to alter his habitual consciousness by allowing himself to be more open to emotion, and by returning the sistrum — the playful music of the life dance — of which he had deprived himself, as surely as he had been deprived of the rattle of his childhood.

As can be seen from the following example, personal grounding was accomplished by separating out and then interrelating archetypal and personal elements within one and the same dream.

A young woman brought a dream:

> While I am walking on the street, I am attacked by a hoodlum, who snatches the purse I carry. I run after him, now over fields and hill and dale; but, even though the man walks exceedingly slowly, the faster I run, the less I can catch up with him.

The motif of not being able to move effectively, either to catch up or to flee in spite of one's extreme effort, occurs quite frequently in nightmares. It images a sense of frightening ineffectiveness or helplessness.

The language of the above dream, by staging the action with the phrase 'over hill and dale' immediately brings out a fairy-tale mood. But even without this detail the magical quality of the paradoxical discrepancy between the inability to catch a slow walker, even while running faster than he, points to a symbolic motif. It is one well known in several mythologies. A story precisely corresponding to, and thus amplifying, the dream lies in the Welsh story of Pwyll, Prince of Dyved. There, the prince beholds an unknown lady pass by on a pure white horse, 'a garment of shining gold around her.' He sends others and then himself tries to pursue, but 'the greater his speed, the further was she from him.' Only when, after repeated failures to catch her, he speaks to her and asks her to stay for him, does she respond: 'I will stay gladly and it were better for thy horse, hadst thou asked this long since.'[13]

This silent assumption that the robber might be a potentially helpful and transpersonal figure was the result of the therapist's amplification. The therapist had read *The Mabinogion*. The dreamer had not. This fact as such does not preclude the validity of the amplification. The dream, operating as it does out of a dimension transcending space/time and individual awareness, routinely uses facts and motifs beyond and outside of the dreamer's (and sometimes the therapist's) present awareness. However, the therapist's assumptions, associations, and even the amplifications he selects, can also apply to the therapist's psychology. It must never be taken for granted that they necessarily fit the dreamer until this is confirmed as the dream is worked through.

In this dream, as in the preceding example, a suprapersonal power is indicated, one which will not be 'caught' or forced by willful ego effort but demands to be addressed and related to respectfully. This may be said to be the general meaning of the archetypal motif in the dream. But what are we to make of the fact that the 'divinity' or transpersonal power happens to be a purse-snatching hoodlum? And how may this all be relevant to the dreamer's psychology?

Association, explanation, and further amplification are needed to provide answers to these crucial questions. First, what is represented in the image of the purse being snatched? The dreamer described it as her wallet. By explanation a wallet is a container for essential personal belongings — in this particular dreamer's case (which always needs to be ascertained), for personal identification, money, and creditcards. Translated into psychological language, we may regard this wallet as an allegorical representation of the container of her sense of personal identity, available energy, or libido (money) and psychological potential value and/or credibility in the world (creditcards). Nothing less than her sense of personal selfness and identity, her trust in herself and her capacities is depicted as being stolen from her in the dream.

What is it in her psychology that is the thief? To find out, the figure and its action need to be 'grounded' — that is, understood and felt in personal, psychological terms. The figure was unknown to the dreamer.

The dreamer immediately wanted to enact the scene as she had learned to do in her Gestalt training group. Her insistent and hurried style — repetition of behavior in previous sessions — was considered by the therapist to be relevant to the dream's message. It could be later used to bring this message to the dreamer's awareness. On the other hand, since the analyst knew the potential value of enactment and fantasy to ascertain whether or not the amplifications and even interpretations were relevant and valid, the imaginal method was deemed helpful. In this instance, too, the dream is relatively unfinished. There is no lysis. (See Chapter 7, Dramatic structure.) As we have seen, waking imagination can be used to continue otherwise unfinished dreams.

The therapist suggested, however, that the dreamer try to address the running robber instead of pursuing him.[14] As the woman called out to the robber, 'Stop, stop!' she felt nothing happened. Frustrated, as she had been in the dream, she became impatient and increasingly loud. Then she fell silent and looked to the therapist for an intervention. In discussing the impasse, which merely repeated the dream action, the therapist pointed out her imperious and impatient tone. The dreamer had some difficulty finding an alternative. She finally managed, 'Would you stop. I really need that purse. It's not yours, so let me have it back. Please.' At that the thief, in her active imagination, turned around. He now looked to her like a professor from her college days, and she imagined that he said, 'Just take it easy; you need to learn a lot.' When she asked if he would give back her purse, he only said cryptically: 'Walk with me, and you will get what you have to have.'

To find out more about the figure with whom she was to walk, associations were needed. The college professor of literature (revealed when she addressed the hoodlum) was, the dreamer said, 'truly inspiring.' This transformation into a positive figure fits the mythological amplification, but needs still more personal grounding. The therapist asked what was inspiring about him. The dreamer remembered his poetic imagination and sense of slow strength and quietly assertive self-confidence. He seemed to know what he wanted and how to get the best out of his students; thus, she assumed, out of life too. He was strong; yet the strength was paired with a quiet, unassuming, highly sensitive, and responsive adaptation to people and situations.

It is of no importance that her view of the man may have been highly idealized or even unrealistic. As her association to the figure, it depicts her projection onto the professor of an unconscious potential and points out to us the ambivalent qualities of the part-personality represented by the hoodlum, who, as long as she actively and desperately 'pursues,' will continue to withhold her selfness and self-potential from her. Although the dreamer felt robbed by what she first thought negatively was a hoodlum, this figure turns out to be a teacher. The dream's message urges the dreamer to revalue and learn from the teacher's sensitive, strong, reflective style. Rather than feeling robbed of her accustomed defensive, willful rush to control, she will get back her wallet and all that it symbolizes — potentially transformed.

For added clarification it is important to do now what should routinely be done at the very beginning of working with a dream, namely to consider the exposition. (See Chapter 7, Dramatic structure.) The dreamer was asked to describe the place where the beginning of the dream occurred: what was the street and what are her associations to that street? It turned out to be the street to her present employment — metaphorically her approach to her life work. Her associations brought her to her driven, ambitious attitude and to her fears that she needed to use will-power, pressure, and political ploys to further her chronically insecure positions in her job and in her relationships. This anxious, compulsive, and manic style could begin then to be further explored in terms of its childhood antecedents, and its effects on the dreamer's current behavior in relation to the analyst and her own therapy.

Throughout the working on the dream, the analyst had silently been wondering about the transferential implications of the image. Had there been a sense of theft experiences in the last session? Was something projected onto the therapist or the therapeutic process that was stealing

94

away the dreamer's habitual sense of identity and energy resources? Even if the amplification implied that this might be positive and a potential encounter with a transpersonal or Self figure, issues of idealization of the therapist as carrier of the projection and frustration with the process might need to be met and made conscious. The therapist remembered that in the previous session the analysand had talked urgently about her current relationship, seeking advice for immediate implementation. When this was met with a reflective interpretation about her style of compelled and anxious rushing to solve the problem on a practical level, the analysand had lapsed into somewhat depressed silence. The dream follows this interaction as a comment from the Guiding Self on the transpersonal life process (the figure of Horse Goddess in *The Mabinogion* story) as this process is manifest also in the therapy. It encourages further exploration of the feelings of the dreamer after the previous session's encounter, imaging them in a mythic context — as a life problem far larger than the therapeutic relationship, but also manifest within it.

Ultimately the conclusions gained from exploring the dream's transferential implications on both personal and archetypal levels should also be cross-checked by other methods such as enactment, guided or active imagination, careful work to elicit associations, explanations, and amplifications to ground the symbolic and allegoric images of the dream. Optimally, as in this example, all will intersect to give the dreamer and analyst the same basic message about the analysand's therapeutic process as it is constellated in the current field.

Since the setting of the dream places the problem in her approach to work, the reference is primarily to her style of work and her obsession with willful active work as her style of life. This needs to be explored first. The problem may subsequently be referred to the transference. Had the setting been a metaphor describing the therapeutic process (see Chapter 12: Dreams of therapy and the figure of the therapist), it would need to be explored in the reverse order. For it is, inevitably, most helpful to approach the problem in the way the dream locates it. In this dreamer's case her obsessive defenses against relationship made initial transference interpretations less acceptable, even though they came readily to the therapist's reflection.

Now, we are able to piece all of that information together into a coherent interpretation. The dream's message — as an integration of personal associations and enactments, explanations, and mythological amplification — may be taken by the therapist to read as follows:

In your attitude to life and work — scheming and always trying to push ahead — your true identity and self potentials and life energy are taken away from you. Thus, your assertive capacities turn against you and you cannot avail yourself of what is yours. Instead of rushing and pushing you need to establish a conscious relationship of 'talking to' and getting to know what is in you. If, instead of rushing and pushing to get back what you have lost, you relate humanly to the thief, you discover that he is a teacher. You discover what he can teach you, by walking with, rather than running after, the figure of the teacher. He has the qualities of the professor who impressed you — qualities of sensitivity, receptivity, poetic inspiration, and also a different kind of strength. These can teach you by opening you to those potentials in yourself, if you will trust yourself to walk with, experiment with the new style.

A like message could, of course, also have been given in an ordinary, personal dream. We may presume that it comes in archetypal, mythic-symbolic terms here, because it is an existential, overall life issue, a 'karmic' problem, that is not yet sufficiently appreciated by the dreamer's present psychological and spiritual context, and perhaps not by the analyst either. This single dream reveals a life pattern that exceeds in significance the present job issue, to which the dreamer associates. It structures her relationship to her partner (the subject of the previous session) and to the analytic process (revealed in her behavior around and during the enactment and in her still unconscious, negative reaction to the analyst's reflective style). Further, the archetypal elements in the dream point to the healing pattern of relationship between ego and Guiding Self, between personal and transpersonal, against which the mis-constellated elements in the dreamer's complexes need to be seen. The myth behind the dream reveals a whole, prediseased or preconditioned structure, which can provide the underpinnings and the lysis of the dreamer's life drama.

What parts of and in what way the message is to be conveyed to the dreamer is, of course and always, to be determined by the style and clinical judgement of the therapist.

Sometimes, dreams that appear in an historical setting — when worked with in terms of current impasses and childhood wounds and amplified by means of fantasy or guided imagination — unfold into or interweave with elements that are felt to be memories of a past lifetime. Such experiences often release powerful affect charges. The dreamer's sense of past life memory should be respected in such cases. But it is also important that the material remain related to, and be understood also allegorically and/or symbolically, in terms of the dreamer's current psychological/existential situation.

A psychiatrist with severe phobic, at times nearly paranoic, authority problems dreamt:

> I am in Spain in a sort of dungeon like place. Black clad men
> are there. I am terribly frightened.

In previous work her authority problems had been dealt with in terms of her memories of a domineering father and her later experiences of being treated by her professors in Medical School with a mixture of patronization and misogyny. After the dream she was invited to focus on the imagery and the excessive fear. There emerged a terror-laden fantasy 'memory' of being interrogated by torture and killed in a prison of the Spanish Inquisition. The flood of terror and despair released in working through this material served as a powerful abreaction. Realizing how she currently reacted to any authority figure as to a threatening inquisitor gave her also a better understanding of her phobia and, hence, some ability to disidentify from its grip on her current life relationships.

DEALING WITH MYTHOLOGICAL MOTIFS

In order to deal with the mythological aspect of archetypal material several steps are always necessary.

First, the mythologem has to be recognized as such. That is not always simple, for the mythological *dramatis personae* do not necessarily appear in the historical costumes, nor in exactly the stories in which we have learned about them in school or in our readings. Usually they present themselves in some fragment or variation of their theme and/or in a contemporary frame of reference. Thus a dreamer was warned by an electrician that he might be accidentally executed by a high tension wire if he did not stop fooling around. This was his symbolic encounter with the transpersonal lord of the thunderbolt and ruler of the energies, Zeus. An 'impressive electrical craftsman' spoke to him, not the bearded Greek god of Praxiteles. Sekhmet appeared as a raging lioness. Cupid may shoot with a gun. The temptation by the devil may be staged as an encounter with a slyly deceitful super-salesperson or job-offering agency. And the victorious Sun hero, threatened by the dark forces of evil, may appear as Superman or J.F. Kennedy. Krishna, the charioteer in the *Bhagavad Gita* (who takes the hero into the battle in which he has to wrestle with his conscience to accept his station in the workings of destiny), may be a wise chauffeur. Building a new apartment house may refer to the creation of a new world. The difficult search for the treasure hard to find may put the dreamer into a ramshackle model-T Ford lugging a Geiger counter through the Arizona desert.

These mythical motifs have to be separated from their past social, political, historical, and cultural encumbrances and recognized in their sometimes abbreviated or even distorted contemporary analogies. This requires adequate familiarity with the chief themes of mythological traditions of the various cultural epochs and cycles, knowledge of comparative religion and anthropology.

Second, dealing with mythological materials requires psychological understanding of their traditional symbolic significances. For, within this amplificatory mode, the range of traditional significance is equivalent to the explanation on the personal level. Thus, the solar hero will refer to some aspect of conscious striving and/or a fertilizing, fatherly principle. Death will usually refer to the dissolution of some existing pattern and/or to transformation through encounter with previously unapprehended archetypal energies. Lunar symbolism generally is Yin, feeling and receptivity-toned, regardless of whether it occurs in a man's or woman's dream, but the dry, weightless satellite of earth, lunar rhythms, lunacy, the old moon–sailor god, Noah–Sin, etc. are also to be considered. Each symbol has a wide variety of possible collective meanings, which require both familiarity and reflective psychological study to help to bring the relevant traditional significance close to its current, particular expression in a modern dream.

Third, imaginative skill is required to adapt those general meanings to the dreamer's specific situation by means of his or her personal associations and explanations. The devil may refer to repressed, 'devilish' stuff that could be redeeming, but it may also be a tempter, a light bringer (Lucifer), or a spoiler. In terms of a particular patient's association, perhaps to Goethe's *Faust* drama, it can be a temptation that needs to be risked for the sake of a renewal of life. As we have seen above, the interlacing of symbolic meaning and personal context is part of the art of psychotherapy. It requires sensitivity to both archetypal and personal dimensions and to their interweavings and points of intersection.

For example, a woman dreamed:

Some men kill a deer. My father is upset, and wants my help.
Then the men come after me. I turn into a boy.

Here we have the motif of Iphigenia,[15] King Agamemnon's daughter. When his men offended Artemis by killing one of her sacred deer, the goddess caused the winds to stop; thus the Greek fleet could not sail forth heroically to conquer Troy. To propitiate the goddess and regain good winds for the journey, Agamemnon decreed that Iphigenia was to be killed. At the time of the sacrifice, Artemis carried the girl away to Tauris as her priestess.

The dream presents elements of the Greek myth, but with a different outcome. In the dream there is no dedication to the goddess. Rather the dream-ego identifies with the aggressor and repudiates her own feminine identity to escape the threat of the controlling, willful father. While such masculine identification was initially helpful for the dreamer's psychological survival, it became a problem in her adult life and was brought into therapy for consideration by this dream.

SOME SPECIAL MOTIFS

There are some basic themes relating to life as a process with particular stages or passages. These occur frequently in dreams when the dreamer's overall life orientation is being presented or re-presented. Among them are the motif of the game, life as a play, the journey or road, the river, the crossing of a body of water by bridge, ford, or boat, alchemical and biological transformations, the dance or ritual, and the themes of vocation, assigned task, household, etc. These motifs seem to occur when problems regarding adequate preparation, commitment, and capacity to decide or participate with full ego intentionality in the struggles set forth by one's destiny are at issue.

Other grand themes around which we create/discover our individual mythologies are those connected to the archetypal rhythms and developments of our bodily existence. Child development and the stages of life, birthing, breathing, touching, being held, feeding, teething and losing teeth, maturing, separating, joining, parenting, dying and rebirthing, etc. all mark the pulse beats of change and transformation. All are dramatic pace setters of our life dramas. In these archetypal experiences, as well as in dreams, fantasies or visions of such experiences, the symbolic and transcendental dimensions merge with and lead to the personal–biographical.

For reasons of space only some of these basic motifs can be discussed and exemplified here. The reader is referred to the vast extant literature on mythological and archetypal symbolism.

THE LIFE PLAY

The drama, at its best, depicts the ritualized, 'just so' of life. Hence its cathartic effect, as well as its attraction in all ages, from antiquity, when it represented the action of the gods or fates, to the present, secularized plays, movies, and TV productions. They all reveal the archetype of life as likened to a show, play, or dream of the deity, a staging of a divinely appointed drama.

The motif of the life theatre (the Greek rootword, *theatron*, meant the stage on which the witnessing audience beheld the spectacle of the gods and goddesses, the creative and destructive forces of life) is an archetypal ritual. In dreams the dream-ego may be shown performing in a play or dance or concert, or watching such performances, at a theater or movie, watching TV, listening to the radio, etc. The dream-ego may be an increasingly distant observer, removed from direct participation in the fated action, and/or a part of a collective or private audience of that action, or may be a passionately involved witness. Participating in the play as one of the actors points toward taking a more conscious and active part in the life drama. However, when the theme is cast negatively (i.e. by repeating the dreamer's conscious identification with a role, it may suggest that the dreamer is acting-out or play-acting a stereotyped part.

When the theatrical motif of 'witnessing the show' appears in dreams — be it in the form of watching a movie, play, TV show, or dreaming a dream while dreaming (a dream within the dream) — an overall Grand Theme of life is presented. The dreamer is confronted with a dominant of his or her overall life pattern. The message is: this is what the 'show,' your life, is all about. Intensely remembered and recurrent childhood dreams have the same significance.

Whatever is played, seen, or heard in these performances points us to the leitmotifs of our life — or at least of the life-situation in which we happen to be at the time the dream is dreamed. Likewise a dream, dreamed in a dream, refers to a hidden, but vitally crucial issue, one with archetypal existential meaning.

Here is an example, the dream of a middle aged woman:

I am watching a movie that goes on and on, ending and beginning all over again. Whenever one goes in one will see it all over again. It is about Richard Burton, who has ruined many women. Now, in the movie, I go into the granary with him. We are to be buried underneath the grain, but I jump out, take him by the hand and walk out, and the whole action starts all over again and again.

The fundamental, existential character of what this dream reveals is here emphasized by its repetitiveness. The dream action seems to imply that the refusal of allowing herself to be buried under the grain with the figure of Richard Burton leads to an endless repetitive impasse.

To Richard Burton the dreamer associated the actor's role in a movie she had seen where he appeared to her as 'a cruel man, cut off from his feelings.' When asked to imagine herself into the state or mood she tended to ascribe to him, she expressed herself somewhat like: 'Everybody is against me. They all are bastards. I can trust no one except myself. So, I'll do anything that suits or is useful to me.'

This attitude, the dream implies, has ruined many women. We might take this to mean that it has ruined her, as a woman, over and again many times and in many situations. Indeed, her tendency to feel victimized, and her grimly resentful, paranoic cynicism had spoiled a great many opportunities for her.

The granary had no personal associations. The therapist's silent amplification was that the granary was frequently the place where the year king accepted sacrifice as the representative of the tribal god. He was killed/buried under the grain to ensure the growth of new crops. The death of the old and outworn was a sacrifice deemed spiritually/magically necessary to bring forth new life.

Unless the dreamer's outworn 'Burton' attitude is given up, she is caught in a repetitive and stereotyped cycle that prevents her life from receiving/finding new meaning. Such giving up would be like a sacrifice. To the dreamer identified as she was with the Burton attitude, it felt like her own death along with the Burton attitude. Her sense of identity had been rooted in this early and precocious defense, which had permitted survival in the face of the hardships of her abused childhood. Thus, she cannot bring herself to give up what feels like giving up herself, and her childhood, with both its defenses and endless hopes for reparation. Since the sacrifice cannot be made, many opportunities are missed and the impasse continues: the show goes on in endless repetitions — until and unless that basic challenge of her life's destiny can be faced.

BIRTH

Birth stages the first incarnation of our life theme. As LSD experimental work[16] has shown, its experience frequently includes a sense of dying or death threat and a sense of what frequently is experienced as memories of past lives and deaths. The transition from intrauterine existence to the onset of delivery is usually experienced as transition from relatively undisturbed cosmic unity to engulfment in a closed system with the experience of 'no exit' or hell. Propulsion through the birth canal has its analogue in a sense of a death–rebirth struggle with ecstasies of aggression, battle, fiery eruptions, blood-orgies, death and sexual arousal with sadomasochistic imagery. The arrival out of the birth canal is analogous to both death and deliverance.

It is not surprising that the particular way the birth process has been experienced and/or is recalled in the course of therapeutic regression, fantasy or dream, carries a fundamental significance for the way life and identity are experienced. Likewise, facing death, either in its ultimate form or in the 'little deaths' of fundamental life changes and transformations, calls forth fundamental existential responses. Similarly, the other biological–archetypal process patterings experienced in infancy (feeding, breathing, being held, etc.) have profound, life-time effects.

Dreams with such mytho-biographical material will call for more than abstract interpretation. They may require direct, even embodied experiencing. Frequently, such dreams are quite cryptic. While they may offer pieces of biographical story mixed with current, personal material, which is helpful in grounding the story, at other times they fail even to elicit associational responses. Often a direct interpretation on subject or current object level is neither possible nor would it plumb the depth of the material. Thus, here particularly, an experiential approach, relying on experiencing in the body and/or fantasy activity, is usually called for.

A middle aged man was uncomfortably stuck in a life situation in which he was unable to come forth with the definite choice it required from him. Avoidance of decision was a life pattern for him. This manifested also in respect to this therapy process, where he spent many hours ruminating about the value of continuing, ignoring interpretations and the presence of his therapist. After some months he brought a dream:

You [the therapist] offer me a treatment, making me curl up and lie on the floor in a most uncomfortable position. After this I feel relieved.

The dreamer did not know what to make of the dream at all and did not, at first, offer any comments or associations. When questioned, he protested that his therapy was not uncomfortable. When asked about being offered treatment, he referred, associatively, to a previous, helpful prescription from the therapist, who was also a psychiatrist.

The therapist had been wondering about the dream's transferential message: whether the dream might be compensating a situation of too little confrontative discomforting or be a warning of the dreamer's feeling himself forced into a potentially destructive 'posture.' However, the above association apprises the therapist of the fact that the dream refers to something 'potentially helpful,' hence, to the therapy process or to the therapist as a representation of the Guiding Self (The inner therapist; see Chapter 12: Dreams of therapy and the figure of the therapist), rather than to the therapist's person and to transference and countertransference.

Seen as a transference/countertransference issue, the situation would be quite serious, indeed, with implications that a sadistic therapist was forcing a regression, which had masochistic satisfaction for the dreamer. Instead, the dream motif is likely to point to a 'treatment' that the Self suggests or demands.

The Guiding Self, represented by the dream figure of the therapist, offers him a situation that is analogous to his own existential impasse, described above. The whole dream can be seen, thus, as a lysis dream, the healing outcome of the therapeutic process. This can be channeled therapeutically by directing it into a Gestalt enactment. His posture might bring out the underlying nature of his defensive refusal to participate in life.

When, as in this case, a bodily stance is directly referred to, it may be helpful to experience it directly. The therapist in this case asked the dreamer to assume — actually and physically — the dream position in order to find out what it felt like. The dreamer shifted around and kept saying 'I can't, I can't.' The therapist noted that he also clenched his fists and that his breathing became labored and tense.

As stated previously, whatever happens when a dream is being worked at belongs to that dream in the same way that an association does. The dreamer was, therefore, asked to pay attention to these tense states, even intensify them, and to keep repeating 'I can't, I can't.' As he did so, his discomfort increased. He became quite spastic, almost convulsive, and eventually rolled on the floor and relived his physical birth in a breech position. His sense of identity shifted between his mother, exclaiming 'I can't' when asked to press harder in order to promote expulsion, and back to himself feeling impotent and unable to move or get out of that stuck position, and afraid he would die or hurt his mother if he made an attempt to 'force' the issue. Thus, the dream did offer him a mirroring simile to his life position by leading him to experience the impasse of his birth process. He experienced how his chronic states of indecision were like being stuck in the birth canal, feeling unable and afraid to move forward.

Eventually with suggestion and encouragement from the therapist he was able to go through to full delivery and complete the birth process imaginally. This brought about a sense of relief and a change of disposition which gradually helped him also to risk making his own decisions. Laboring through an arrested birthprocess was shown him as the grand theme of his life, his life's myth.

CHILDREN

Insofar as they may not fit object level significance, that is, do not apply to any actual children or problems the dreamer might be having with actual children, children and babies in dreams refer to the 'inner child' — the child level within the dreamer, to everything that is unfinished and/or in the process or need of growth, and to the fruits of relationships to other people, and to productive skills. Positively, this may point, according to the dreamer's associations and explanations, to potentialities and possibilities, to whatever is not yet matured or fulfilled in the dreamer's life, to growth and renewal capacities, to the sense of wonder, to the connection to the transpersonal realm, to freely spontaneous emotional expression, to positive exhibitionism, etc.

Negatively, it points to immaturity, childish omnipotence, and infantilism.[17] Frequently, also, it may refer to the hurt and wounded child in the dreamer and to traumatic memories of childhood that he or she still carries psychologically and, usually, tries to forget and repress in favor of 'adult' ego-ideals.

When determining the significance of a child in a dream, it is helpful to elicit the age of that child. If this is not obvious from the dream itself, the first fantasy or association coming to the dreamer's mind, upon being asked how old the child is, is likely to turn out to be relevant; for there is a reliable and rather exact timing sense in the unconscious psyche. Using this age as a pointer, a 3-year-old dream child may relate to some experience of the dreamer at approximately age 3; or it may refer to something that started, came into being (was born) approximately three years prior to the dream.

In view of the so frequently repressed and traumatic memories that the child figure tends to connect us with, it is especially important and helpful to have the dreamer 'feel into,' try to embody or attempt to explore in fantasy what the dream child experiences or feels, to try to look at and communicate with the world or the other dream figures in terms of the dream child's eyes and mind. More often than not, this process will bring forth memories that might otherwise not be so easily accessible.

There is a baby lying in its crib.

There were no further details to this simple dream. But, as the dreamer told it, he noted an anxious, oppressive, and nightmarish feeling, that had plagued him repeatedly and never been understood. He was asked to try to imagine or feel himself as the baby, feeling that nightmarish anxiety, then to report what he experienced as the baby. As he eventually succeeded in getting the 'feel' of the baby, he became tense and felt something like suffocation. Intensifying the fantasy he felt a pillow pressed upon his face that threatened to suffocate him. The therapist asked him to stay with the fantasy and see if he could find out who was doing that to him. With horror and disbelief, the dreamer realized that it was his own mother who seemed to be suffocating him.

This was too important and fearsome to leave at this level; so the therapist suggested now that the dreamer imagine himself moving out of the dream baby's body, to watch the whole scene from a bird's eye view, and to describe what he saw, and, particularly, what made her do it. Now the dreamer 'saw' and recalled memories of fearful anxiety pervading the atmosphere as his parents were hiding somewhere in occupied France in flight from the Nazis. Apparently, there was a search going on in the neighboring apartment and, in order not to betray their presence through the baby's crying, the mother pressed a pillow on its face. To the infant these rationales were, obviously, not evident. All it could feel was the frighteningly traumatic threat of suffocation, the unconscious memory of which profoundly affected his overall attitude to life. Needless to add, this memory was allegoric/metaphoric and symbolic as well as, probably, actual. Metaphorically, it brought to the dreamer's awareness the quality of his relationship to his mother which felt suffocating to him. Symbolically, the image of the helpless child, overwhelmed by what it felt to be crushing and superhuman power, gave the dreamer an image of his existential relationship to, and feeling about, life as a whole. Work on the dream helped to open the dreamer also to the reality of holocaust events behind his personal mother complex and fear of life, and permitted a breath of objectivity and perspective.

Another aspect of the dream figure of the child is brought out in the following dream:

> A child has wrecked my jewel box and scattered the contents around. I yell and scream at the child. Now it is sick in the hospital and my therapist tells me I must take charge of the tonsillectomy.

Upon being questioned the dreamer felt that the child's age was about 1 year old. One year ago, her analysis had begun. Thus, it might be suggested that the child represents a development that is the 'child' of the analysis. A child aspect of the dreamer has been brought to life but not yet adequately dealt with by the process. The likely reference to the therapy process is also reinforced by the fact that the therapist appears in the dream.

The jewels, something of precious value (explanation), are being spilled out of a damaged box. Valuable psychological contents have been spilled out of the 'wrecked' analytic container. The dream indicates that something is amiss or 'sick' in the present state of the therapy process or the transference.

When asked what were the child's motives for breaking into the box, the dreamer responded, 'want and need.' This want and neediness reached back into the dreamer's earliest childhood memories of feeling unaccepted and unwanted by her parents. The tonsillectomy evoked memories of feeling abandoned and terrified and hurt in the hospital, at the mercy of strangers, and feeling that no one could be trusted to protect her. Hence she had to bear up stoically.

Her response to her denied dependency is represented in the dream as that of screaming and yelling at her child self. In identity with the parental attitude, and in response to the sense of there being no one to rely on, she brutally repressed expressions of neediness. Thus, she controlled and avoided any expression to the therapist of her growing dependency. Projecting the parental complex onto the therapist, she felt that she was expected to be 'responsible' and take care of what she considered her 'sick' feelings herself, rather than to let them show. Thus the dream figure of her inner therapist expects her to take charge of the tonsillectomy as surgeon — in metaphoric terms, to take responsibility for the therapy, a task which she accomplished by cutting off her dependency affects. The unrealistic demandingness of the dream therapist was projected upon the actual therapist and also induced as an aspect of the countertransference.

The dreamer's neediness, repressed and in the charge of her negative parental complex, damages the analytic container by allowing contents to 'spill' outside it. This spilling turned out to be the dreamer's unconscious, compulsive acting out of excessive and unrealistic demands for caring support from her husband, including expecting him to listen to her complaints and revelations about her analytic sessions. He was to take care of the 'child's' affect expressions that, thereby, were kept out of the therapy process.

The countertransference aspect, which had provided a hook for the projection, was brought to the therapist's attention by the dream. It lay in the therapist's patiently waiting stance — waiting for a dream to raise the issue, rather than confronting the analysand's withdrawal of affect and making an intervention himself. In the face of the dreamer's careful emotional distancing a temporary collusion had occurred. This would have prevented adequate therapy had it not been brought into the open through the understanding of this dream.

Another, more serious, prognostic example of the child motif is the dream of a hospitalized patient:

A tidal wave engulfs my house. I and most of the occupants manage to get out; but the child was already dead.

This dream portended an imminent acute psychotic episode, from which it was possible merely to restore an average reality adaptation (the dream-ego escapes). The finality of the dream tone announcing the child's death suggests that developmental possibilities had been already destroyed. Little further personality growth was possible.

ANIMALS

Animal figures refer to the prerational affect and drive level. The particular nature of the drive quality is expressed by the character associated with the dream animal by the dreamer, as well as archetypally and mythologically by folklore and collective, religious traditions. As mentioned before, the pre-Judaic and pre-Christian animal cults postulated a god-like, transpersonal, and relatively pure essence structuring and filling every particular animal. Archetypally a falcon or hawk, for instance, 'is' sharpness of insight, hence, solar consciousness, in Egyptian mythology. The male wolf 'is' sheer aggressive strength for the Roman; the fox, a cunning trickster and guide in many fairy tales. The serpent 'is' a source of healing wisdom and power of transformation and immortality in many cultures, but a dangerous, devilish tempter in the Old Testament. The pig 'is' earthiness, fecundity, orality, and it is related to the Great Goddess in many cultures.

In dealing with animals, then, mythological amplifications will always have to be considered in addition to the dreamer's personal associations and explanations. For the sake of facilitating the dreamer's explanations it is sometimes helpful to suggest that she or he imagine an animal theatre, or a play, in which every part were to be played by an animal: suppose the lion is king, the fox a sly councilor, the dog a faithful follower, etc. Given those, what role would then be assigned to the animal of the dream?

As in every other instance, personal explanations and associations will have to be interwoven and blended with those biological and behavioral explanatory facts and mythological amplifications about the animal that seem most relevant to the personal responses. Sometimes these are similar to the personal material, but sometimes they complement it, by pointing to important motifs that the dreamer did not know. In the case of a dream about 'a dangerous female alligator swimming around in a muddy pool' it was important for the dreamer to learn that female alligators provide unusually attentive maternal care to their young. The 'dangerous' oral 'aggression and powerful lashing tail' could then be seen in the service of defending new life. This provided a perspective on the image that touched the dreamer deeply.

It is not sufficient simply to call the animal the representation of an instinct. In every instance, if an important message is not to be missed, the particular quality or type of affect or instinctual drive that wants to reach consciousness in the form of the dream animal is to be considered.

Also, mythologically, in fairy tales and folklore, the ways the animals need or demand relationship vary widely. Sometimes they are to be feared. Sometimes they are to be trusted, avoided, sought out, killed, or protected. There is unanimity in all traditions and versions on only one point — that they are never to be disregarded with impunity. Always it is important to pay attention to their message or intents, for they have some important contribution to offer, one way or the other.

In the recurrent nightmare of a young boy a fox incessantly stared at him. The dreamer did not have any personal associations, but he did remember a fairy tale in which a cunning fox helped the hero out of an impasse. The therapist asked him to imagine that fox as though in a fairy tale or animal theater (as described above) and to listen to the words the fox would speak to whomever he was trying to help. What he imagined/discovered the fox to say was, 'Be smart, use your mind!' This, then, was taken to be the dream's message to the boy, who was quite passive and naive, unaware of his own 'smart mind.'

Monsters and dinosaurs are not uncommon in dreams. They refer to pre-human energy that is, in actuality, or felt to be, 'monstrous' or archaically primitive. Often the figure is an unnatural combination of qualities, horrible, wonderful, fabulous, and unusual to the dreamer. These qualities, then, demand to be looked at and related to.

INTERPRETING MYTHOLOGICAL MATERIAL

Whether or not to interpret mythological material to an analysand in a given situation is a matter of clinical judgement. Generally it is not advisable to point to or elucidate amplificatory material with story telling unless there is a cogent reason to do so, and until personal, reductive, and transferential issues have been dealt with. Otherwise amplification can detract from the here/now dynamics of the situation and even be used to distance from or rationalize a problem. It can be used to provoke idealization and envy of the knowing therapist, or to avoid difficult transferential/countertransferential issues by aiming away from the therapeutic relationship. Thus it can be a poor substitute for working through the personal material needed for ego-building and exploration of unconscious complexes.

On the other hand, mythological amplification points to transcendent meaning patterns. This is invaluable, especially when there are insoluble life problems, for it provides orientation and relates ego discomfort to its collective and spiritual matrix. Further, while amplification easily can be 'inflationary,' in that it can encourage identification with grand mythic patterns, moving the dreamer's ego closer to the Self, by virtue of connecting her/him with existential themes, may be at times desirable.

Amplification may shore up a very fragile ego state. When the transference is not yet formed or is endangered by severely negative projections, pointing to a universal theme, which can then *hold* the patient's psyche, may be therapeutic. Sometimes, in such cases, simply telling the story of the dream motif can give the dreamer a sense of meaning that bridges across the painful work of personal analysis and lets the dreamer feel the analyst's understanding. The tale speaks directly to the analysand's unconscious, presenting a healing pattern. It can also serve to create the sometimes necessary atmosphere of parent/wise storyteller/healer securely holding the confused and wounded 'child'/ patient. Such was the case with a dream presented in the first session by a near-psychotic, depressed woman. She dreamed that:

> A glass of wine has spilled and keeps pouring out endlessly no matter how much I wipe it up.

Her fear of revealing (spilling) anything incriminating about herself prevented her speaking, and she sat in agonized silence once she had told the dream. After interpreting that she seemed very frightened about making a mess and letting anything spill out, the analyst felt a strong increase of fear from the dreamer, who now felt scolded even for being afraid. Since the analyst had heard that the patient tended to have accidents on the way home from therapy, and had broken several limbs after the initial and final sessions with two previous therapists, this time the therapist decided to tell her a fairy tale of the overflowing pot. It is one of many variations on the theme of the ever-flowing transcendent vessel, the cornucopia of life, analogous to the dream motif. It was hoped that the story itself would hold the patient's psyche until another meeting could be arranged. In this case the telling of the mythological amplification served its purpose, refocusing the dreamer's attention from her culpability before a sadistic superego to the archetype of an ever-flowing 'good breast' source of life, with which she might come in contact. The idealizing transferential implications of becoming identified with this rewarding source, even through telling the story, had been weighed consciously by the analyst and accepted.

Always the analyst needs to weigh such implications, as well as the potential psychological effects of dissolving or supporting personal material in the archetypal level. Amplification is a potent therapeutic method. The therapist needs to be able to use it as part of his or her therapeutic repertoire, for it is invaluable for his/her orientation. But when there is a question of revealing the amplificatory material to the analysand, the therapist needs also to consider carefully the serious con- sequences — both for good and ill — which are inevitable with any potent medicine.

Chapter Nine

TECHNICAL POINTS

TIME SEQUENCE

In the dimension in which dreams operate, time and space are relativized
or suspended. What to our waking consciousness appears separated in
time or space may, in dreams, appear in temporal or spatial simultaneity.
Events that usually follow each other — possibly in terms of cause and
effect relation — may, in dreams, be presented as occurring simultaneously. On the other hand, what waking consciousness finds to be
an obvious cause–effect relationship may be presented in dream
mentation as a sequential one.

Frequently, therefore, sequentiality and (at times) even simultaneity
are to be considered to represent a causal relation. X and Y occurring
simultaneously or in direct sequence to one another, either as a clump
or a chain, means that they are linked: given X, Y is there too. When
X is placed simultaneously, that is, concurring timewise with Y, it may
imply that there is some coincidental or cause–effect relation, the exact
nature or direction of which is still to be determined between X and
Y: Y following X may mean that X is the cause of Y.

Here is an example:

> I am trying to maneuver a difficult piece of trail. A man offers
> to help me. I refuse, fearing to become too dependent on
> anyone. Then I am on a lonely spit of land. I notice I am
> crippled.

To the man the dreamer associated her lover with whom she was having
difficulties, precisely for the reasons which the dream mirrors back to
her: she was so anxious about defending against her dependency that
she could not, or would not, accept any emotional support and closeness.
Beyond the concretely personal, object level, however, the dream also

111

allegorizes her existential orientation. Subsequent to — meaning in our rational language, in consequence of — always refusing help from others, she becomes isolated, lonely, and 'crippled' in her capacities. Carried a step further, at the subject level, the dream may also be read as saying that her capacities to maneuver her life path are crippled in consequence of refusing help from the elements of her unconscious psyche (the 'inner' masculine or animus) and thus isolating herself from her own depths and potential.

Another example also shows the importance of carefully considering the implication of the exposition, lest one get misled by the imagery of the dream:

> I am with my husband, and we live in poor circumstances and are hungry. We realize that there is no way out: we have to die, and we have come to accept that fact. Now, we are contented and get along quite well.

In terms of external, concrete reality, this dream was irrelevant. The couple was quite well off, materially. To the husband, the dreamer associated her 'relationship problem.' She perceived him as utterly perfectionistic and overcritical. Looked at on the subject level, then, the dream's exposition mirrors the poor circumstances of the dreamer's relationship problem in consequence, or *because*, of her critical perfectionism.

Death the dreamer called the 'inevitable limitation of everything,' something 'difficult to face and accept.' Symbolically, it points towards radical transformation.

In the dream, she is prepared to accept the transformative fact of inevitable limitation. Then, suddenly, the dream-ego and the inner husband 'are content' and can 'get along quite well.' *Because* limitation is accepted as existential reality, implying that she is enabled to find standards that are less perfectionistically critical, the relationship problem will improve. On an outer level this relates to her relationship problem with her actual husband. On a subject level such change in her 'inner' perfectionist critic permits her to be more self-accepting and less self-critical as well.

THE RE-EVALUATING FUNCTION OF THE DREAM

Dreams often tend to reassess or correct a faulty viewpoint. It is a special instance of compensation; however, rather than showing a generalized view of the 'other side,' it directly points out the error. The dream may, for instance, show that something valued favorably is of no value or even detrimental. Alternatively, something that may be rejected and/or feared may be represented to be of high value. A supposedly protecting or supportive figure may be cast by the dream into the role of the criminal or robber, while a dreaded intruder or suspected criminal may be shown to be innocent or even helpful; the hoped-for medicine is seen as poison or even the cause of the illness. At times, the dream may even depict a full-fledged 'who done it' story.

Such material needs to be carefully evaluated both in terms of the dreamer's and general explanatory value standards, as well as in terms of dramatic context and likely compensatory function (in relation to the conscious position). Only then can the interpretation establish what is meant to be shown as 'right' and as 'wrong.' Needless to say, when this can be successfully done, such dream motifs are of diagnostic and directive significance in that they directly indicate which way attention and development are, and are not, to go.

An instructive example of this 'disentanglement' need is furnished by the following dream:

It has become necessary that *Time* magazine take over *US World Report* because *US World Report*'s labor relations are dominated by the union and are, therefore, utterly inadequate and destructive.

The tone and metaphors of this dream are quite impersonal and collective, already telling us something about the dreamer's psychological distance from and attitude to his problems. The dreamer was a rather traditional and conservative business man. He read both journals mentioned in the dream but had no connection with their management, nor was he in favor of liberal policies. The rather terse and emphatically directive dream makes no sense on the object level. To labor unions, the dreamer associated 'egotistical, work-shirking self-indulgence and laziness.' *Time* magazine was a representative of 'a degenerate, liberal and destructive establishment.' *US World Report*, on the other hand, he hailed as being in 'the best of traditional American values' of 'austere competitiveness' and 'every man for himself.'

In terms of these associations it is quite obvious that this dream is at variance and directly contradicts the dreamer's conscious value system. It shows the conservative stance allied with what he considers 'lazy' and 'egotistical self-indulgence;' therefore it is inadequate and possibly destructive. Whereas a more liberal attitude, which the dreamer views as 'degenerate,' is really called for. Since his interest in the actual journals and their policies was rather minimal, the images are to be understood metaphorically in terms of their psychological meaning. We must look for subject level interpretation.

And here the compensation became quite obvious. The dreamer believed in austere self-denial to the point of rigid, emotional sterility. Working hard was his supreme value. This attitude, the dream signals to him, is too conservative, self-indulgent, and even self-defeating. It interferes with 'labor relations,' that is, with work efficiency and productive relations between goals and means. Instead of this restrictive stance, and in order not to jeopardize his living and working capacity, the dream calls for a change in his values. What he views as degenerate — namely a greater and more 'liberal' concern for his personal and emotional needs — must take charge of his affairs.

This abstract dream had to be dealt with first in terms of its abstract, philosophical outlooks and convictions, since that is where the dreamer happened to be. Only then could it be brought closer to the inner and emotional level.

Another, rather poignant example of re-evaluation occurred in the following dream:

A terrorist, filled with liquor and LSD, points a gun at me and screams: 'You must have self awareness!'

Here, the call for awareness is uttered in an unacceptable and absurd form by a fanatical, obsessive, and dangerous figure. One cannot become more conscious at gunpoint, nor 'filled' with mind-altering substances.

The dreamer's fanatical striving for awareness is here shown to be a 'wrong' and ineffective approach. The dream drama itself serves as a subject level message. The dreamer is called to awareness of the murderous fanatic within himself, and to reassessment of his own use of 'mind-altering' substitutes for confronting his psychological pain and spiritual reality. On a subject level this turned out to involve forcing himself to become 'individuated' by thinking about it, seeking 'teachers,' etc. The dream needed consideration by the therapist, as well, for the one who calls to awareness is an allusion to the figure of the inner therapist. Since such qualities may be projected and induced or defended against in the transference/countertransference interrelationship, the therapist needs to consider and explore their presence or potential presence in the therapy and in himself. (See Chapter 12: Dreams of therapy and the figure of the therapist.)

A particular variation of re-evaluation dreams is structured upon the theme 'not this but that.' An example:

> My nephew comes out of what I believe to be my sister's house. But it turns out to be not my sister's but Ruth's house. From there he goes to what really is my sister's house.

To the nephew, the association was 'inferiority feeling.' This the dream expressly places into a location different from the one the dreamer assumes. The association to the sister was fear-motivated 'passivity,' to Ruth it was 'overdemanding, fierce competitiveness.'

The dream, in metaphoric fashion, corrects a diagnosis. The inferiority feeling emerges not, as the dreamer assumed, from passivity and anxiety but from the opposite. He feels inadequate, the dream shows, because he expects and demands too much from himself. Only secondarily, this leads to anxiety and passivity (going into the sister's house) as a result. What is called for is not more but less pressured competitive effort.

A special variant is the 'who done it' type of dream which often reads like a veritable detective story.

A young man from a conservative, conventional background had homoerotic feelings, which he rejected with self-hate. He vigorously tried to make himself more 'manly' by repressing his 'effeminate' sensitivities and identifying with the most traditional macho attitudes. This functioned to make him feel increasingly self-alienated. He had the following dream:

> My friend warns me to beware of the homosexual haters who would do me in and points them out to me. But I did not listen to him, and they now waylay and catch us. They take away all of our identity papers and possessions and proceed to torture us. I ask how they happened to know about us. They tell me that G, an early school friend of mine, put them on our tracks. I try to give them a false name in the hope of being released by them. But I know that will not work, since they hold our papers.

His friend who tried to protect him, he described as a warm, intuitive and sensitive person. G, a schoolfriend, whom he had detested, he called a 'stick in the mud,' an 'unimaginative, conventional, and brutish fellow.'

This dream points out to the dreamer that his sensitive side, of which he is ashamed and which he tries to repress, would protect him from self-hate, if he would accept and listen to it. Instead, trying to be what he is not, he tortures himself and is threatened with loss of his identity. But

115

the culprit — the force that 'puts [the threat] on [his] tracks' — is the very attitude, here presented to him in the most unsavory re-evaluation, that he was trying to invoke as his ideal of manliness. Here it is depicted as an insensitive 'stick in the mud.' Trying to get out of the impasse by relying on a false identity, claiming to be what he is not, and pretending at tolerance and self-acceptance, will not help. The homosexual haters have his number. His identity is held, the dream puts it, by his self rejection, and he cannot evade the torture of facing up to that problem.

A young woman after several years in a rather dull and childless marriage of convenience felt, for the first time, deeply emotionally stirred by another man. She felt she should not 'start trouble,' however. She dreamed:

> I am a soldier in the army. I don't want to fight or to have
> anything to do with the war. I seek help from my friend who, it
> turns out, can do nothing for me. Then I am taken prisoner by
> the enemy, who wear blue coats and are all women. They doom
> me to death by starvation. The only way I can gain my freedom,
> I am given to understand, is by accepting scarlet clothes.

Here, the exposition depicts a 'pacifist' attitude which gets the dreamer into trouble. Hence, this attitude, whatever it signifies psychologically, would seem in need of re-evaluation.

The dreamer's associations to soldier and army were that she did 'not like fighting and getting into arguments, because she believed in universal love.' This merely repeats the setting of the dream. To the friend, to whom she appealed for help, and who 'can do nothing' for the dream-ego, the dreamer associated 'an escapist.' To the color blue (the uniform of the enemy) she associated 'spirituality.' Women, she felt, 'would never fight if they could help it.' Scarlet, which would gain her her freedom, she associated with passion, fire, blood, and with Hawthorne's *Scarlet Letter* as the mark of an adulteress.

A mythological amplification relevant to the theme of this dream is the opening scene of the *Bhagavad Gita*. There, the protagonist Arjuna, the leader of an army drawn up in battle formation, feels he cannot enter the fight because his friends and kinsmen are in the enemy's ranks. To join battle against them would be fratricidal. As he holds back from action pondering these thoughts, he is addressed and reprimanded by the Lord Krishna, through the person of his charioteer, for shirking his appointed role in life and his *dharma*. He is given to understand that his human task is to act in terms of what his destiny as a warrior requires. The 'fruit of the action' is not in his hands. It is the concern of the gods or of the Divine Self.

This amplification, confirmed by the associations and dramatic development, sustains the exposition's pointing to a tendency of escapism. The dreamer's love of peace is represented by the dream as an attempt to avoid involvement in life and its conflicts. The dream-ego is captured by blue clad women — her escapism is taken over by a collective identity 'dressed' in rationalizations and pseudo-spiritual idealism about femininity. Wearing scarlet — 'passion, fire, blood,' and even adultery — would gain her release. Hence, by implication, the dream makes it quite clear that it is not concerned with merely abstract, philosophical considerations. It points rather toward a re-evaluation of the dreamer's specific moral and spiritual assumptions, which have been misused in the service of escapism to help her avoid living more fully and emotionally and suffering the conflicts of her concrete life situation.

Another special form of the re-evaluation dream is that of the intruder. Often the intruder represents a quality of psychic energy, which has been feared and dissociated from consciousness. Its appearance in a dream usually serves first to enable the dreamer to become aware of the fear and/or devaluation, and to confront the qualities represented by the intruder. This begins the slow process of establishing a conscious relationship between the dreamer's sense of identity and those qualities. A striking example of this category is the dream of a relatively young woman, close to death from terminal cancer and fearfully trying to deny that fact. She had a nightmare of a stranger trying to get into the house. For lack of associations, the therapist asked her to imagine looking out through the peephole to see who it was. She described the stranger as a Chassidic student. But she could not account, rationally, for her fear. This dreamer came from a religiously orthodox Jewish background, yet had managed to live without any sort of religious or spiritual connection. Close to death, some sort of a spiritual connection 'demanded' to be established. For lack of a personally individualized form, the spiritual dimension presented itself in ancestral garb: the spirit of her ancestors wanted to be heard and seen at this juncture. It came as an intruder and was initially feared and resisted for what it implied to her.

THE DAY RESIDUE

In the process of depicting its intended messages, the dream freely avails itself of appropriate imagery regardless of time sequence. On the unconscious level space relations are relativized and there is no differentiation between past, present, and future. Hence, suitable imagery may be drawn from any place or time. Consequently, also, whatever may have happened the day before may serve the dream's purpose and be useful material for its metaphors or symbols, no matter how important or unimportant the day event itself may or may not have been for the dreamer.

Like every other dream image, the day residue will have to be viewed relative to the blind spot, on the object or subject level, to which it is pointing. However, it is important to consider its similarity to and/or difference from the remembered version of the particular event. Any deviations usually provide the key to the pertinent point of the message. When the dream reproduces the day event as it actually occurred, without any significant deviation, it usually points to a subject level content allegorized by the day residue image.

For instance, suppose the dreamer had an argument, the day before, with R who behaved in a rather rude fashion. In the dream that event is repeated; but in the dream R appears as rather kindly. Such a deviation from the remembered scene would have to be considered the significant message of the dream. There is a blind spot related to how R was consciously experienced. Either R is, actually, more kind than she or he was seen and the rudeness is in the dreamer and was projected upon that other person, or the opposite. The dreamer may be seeing R in too kindly a fashion, projecting kindness upon R, who is even more rude than perceived. Which of the two interpretations happens to apply would be determined by compensation or complementation. If the dreamer's conscious position is annoyance at what he considers R's rudeness, the first contingency (the projection of rudeness) is more likely to apply. If the dreamer attempts to take a charitable view of the situation, it is probable that the dreamer's kindness is distorting the facts.

In another example, the dreamer is back in the dentist's chair where he was yesterday. The dream dentist asks him to 'open his mouth and keep it persistently open.' At first the dreamer felt this was an exact reproduction of what he remembered of his dental session. When pressed by the therapist to check carefully if there really was no difference in any detail, he remembered that what the dentist had said was, 'Keep it *wide* open.' The substitution of 'persistent' for 'wide', then focuses this dream's message. A need for persistence is emphasized in respect to opening himself to the work upon the teeth: metaphor for the means of grasping and integrating reality to begin its metabolization. Since such imagery frequently refers to the therapy process (see Chapter 12), the need for a more 'persistent openness' in relation to therapy had to be explored. The dream did, in fact, open the dreamer's unconscious doubt about his capacity to sustain the sometimes painful difficulties attending self-discovery.

A physician of a rather hypochondriac disposition who was prone, rather frequently, to 'discover' some new illness in himself had just had a general physical checkup with a Dr X, in which he had been given a clean bill of health. The following night he went through the whole examination process again, but in the dream Dr X diagnosed him as seriously ill and commented to the dream-ego. 'How, while being so seriously ill, can you take care of other patients? Is that not awful?'

Here, the difference between day residue and dream version is the nature of the diagnosis and the doctor's alarm. First, the interpreter would have to consider such a dream on the object level, as a possible warning of something that the examiner may have overlooked. A review may be in order. Perhaps the dreamer *is* more seriously ill than was assumed. In view of the dreamer's hypochondriac alarmism, however, it is more likely that the dream confronts the dreamer with a situation to be investigated on the subject level. His 'inner' Dr X may be represented as an alarmist in the face of a good state of external health but possibly correctly pointing to serious disorder on the psychological, 'inner' level.

Associations were asked for. Dr X, the dreamer felt, was a 'superior person,' who 'looked down on people [like himself] whom the specialist would consider insignificant.' Applied to the dream, we have here an inner 'spoiler' figure, identified with a 'superior' snob standard. This acts as a force of self-rejection and self-doubt, imputing illness to his very being. This causes the dreamer's tendency to overdramatizing panic as a means of giving himself the attention he easily accords to others, on whom the need for care is projected. The possible reference to the therapy situation, where such a patronizing attitude may be projected onto the analyst, needs also to be explored.

DREAM SERIES

Until now, we have been dealing with single dreams. However, there is a continuity, we might almost say, an extended story, as dreams unfold sequentially as part of a steadily evolving series. They tend to tell a running narrative, which feeds the conscious ego the kind of information it requires and is able to assimilate, given its particular position in the developmental process. As consciousness takes in and responds to the dream's messages, the dreams again respond to the newly gained positions of consciousness; thus a dialectical play develops. When it is a matter of vitally important or fundamental life issues and consciousness does not respond adequately to assimilate the message, dreams will recur. Sometimes they repeat in the same form; sometimes the images become more numerous, larger, or threatening. This kind of recurring dream series may even lead to nightmares. Such nightmares and recurring dreams — and particularly those that have been recurring since childhood — deserve urgent attention.

Dreams should be considered not only singly but as part of a steadily evolving series. When a dream journal is kept,[1] one gets the impression of an unfolding continuum of views, and of a seeming intentionality in the selection of themes for each given moment.

Indeed, in the instance of a specific, organic symbol, birth in dreams can usually be seen to refer back to a process seeded some nine months before. Or the age of a dream figure will refer to some energy that was 'born' those many years before. But more than that, it is as though dream number six in October knew what dream number twenty-nine in April was going to raise and was preparing the dreamer with preliminary insights. Subsequent dreams quite often, therefore, need to be considered in the light of preceding ones, that might have dealt with the same or similar subject matter. A central theme or themes are developed in sequence over time. Often, one cannot avoid the impression that the series operates as though the unconscious could 'anticipate . . . future conscious achievements,' no less than future unconscious dilemmas, for an early dream seems already to 'know' or 'plan' what a later dream is to pick up and carry further. This is an aspect of what Jung called the 'prospective function' of dreams.[2]

Usually, such an elaboration occurs not in linear progression but rather like a circular or spiral movement around a central thematic core,[3] casting light upon the central theme from, what might be considered, different psychological angles. It is as though dream one raises a theme; dream two raises a seemingly different one; dream three presents again another angle and so forth; while dream twelve may perhaps pick up on one, and fourteen may link up what was raised by three and twelve — or whatever. This circumambulation of the dreamer's psychic field thus repeatedly brings up crucial complexes, and elaborates on them, building on previous consciousness. Gradually a sense of 'wholeness pattern' develops through the process of being shown the various aspects of the themes, presented with all their variations from a variety of viewpoints. In keeping up with the images of the dream series, one can keep up with the life — and individuation process.

An example of three dreams from the same dreamer over a period of one year, dealing with the motif of unconscious and spoiling rage, shows the development of the ego in its relationship to the transpersonal archetypal drive:

(1) There is a tornado, from which I have been hiding in a cave. A vortex of black energy grabs me and swirls me away.

The dreamer did in fact tend to hide out from life's emotions in the illusion of maternal protection. He had just lost the manuscript of a story he had finished, after drinking to the success of its completion. The dream complements the situation by showing the dreamer in a dramatized form the dynamic of his self-destructive acting out. It shows that he is endangered not by what he had assumed, with masochistic self-berating, to be his own 'stupidity,' but by an unconscious force which spoils his sense of reality. The image aroused his fear and showed him the archetypal power he was up against; thus it began the slow process of separating him from rage, split off and turned against his fragile and imperfect human existence. It began to coalesce his ego.

(2) A killer is loose in the cellar. It's tearing off the insulation on the furnace to explode the house. I am afraid and run away to hide.

In this dream the fact of fear is noted by the dream-ego; hence the affect is beginning to reach consciousness. The fear is connected to by the dream-ego, but the rage is projected onto the killer. The attitude of the ego now became the focus of the dream work: why did the dream-ego feel unable to get help to confront the raging energy? The dreamer still denied that the killing rage was connected to his emotional reality. The killer is an impersonal 'it.' Fear in the dream-ego was the only emotional symptom of its presence. The unconscious affect was in the cellar, which reminded him of his parents' house. In the dream he ran from it, terrified. In working on the dream he recalled that he had experienced similar terror and hidden under the bed before his father's drunken outbursts. The dream pointed out that the rage which might legitimately be his own was still held in the feared father complex. Unconfronted, the hidden affect still threatened to destroy his psychological space.

It was possible in working on the dream to relate it to an event in the preceding therapy hour. The dreamer had had to wait outside because the analyst forgot to unlock the consulting room door on time before the session. The dreamer had not been aware of the extent of his anger and denied all but slight 'annoyance' as he expressed empathic 'understanding.'

He could see that he feared the therapist would retaliate if he expressed his feelings. Thus he became able now to find his rage in projection on the therapist. Further work uncovered and legitimized his own anger at being locked out. He could begin to feel that it belonged to him personally as he differentiated this anger from the father complex and what he had feared as killing rage in himself.

> (3) In the subway a man grabs my arm and starts to push me. I shout, and shine my old camp flashlight in his face. He steps back and I look at him.

The tendency towards raw aggression is still underground and somewhat compulsive, but the dream-ego is now able to use the light of awareness, which he had begun to develop in a short experience with peers who were rowdy in summer camp when he was 9. Through the memory of this experience which taught him that within certain limits some amount of rowdiness can be acceptable as part of his identity, he is enabled to confront the automatic rage reaction. When finally asked of whom the pushy man in the dream reminded him, the dreamer described an acquaintance who lost his temper when he became insecure. Without much difficulty the dreamer was able to become aware of his own belligerent defensiveness during a recent confrontation with his wife.

VARIATIONS ON A THEME

There is another kind of temporal dream grouping. Its development is in terms of variations on a central theme, but the dreams may occur simultaneously, synchronistically or anticipatorily.

Dreams that occur during the same night or, less obviously, dreams that happen to be remembered and brought up for discussion at the same time (even though they may have been dreamed on different nights, even years apart) are likely to cluster about and elaborate a common theme.

Equally so, behavioral or event patterns that coincide with dreaming or relating a dream are to be considered and treated like relevant associations or amplifications. (See Chapter 5, Associations.) In the dimension in which dreams operate, our rational standards of space, time, and causality do not apply. Thus, also, dreams referring to or commenting upon events in daily life frequently occur not after but prior to the event, even though the dreamer may have been quite unaware of what was about to happen.

An example occurred with a relativley new analysand, who walked into her therapist's office without shutting the door to the waiting room behind her, as she had done previously. This time she left it wide ajar. As the session developed, she raised the problem of her 'fear of success' and its effect in always hampering her life and relationships. She then suddenly remembered she had had a 'rather trivial dream:'

I am in my childhood room, and the door is wide open.

The connection with the previously noted behavioral event struck the therapist immediately. In discussing the context of the open door of her childhood room, it developed that she was never allowed to close it, for this was taken as a sign of unsociability. To the dreamer, however, leaving the door open felt like the denial of her privacy, and the threat of impingement. She found it impossible to focus on 'doing her own thing.' While eventually she learned to accept the requirement and even developed the habit of leaving doors open behind her, both literally as well as figuratively, she felt nothing could be claimed as her own. Nothing could safely belong in her own space; nothing felt connected closely enough to herself to merit finishing. Things were always left 'open-ended,' widely ajar. Hence, her projects and thoughts and relationships felt inadequately closed and were prematurely abandoned. The open door, not the fear of success, was the issue. And in this the 'trivial' dream as well as the 'trivial' event in entering the office cooperated in elaborating it, serially and synchronistically.

Different dreams told or remembered together are likely to elaborate the same themes, even though their imagery may not, at first view, reveal that fact. Likewise, dreams occurring in time sequence tend to pick up and develop issues raised by previous — even though not necessarily immediately preceding — dreams. In either case that development occurs by means of variation, extension, or amplification. Consequently, based on the assumption that another dream is likely to convey the same or a similar message from a slightly different viewpoint, it often is possible to shed light on an otherwise obscure dream by looking upon the other one that is connected with it either sequentially or simultaneously. Always then, in dealing with dream series, it is important to look for common denominators, central themes, and/or polarization of opposites to which the individual dreams relate like variations upon a theme.

The following three dreams were brought together to the therapy session. They all occurred during the same night.

(1) I put a fish onto a raft that is too small, in the hope that the sun will cook it.

(2) I am eating fruit salad. But I had poured out the juice. Now I am drinking the juice but find that it is contaminated with sea water.

(3) I ask my wife to get an instruction booklet for me.

The first dream, even without yet getting personal associations, reveals a rather unrealistic expectation: the 'hope' that the sun will cook the fish, rather than spoil it. A task that properly is to be performed in person on a fire or cooking stove is relegated here to a cosmic force, the sun. Moreover, the receptacle is inadequate; the raft is too small.

We can readily pick up a related theme in the third dream. The wife is asked to get something for him. As such, this might not be necessarily unrealistic, were it not for the similar motif of the first dream. Upon questioning, the dreamer admitted that he did tend to rely upon his wife to do things for him. He liked to 'pass the buck' to her, particularly in practical matters.

An unexpected confirmation of the 'buck passing' motif turned up during discussion of the second dream. The therapist asked the dreamer to associate or imagine how or why the juice might have become contaminated with sea water. He responded, perhaps, because he had rinsed the bowl in the ocean rather than in the kitchen sink. There we have again a repetition of the first dream's cooking by the sun rather than the kitchen stove. Again, a personal effort is shunned and passed on to a cosmic — hence in this context rather abstract and inappropriate — level.

Associations are needed to understand those general meanings more concretely. The association to fish was: food against arteriosclerosis (a rather unexpected association, but the more significant, for that reason). The therapist asked, What is arteriosclerosis? (Explanation.) The answer was, 'inability to think.' So, we know that the processing of the protection against inability to think is passed onto a cosmic order rather than upon personal effort and, moreover, it is held in too small a container.

All three dreams, then, agree that the task at hand — something expressed as protection against inability to think in dream 1 and as easy care in dream 2 and as getting instruction in dream 3 — is passed onto sun, ocean, and wife, respectively. Presented with these images, the

124

dreamer responded and admitted that, indeed, he liked to avoid having to deal with or think about practical issues. He hoped they 'would go away' or that somebody else (foremost, his wife) would take care of them. So far so good, but why this equivalence of wife with sun and ocean? Clearly, this equivalence points to an archetypal principle beyond the personal one. Mythologically, the ocean is the 'world mother,' the sun, in alchemistic representations, the world soul, 'anima mundi.' The World Mother is expected to do the practical problem solving for the dreamer, and the wife is expected to function as a stand-in for the World Mother or Great Goddess. This role, it turned out, had been filled by the dreamer's own mother.

The three dreams then point to the dreamer's escapist attitude toward concrete and practical life problems, responsibility for which was delegated to divinity, providence, hope, chance, mother, and wife.

An additional fine point is added when we attend to the theme of the fruit juice. Fruit salad was to the dreamer 'a healthy food,' somewhat analogous to fish; and juice represented 'the tasty, pleasurable part of it.' Thus, it is implied that the pleasurable aspect of life-planning, the joy of living and striving is lost when it is 'contaminated' by buck-passing avoidance. In running away from life's problems, the dreamer ran away from himself; in avoiding, he avoided the experience of his own reality; thus he did not feel himself as fully existing.

That much can be read through the careful evaluation of the 'variations on a theme' of a dream series.

NIGHTMARES

Nightmares are dreams which frighten the dreamer and/or dream-ego. They usually constitute urgent messages from the Guiding Self of the dreamer about hitherto unheard, denied, or inadequately considered material. They may point to new problems and adaptations far from the dreamer's ego attitude which come as frightening intruders into the habitually comfortable psychological space of the dream-ego. They may expose outgrown limitations and/or constitute invitations to development that the dreamer fears to risk. Nightmares serve to support the death of the currently held ego attitude; and as such they may include dreams of dying or dismemberment.

Other nightmares may point to spoiling elements attacking newly integrated capacities and attitudes. Sometimes they even use the image of threatening monsters. They can serve to coalesce the new ego position by presenting the threat or backlash of inertial complexes as a danger to be confronted and stood against.

Other nightmares repeat traumatic situations as if to force their confrontation by the dreamer and to assist in the process of reaching some conscious relationship to the stressful and threatening energies on the object and subject levels.

Nightmares need to be handled with the same techniques applied to any other dream, but in view of the urgency of their message, they usually need to be given a high priority of attention.

Chapter Ten

PROGNOSIS FROM DREAMS

In presenting the situation as it is, with implications for potential development, dreams provide us also with invaluable diagnostic and prognostic evidence. Often the images speak for themselves. At other times it is the emotional atmosphere which the sensitive therapist apprehends that offers a clue.

The following is an initial dream brought by a young man who wanted to be a lawyer, but whose presenting issue was 'having problems getting work done:'

> I live in a house that is a ghost ridden, decrepit shack built on rotting stilts over a swamp. The muddy road leading to it is booby-trapped with land mines.

This dream depicts emphatically for his analyst-in-training the prospective client's highly unstable psychic situation. The dreamer's 'shack,' namely psychological structure, is 'decrepit' and ready to fall to pieces. Any approach to his problems is 'mined'. The dream warns of the need for utmost circumspection in dealing with a potential psychosis.

The implications of these images are self evident. (Other examples of images of this kind may include such motifs as being walled in, enclosed in glass, mutilations, and other serious biological threats.)

After being referred on by the trainee who took the dream's warning quite seriously, this patient brought to the other, more experienced analyst another dream — one from the night before the first session with the new therapist:

> I see a terrible animal face in the corner of my bedroom. Then I am in what I think is your office and see a picture of that fierce face in a frame on your bookshelf.

This dream is more subtle and ambiguous. At first sight it would seem that the unconscious terror can be 'contained' and held in a framed picture, hence recognized and dealt with, at least to a degree, by the analytic process.

On the other hand, the image is on the bookshelf and is reduced to a glass-enclosed abstraction which, when asked to draw, he rendered only as a stick figure.

The subtle implication points to a likely tendency of using intellectual defenses to reduce the fierce affect to bookish abstractions. As it turned out the therapy did bog down on his insistence, or possibly, need, to maintain an intellectual and thinking distance from his 'fierce animal,' the unconscious rage in him.

Another obvious example of a very serious warning, conveyed by atmosphere as well as specifics of content, is found in the initial dream of a 50-year-old nursing teacher. She sought therapy in order to become a therapist and considered herself quite competent and stable.

> I am walking in a deserted city, everything is empty. Suddenly a great blackness comes down and I try to jump around and stay out of its way, to avoid being crushed, but I only go up and down in the same spot. It feels like I am dying of fear. I start yelling for my older sister. Then I remember she is dead, and I collapse.

In a deserted place, instead of finding collective help, civilization, and adaptation potentials of a city, she finds emptiness. She is threatened with natural disaster, inevitable darkness, a crushing increase of unconsciousness. Her recourse is to try vainly to jump in an old manic defense and to call for help from her 'pampered, sickly little sister, who died before [the dreamer] . . . was born.' The dream offers no means of support for the dreamer; although she described herself as 'generally cheerful and a good worker with lots of acquaintances — nobody I really like, though.' The dream-ego's attempt to bring about a lysis ends in a collapse. This dream is to be taken as a serious warning to the therapist. It points to severe difficulties in respect to the possibility of a psychotic depression and a doubtful therapeutic prognosis.

Extreme polarizations between the unconscious and conscious positions and imagery, such as in the case above, may suggest an inability to undertake any creative dialectic unless and until a more stable psychological identity can first be built.

A dream reported by Jung of 'an entirely normal' doctor seeking to become an analyst shows such an extreme polarization. The man felt himself already an accomplished and mature professional and said he had 'no problems.' His dreams, however, pointed to a different prognosis.

His first dream was of travelling by train and arriving for a two-hour stop in a strange town. The dream-ego found a medieval building, perhaps the town hall. It was full of old paintings and precious objects. As dusk approached, he realized that he was lost and that he had met no human being. A door, which he hoped led to an exit, opened into a large dark room. In its center a 2-year-old idiot child sat on a chamber pot smeared with his own feces. The dreamer awoke with a cry of panic.[1] As Jung remarked, the idiot child smeared with feces is not, as such, pathognomic. It could represent a two-year-old partial personality of the dreamer that needs integration. But the child's placement in the center of a gloomy, huge, uninhabited space at the center of the town, the uncanny atmosphere and the dream-ego's dramatic realization of the sun's setting and his own lostness and loneliness — all of these as well as a later dream of pursuit by a dangerous psychotic (*Geisteskranker*) justify Jung's assumption of a latent psychosis.

By contrast, an early analytic dream of another woman who was very obsessive and self-controlled portrayed her in a dangerous position.

I am lying in a stream that ran through my house, floating like Ophelia.

She said that the dream experience felt good, like a relief, unlike her conscious sense of miserable rejection and 'driven craziness and need for control.' The dream compensates her conscious position, but also shows danger to the dream-ego.

Unlike the preceding initial dream, this one, dreamed in the course of work upon her compulsive obsessive state, is to be seen as a complementation as well as a warning. It reveals the fact that the naturally compensatory factor against her obsessive control tendencies is of a potentially harmful nature: it goes too far.

Like the preceding one, this dream also shows a dangerous situation (the image is akin to Ophelia's in Shakespeare's *Hamlet*) of being prone to a suicidal floating and giving up and feeling 'good' about it. But unlike the situation of the preceding doctor's dream, the impasse is in the exposition, not where the resolution ought to be; it does not at present lead to a potentially catastrophic deadlock, but is a situational picture that, showing neither crisis nor lysis, leaves open which way response and development might go.

In this case, the dreamer was able to assimilate the image the Guiding Self had created of her and to acknowledge her suicidal escapism which in her case was a rather extreme form of acting out the desire to give up her obsessive defenses by floating away peacefully into romantic fantasies — her old autistic solution to the abuses of her childhood environment. Her dream points to the danger of such escape and the need to build a more stable and boundaried, interior psychic space.

Always, in the face of such dream material, the therapist is faced with clinical decisions about the client's ability to bear the pain and conflict necessary for analytic work. If the ego is too fearful, rigid, brittle, chaotic, fused, unboundaried, it may not be able to undertake a dialogue with the unconscious without somatizing or cracking into psychosis.

States of ego deficit will be reflected in dreams. Chaotic, irrational jumps in the dream imagery, for example, may suggest borderline pathology. The initial dream of a computer engineer imaged his confused and humanly unrelated state and showed his therapist his profound borderline-schizoid problem.

> All the computers are down; they are mixing up all the programs, so it is impossible to read what was what.

A perfectionistic housewife, with her self-esteem injured by the complex of a domineering mother, presented herself to therapy with a dream:

> I am lying on the ground. A lion is eating my hand; then my arm.

She could not relate to the image of instinctual energy symbolized by the lion, except to remember that 'lions ate Christian martyrs, didn't they?' Her own rage was so unconscious, hence projected and/or identified with and turned masochistically against herself, that she lived the role of a virtuous Christian martyr. She did not even feel endangered when the dream was discussed. Only when contemplating what her reaction would be if it were her daughter lying there instead of herself did she begin to sense any problem with the image as a depiction of a way of life. Her Christian martyr role substituted for a lack of individual ego consciousness.

Dreams can also show the fact of ego strength. A woman so depressed and anxious she could hardly talk dreamed:

> An old man shows me that I own a flourishing garden. I did not know it was there.

Later, she dreamed:

My friend's cat is drowning. I am able to save it.

In the first dream the fertile creative space is shown as already present and ready to be claimed by her. She needs help to make this fact consciously her own. Her associations to the garden were to a bouquet she had been given at work. Hence, the dream pointed to the available area of thriving as her relation to her work which had been devalued by her in terms of purely financial considerations.

To the friend she associated a person who was able to restructure her own independent and creative life. The cat was considered obnoxious by the dreamer, because it tended to make its needs abundantly and noisily clear. The dream shows her capacity to revalue and actively support this survival instinct.

Sometimes the initial dreams point precisely to how therapy needs to proceed, and give much information to the analyst even if they are barely discussed with the analysand. One young man brought two dreams to his initial session. In the first:

I am starting to walk across a beautiful oriental carpet in an unknown living room. It sinks. I pull it off and discover that it concealed a carpet-size tank of piranhas.

In the second:

I find myself in my childhood bedroom throwing my old teddy bear repeatedly at an empty rocking chair. As the result of this, I begin to discern the form of a common-looking woman in the chair.

The two dreams presented the problems that were to underlie the course of several years of therapy, as he discovered the vicious, devouring sadism under the elegant, narcissistic facade of the mother complex. Initially, however, as the carpet-covered piranhas dream suggests, he had such intense fear of falling through the floor to confront the voracious devouring contents of the unconscious (piranhas are small fish known to attack and devour large animals speedily) that he had difficulty entering analysis for his own sake. He warded off dealing with his personal problems by focusing on 'the wonderful images' of dreams analogous to the beautiful patterns in the rug — just as, it turned out, he felt his mother had focused on his 'beautiful' accomplishments for her own aggrandisement. He entered analysis, ostensibly, to become able to use them in his film work.

There is no securely holding floor in the first dream. The second shows that as a result of his claiming his own rage — transforming the piranha energy — a holding maternal figure appears in what was a space of psychic emptiness.

The positive result of hurling the teddy bear could be taken by the therapist as a message regarding the positive result of accepting the expressions of the dreamer's infantile rages. These erupted when his defenses and idealizations were challenged, but the confrontations served as a means of bringing forth the 'common-looking woman.' To this figure he associated a mother figure — a far cry from the demanding, elegant and narcissistic mother he had known. In the further course of therapy, it turned out that this figure represented his potential for a more serene self-acceptance.

In the first dream, destructive aggression is shown on the level of primitive instinctual voraciousness and oral aggression — piranhas, specifically.

In the second, it is humanized into a relational context of expressing infantile rage at maternal emptiness. Thereby, a new quality of humanity, first contemptuously scorned as 'common,' is called forth.

These dreams depict a transformation of energy from the primitive, unconscious and obsessive (piranhas) level, through infantile aggression, to a potential for acceptance as part of common humanity.

DREAMS OF DEATH OR ILLNESS

A special category of prognostic dreams are dreams that deal with death or illness.[2]

While every dream may, potentially, point to future development and can thus be used prognostically, dreams of actual death are rarely to be taken literally. Most often they refer to a symbolic death and rebirth process, inherent in any psychological development. The old position must 'die' to enable the creation/discovery of a newly felt-identity.

On the other hand biological threats may be imaged in dreams. An example of such a prognostic dream was brought by a woman who came into therapy because she had recently discovered a lump in her breast. She dreamed:

I met my husband who told me that everything will be all right, and that I need not worry. Then I bade him goodbye and found myself at the seashore. The beach was lonely, and the light darkening. The shore was empty except for some barges.[3]

To the husband her association was 'a silly optimist who never wants to face up to reality.' The barges reminded her of Egyptian death barges which she had seen in the museum. The darkening light, the lonely beach with the waiting barges, and her description evoked an atmosphere of eerie gloom in the therapist. This was not a part of his own mood but was induced by the dream. Together, all of this clearly conveys a message of death. The setting or exposition, which shows the situation as it is, refers to unrealistic optimism, which is followed by an image of death. Indeed, the lump turned out to be cancerous and did lead to her death. Whether confronting the unrealistic optimism that avoided facing reality might have led to earlier diagnosis and perhaps a better outcome is conjectural. In terms of the structure and sequence of the dream's events, such a possibility cannot be excluded.

Another client dreamed of:

A man in formal evening dress is on horseback. He encounters and tries to ride down a strolling minstrel. Angered and panicked by the threat, the minstrel grabs an axe and starts pounding and maiming the horse.

To the man in evening dress the dreamer associated social formality, conventionality, and the resulting ennui. The minstrel, a strolling player, represented to him his romantic nature and his emotional longing, as well as his healthy exhibitionism. To the horse he associated 'animal strength' and 'horsepower.' Here is an instance where the personal associations are in keeping with universal and archetypal meanings. Already Freud used the image of horse and rider to illustrate the relation between conscious psyche and unconscious body dynamics. Mythologically, the horse appears as an image of instinctual energy and motive power. Thus, Poseidon and Mannanan mac Lir, lords of the seas, are masters of horses as well; the solar chariot with its life-giving energy is drawn by horses.

The dream shows that the life energy is 'ridden' by an attitude of stiff formality and social conventionality. It threatens to run down his emotional side, his need and longing for recognition. In turn the threatened emotional dynamics retaliate by self-destructiveness — attacking the life energy. Indeed the man appeared to be meek and self-effacing, but was filled with seething fury, self doubts, and passive–aggressive rage.

133

Besides depicting his psychological situation accurately for him to relate to, the dream contains a warning of the danger of somatic threat. If maintained, the continuing repressive and self-denying stance may pose a threat on the biological level: the life force, or the will to live, is being mutilated.

Other examples of actual life-threatening motifs are expressed by dream images depicting floods, tidal waves, sandstorms, earthquakes, or other natural catastrophes. A threat to psychological and/or biological life exists when these actually injure or destroy in a dream the symbolic image of the dreamer's self, or his or her child (as future life — not childishness), or personally related animals (as instinctive life), or some images that would represent basic life entities such as forests, fields of wheat, etc,. or basic containers of life, one's house or bed. Most other figures, including the dream-ego, since they represent part personalities, or complexes, are 'expendable;' although the loss or disruption of the fixed complex they represent may feel painful to the dreamer.

Some motifs associated with realistic dangers, that may also include external event patterns, occur in dreams as symbolic eruptions. A woman's dream of 'City buildings falling' occurred two days before a stock market crash. While its imagery anticipated the external event in which the family finances were shaken, the actual breakdown pointed to by the dream was a psychological one. It related to the effects upon her psyche of the unexpected rejection of their marriage by her husband.

Nuclear war usually appears as metaphor for radical, 'nuclear' upheaval and annihilation and temporary ensuing chaos, which is felt as terrifying by the dream-ego but is not necessarily objectively destructive — depending, of course, upon the overall context and possible compensation factors. Diseases in dreams need usually be seen in terms of their metaphoric meaning, although there are instances of literal prediction, also. Leukemia, for instance, a proliferative excess of defensive white cells, often indicates a psychological defensive system that is excessive, but thereby ineffective and out of control. AIDS, by contrast, seems in dream work contexts to point to a general inability to defend one's own psychological integrity. Cancer may be a metaphor for any autonomous unconscious proliferative process whatsoever — split off and unattended life energy — hence energy out of control and destructive.

The 'personality' of the disease pattern needs to be imaginatively experienced in terms of its symbolic implications. For every biological theme of illness conveys a critical archetypal motif in need of adequate embodiment. It presents an as yet unassimilated conflict between archetypal dynamics and ego which requires realization of the archetypal problem and its meaning. It is represented as illness because every crisis constitutes a 'dis-ease' for us.

The dramatic implications within the dream are also pertinent. In dreams destruction may be followed by rebirth, provided the images of life energy and integrity are preserved. Moreover, in any dream depicting destruction, the dramatic development may also indicate under what circumstances, or given what attitude, the threat could be avoided. In a flood the dreamer may manage with effort to swim to a safe shore. Or she or he may manage to keep the head above water until the tide recedes, or happen to discover that she or he is situated safely at a real-life spot on shore or in a sturdy building, etc. All these details of the dream's dramatic story need to be taken into consideration to arrive at a clinical assessment regarding the dreamer's situation and prognosis. The dreamer's associations, including those to the part of the body affected, are always, also, to the point. (See Chapter 11: Body imagery.)

It is important in view of all of this to keep in mind that ominous motifs are to be treated as warnings but never as definite or final predictions. In particular, as mentioned above, death and transformation are equivalent, as far as the unconscious psyche is concerned. Hence death and transformation dreams are indistinguishable from each other in terms of their imagery. Transformation motifs may portend death, given the appropriate dramatic setting, and apparent death dreams may refer to fundamental transformation. We may avail ourselves of intimations or warnings for what they are worth, but only hindsight can tell for sure.

Moreover, no dream ever tells a final or unalterable story. It depicts the 'situation as it is,' given the present circumstances of the dreamer's position and awareness. As that position changes, possibly owing to an increase of consciousness gained through understanding the threatening dream itself, the next dream will usually paint a different picture. Dreams express potentialities, even probabilities, through their dramatic form. Only in rare circumstances do they indicate finalities. Then the motifs 'chosen' by the dream simply state a situation that, by its own nature, cannot be changed. The woman who stood at the shore by the barges of the dead might still retrace her steps and deal with the foolish, optimistic attitude in herself, one from which the way led to the death shore (sequence of events often depicts causality; see Chapter 9: Technical points). But neither she nor the dreamer of the descending darkness dream is depicted in situations with much chance of restructuring. Contrary to her initial optimism, this woman found that her analysis turned out to be a preparation for dying.

Yet, even when no overt alternative is given, it is wise to wait for what subsquent dreams have to say. The insights may bring changes or the possibility of different approaches. Inadequate or erroneous interpretations or understandings will result in repetitions and perhaps in modified forms of the same message or even in the form of nightmares, when an important message is not 'heard.' Vital points that have been overlooked or not given enough attention may become the subjects of new dreams.

Chapter Eleven

BODY IMAGERY

Mind and body are presumably a pair of opposites and, as such, the expression of a single entity whose essential nature is not knowable either from its outward, material manifestation or from inner, direct perception . . . [the] living being appears outwardly as the material body, but inwardly as a series of images of the vital activities taking place within it. They are two sides of the same coin.

(*CW*, 8 para. 619)

In the view of the unconscious psyche the body is experienced as the vehicle or locus of incarnation. (Incarnation, as an archetypal process, implies the existential expression of the personality living here and now.) This vehicle has its own biological dynamic and rhythms, which reciprocally resonate with psychic dynamics, and which are, for the most part, not subject to direct ego control. Hence, body dynamics represent forces of organic living, functions expressive of, and akin to, animal life in affect impulsivity and to vegetational life in growth and decay. These dynamics have to be related to as an *a priori* given; they cannot be deliberately changed.

References to the body, bodily functioning, bodily needs, or bodily pathology can occur in dreams in the imagery of solid structures of all sorts — edifices like houses or huts, vehicles like automobiles, boats, etc. The common denominator of all of these is that they are habitable, or usable as containers of life. And in terms of their containing, they can also function as vehicles for expressing human activity.

Body reference may also occur in terms of animal or plant images. In such cases the particular qualities, drive or form patterns associated by the dreamer, or metaphorically or symbolically linked to that particular animal or plant, will point to the specific meaning of the particular body or affect function to which the dream image refers.

As an example (but only as an example, not as a fixed or stereotyped formula) we may consider a horse as depicting vital force and power ('horse power' that can enable feats we cannot perform on foot). It sustains and carries its rider, the human person, much as the body sustains and carries the personality. The horse image may of course also refer to a mythological horse god or goddess, which in turn would express those same forces of vitality and carrying power with particular nuances of masculine or feminine qualities. And/or, for that matter, the image of the dream horse may also have associations to the qualities of the horse that the dreamer rode at the dude ranch last summer.

A tree may associate to a particular tree in the garden of one's childhood, to the ancestral tree, to verticality and connection between natural and transcendent realms, and/or to vital strength and the capacities for growth and endurance.[1] The felling of a tree in a dream may represent an image for the ending of a particular phase of life process. If the tree should, instead, be represented as dead, damaged, or stunted, the interpreter might consider the possibility of corresponding harm on the biological level: namely physical illness that has not yet become manifest or detected. Or the harm may be to psychological or spiritual factors in the dreamer. For clarification the analyst would need to explore what the image refers to or compensates in the dreamer's life and what contributed to the tree's condition in the dream.

A dream containing a serious warning of bodily disruption was dreamed by a woman the day before she had a stroke. In the dream she saw her house roof pierced by the branches of a tree torn loose in a windstorm.

In the category of images that allegorize the body, we have also to consider dreams of seasonal or diurnal rhythms, both in terms of their changes and/or of the dream-ego's failure to adapt to those changes. Such images might point to the morning or evening or to the spring, summer, fall or winter of the dreamer's life.

An example of such a dream that actually prefigured the dreamer's death came the night before he died. In the dream he is addressed by the voice of his long deceased grandmother, who tells him that it is five minutes to four.[2] To four o'clock he associated 'time for a coffee break,' and coffee break meant to him 'the time when one stopped working to take a temporary break in order to return to work again, rested and refreshed.' The image implies that the biological clock has run out, and that the dreamer is being called by his ancestress, the Grand or Great

Mother (a common mythological figure for the goddess of individual fate;[3]) yet it contains also the implication of rebirth or reincarnation as a cyclical event.

When we meet body imagery, for instance in dreams of having heart or skin disease or cancer or weak bones, or when we find dream images referring to particular bodily functions, such as sexuality, excretion, eating, sleeping, etc., the allusion has to be first explored on the literal object level. Is there an actual problem to which the dream points? What is the dreamer's conscious relation to the particular bodily function? When the object level interpretation does not seem to fit — but also when it does, and in addition to it — the allegoric or symbolic subject level implications of the psychosomatic dynamics need exploration. This would occur in terms of personal associations or explanations to the parts of the body in question, as well as in terms of collective (or mythological) comparatively fixed traditional associations or explanations to those parts. Examples of such collective explanations are firmness and structure for bones; aggressive anger, bitterness, or rage for gall or bile; depression for black bile; feeling and connection to what is 'felt' as a transpersonal spiritual center for heart; an autonomous destructively 'infiltrating' or proliferative activity of a psychological complex for cancer, etc.

In this category one may also consider dreams of the dreamer's death and of dying. In contradistinction to the examples above of biological or temporal rhythm change, dreams of death rarely refer to the literal event. As stated in Chapter 10: Prognosis from dreams, they usually point to a radical, existential ending of a cycle, hence also to a new beginning. Such dream images refer to drive and affect dynamics which are deeply rooted in bodily and instinctual patterns; hence, they cannot be expected to change easily or without the psychological 'death' that transformation often requires.

SEXUALITY

While we commonly think of sexuality in terms of gender, archetypally its range is much broader. The Yang-Yin, Lingam-Yoni symbolism seems archetypally ingrained in our psyches, as a representation of fundamental polarity both between partners and within the individual psyche. Outgoing-indwelling, light-dark, initiating-responsive, creative-receptive, assertive-adaptive are but a few of the possible meanings which may be implied by gender images in dreams, regardless of the gender of the dreamer. The dreamer's personal associations and explanations need also to be taken into consideration.

Sexual symbolism is a frequently encountered form of body imagery in dreams. In its widest meaning, it refers to the attraction to and urge toward merger and union with whatever happens to be felt as a polar opposite. Such imagery often occurs when there is a problem in bridging emotional distance between positions (for example, between analyst and analysand). Thus, positively, it may point towards psychological completion, or, negatively, towards a state of being attracted to or 'involved' with dynamics that may hinder psychological development and/or genuine relatedness.

An example may illustrate this. A young man with slightly obsessive traits had the following dream:

> I am in my car, ready to step on the gas, when I notice that a
> woman on my right is passionately stroking and arousing my
> penis to repeated ejaculations. The sensation feels familiar and I
> like it, but I am slightly concerned about driving that way since
> in the long run it might drain my energies and confuse me.
> Then a man who was sitting behind me gently touches my
> cheeks in what feels like a loving caress. I decide to turn to him
> to see who he is, for I like the feel of his touch better than her
> intensity. But, if I am to turn around toward him and see what
> he wants, I have to disentangle myself from her and also to take
> my foot off the gas pedal.

To the woman on the right he associated an acquaintance for whom he felt no particular attraction; if anything, rather a slight degree of irritation. He described her as an amazon type, very ambitious, competitive, and pushy, but also prone to what he called 'hysterics and tantrums if things would not go the way she wanted.' Her personality reminded him of his mother, whom he characterized as a similar type.

The man did not remind him of anybody he knew. When asked to visualize the figure in fantasy, the dreamer described a quiet, warm hearted, and sensitive artist. Such a man was very much the opposite of the way the dreamer regarded himself. His self-image was of a rational and coolly effective business man, occasionally rather excitable and ambitious, but primarily solid and practical.

On the object level there was no issue of homosexuality. Nor was there any attraction, incestuous or otherwise, to the actual woman figure of the dream. Subjectively, however, looked at in terms of libidinal merger and attraction, this dream led to important insights.

The setting and development show the dream-ego in the 'driving body,' the automobile, ready to step on the gas. The image is an embodiment of alert, drive readiness. At the same moment, the dream-ego discovers he is libidinally merged (sexually aroused) on his right side (left brain: rational action) with an embodiment of ambitious, competitive pushiness and propensity to hysterics and tantrums (his associations to the woman). He is getting a familiar, repeated, and pleasurable 'jerk off.' This figure arouses his phallus, the potent, assertive expression of what he feels to be his maleness.

The critical highpoint in the dream drama is the unexpected intervention of the young man in the back seat. The dream-ego finds himself being touched by qualities in himself of which he had been totally unaware. The sensitive, warm, and artistic young man in the back seat is a figure allegorizing his own unconscious potential. This he can reach, the dream puts it, only by distancing himself from the arousing figure and taking his foot off the gas. Both images refer to his problem with impulse control.

The dream images a deviation from the dreamer's cliché standard of what he, and much of his collective, considered to be masculine and feminine. The attraction to the young man behind the dream-ego expresses an urge toward achieving a fuller masculinity. This, in terms of the dream, is to be reached by connecting with sensitivity, warmth, and artistic qualities, which the dreamer commonly considered 'feminine.' In turn, the heroic, macho attitude is here represented by a female figure. It represents a function of the self-indulgent 'feminine' side of his being, an expression of early libidinal merger with mother and her ambitions for him that still drains his energies.

This dream illustrates some differential nuances in the qualities of involvement between dream-ego and attracting partners. With the figure of the woman there is a directly arousing sexual contact. The anima is 'jerking him off;' he is not participating consciously. The sensitive man merely touches him and evokes an as-yet distant response of attraction. The former actual close involvement expresses exactly that — a state of *identity* with a complex. Here it images the dream-ego identity with the obsessively ambitious and hysterical, arousing anima figure. The sexual or emotional attraction that has not, or not yet, resulted in intimate bodily contact points to an existing, unconscious pull. It represents a libidinal vector in the direction of the featured entity, a pull, however, toward a potentiality which has not yet been consummated.

Here, paradoxically, we may note a relation of polarity between

141

sexual dreams and dreams of intruders and of persecution. While sexual dreams show what draws the dream-ego, intruder or persecutor dreams show what is drawn toward it — what 'wants to come to me.'[4] These represent contents of the unconscious that urgently press toward awareness against the dreamer's fear and/or resistance.

So called sexual 'perversions' represent variants of the form or content of libidinal attraction. We must keep in mind that any attempt to define what is supposedly 'normal' or 'abnormal' on the level of instinctual dynamics applies social norms to a presocial drive level. An overt, acting-out behavior we may, perhaps, judge as abnormal; but we cannot apply any such standard to an image or dream, which simply describes the nature of libidinal pull along archetypal, instinctual lines. That is not to say that such dreams may not depict pathology, particularly so when they point to the tendency of destructive acting-out. Yet, this equally applies to any dream, whether sexual or non-sexual.

Homoerotic motifs, as our example has shown, express an attraction toward features expressive of, or tending to complete the character of, the dream-ego's own gender. Such features, if fully connected with, would make the dreamer more fully a man or a woman in terms of the Guiding Self's image of what he or she is 'meant to be' on the path of individuation.

Masturbation is self-arousal, literally. It may suggest the pleasure inherent in a capacity to 'turn oneself on' by becoming more positively autonomous, self-reliant, and self-loving. Such turning into self and self-arousal may image creative potentials to be aroused from the dreamer's individual depths, leading to an ability to bring more pleasurable will and individual creative effort to bear on the life task at hand. (In an Egyptian myth the world was created by a divinity's masturbatory act.[5]) Or it may point to autistic or solitary addictive tendencies, which contain the archetype of self creation in still compulsive form.

Sadistic motifs may sometimes show the unconscious urge or need for more assertion, dominance, and control. At other times they may image the way one aspect of the psyche takes pleasure in dominating, raping, or 'fucking-over' another. Masochistic motifs may depict the need or 'call' for more submissive adaptation to whatever is allegorized by the partner, or conversely too much of a tendency to misapplied submissiveness. Such motifs require careful scrutiny of the partners involved on both object and subject levels and must be seen from the perspective of the principle of compensation.

A middle aged woman dreamed:

I am in bed with an elderly man, somewhat like my father. He brutally beats and rapes me. I am horrified, but nevertheless I experience intense pleasure and orgiastic sexual arousal.

Her father she remembered as 'an exciting and inspiring figure, a bit severe at times, and with strong convictions,' but, so she thought, essentially benign and helpful. Only upon intense working-through of relevant memories evoked associatively by this dream could she remember how she actually had been brutalized physically and mentally and not allowed her own ways of feeling, thinking, and acting. Yet, since this was the only way in which the young girl experienced her father's attention, all this was glorified and felt to be fatherly love and guidance. As the result she became a replica of father's outlooks and opinions, rarely thinking a thought of her own, and she married a similarly domineering man whom she bitterly resented without yet being able to free and assert herself. While consciously resenting, unconsciously she glorified in being victimized.

Paradoxically, however, and contrary to the dreamer's view of herself, others experienced her as quite willful, domineering, and strong. Her husband, who underneath a bluffing, bullying surface was a rather weak man, admitted in marriage counseling that he feared her. So did some of the members of her therapy group.

Here, the subject level implication of her dream becomes significant; indeed, a careful reading of the dream should make us suspect that it is the subject level implication that is of primary significance. The rectifying of her views of her father and of his effects upon her were of vital importance. But in terms of the dream, they are to be viewed merely as associative material. For the dream shows her sadistic sexual partner not as her father but as an unknown stranger who merely resembles her father. The figure represents an inner, partial personality (an animus figure in Jungian terminology). The figure represents a likeness to her father, as a part of her own personality; in other words, her own unknown strength — indeed brutality and dogmatic dictatorial-ness — with which she is shown to be in a state of psychic identity (in bed: intimately and/or sexually involved). To such dominance by her inner brutal dictatorialness she joyfully submits; and unconsciously she acts it out in passive aggression. She dominates by means of her role of suffering and abused victim. And projectively, she induces and brings out the complementing role of active aggressor in the men around her, including her therapist. Thus, feeling ever and again confirmed in her 'helplessness,' she cannot avail herself of her own hidden strength. She remains helplessly tied to the force which 'rapes' her but is not available to her as her own disposable strength. Were she able to assimilate the dream's implication, by consciously accepting and connecting (sexual image) with the potential, assertive capacities depicted by the dream figure, she would be able to integrate a missing piece of her psychological wholeness, one relevant to her individuation.

So called sexual 'perversions' in dreams are to be taken as passionate attempts to connect with or being in identification with the tendencies allegorized by the image. While they first need to be checked out on the object level, they also point to psychological dynamics and often to spiritual cravings. Vampirism, for example, depicts the 'thirst' for 'lifeblood.' It images the drawing of intense, vital life energy (rightly or mistakenly, depending upon the dream's context) from the object of the vampiristic desire. On the object level it may point to psychological vampirism, to the tendency of passive overreliance on others for support, initiative, and psychological strength. Such a tendency is capable, by virtue of psychic induction, of draining the vitality of the persons chosen to be the objects of the vampire. It is a common theme in children's dreams when parental narcissistic needs are draining the life energy and autonomy of the child. On the subject level, as an oral craving, it often allegorizes infantile symbiotic needs that are split off and attacking the dream-ego.

Fetishism expresses a devotion — called for or fixated and/or over-involved — to the qualities depicted by the fetish. A relatively common example would be male shoe or panty fetishism, usually depicting an unconscious attraction or urge to devotion for the feminine 'standpoint' (shoe) or to the feminine 'veiled mystery,' that which covers and conceals the feminine 'secret' and 'sacred' parts. Voyeurism has a similar connotation, and its allegoric meaning depends on the dreamer's object of focus. Each dream with its images of 'perversion' would need to be explored fully. Such general indications of meaning as are suggested here are to be taken as simple pointers toward the amplification of general archetypal trends — no more, no less. The specific application of these contexts will always depend, and have to be modified by, the individual dreamer's explanations and associations.

IMAGERY OF BODY ORIFICES

The body orifices, foremost mouth, vagina, nipples, anus, and urethra, but also eyes, nose, and ears, carry a significance that seems to pertain to a phylogenetically very early (reptilian brain) level of reality relation. They function as portals of entry for, as well as toward, the external world. Much has been written on these orifices and the dynamics found and projected onto their images. When their images appear in dreams it is important that the interpreter has some understanding of the clinical literature, but equally he or she needs to have an imaginal and experiential understanding of these body metaphors. The literature and arts of the world are replete with these images. They can be studied profitably for the therapist's fuller imaginal understanding of the rich and polyvalent meanings of body symbolism.

Through mouth, nose, and ear, solid and fluid substances, air, scent, and sound enter; through urethra and anus flowing and solid substance are allowed and/or urged to leave. Through nipples flow primary nourishment, beneficent milk, or 'sour poison.' The vagina is entry into the powerful and numinous feminine, for pleasure, insemination, or fearsome devouring. From its darkness rhythmically flows the potent blood of menstruation that marks one stage of womanhood, and that brings problems of catching the flow, fertility, mess, communion with other women and nature. From it struggles all newborn life, and its image is, also, found as gateway to the return to darkness, that is death. Each of these images needs to be seen in relation to object and subject level dynamics.

The mouth functions as an organ of taste, the entry for life-sustaining food and the primary means of incorporation. It can serve as metaphor for all of these, as well as for willful expulsion of breath, spit, vomit, and the expression of feeling in sobs, kisses, yells, song, and speech. Oral motifs suggest variations on the themes of receiving life-supporting or life-damaging material, as well as of primal self-expression and assertion. They often refer to dependency needs, to the capacity to take in, or close against, what is offered, needed, or requires metabolization. (Oral sexual motifs may depict the urge to 'take in' phallic or yonic energy.) Teeth sharpen the oral capacity to grasp, to 'get one's teeth into,' to 'chew up.' They prepare the stuff of the external world for assimilation. They bite. Hence, teeth may also refer to oral aggression, to greed and devouring envy. Losing teeth may refer to the loss of a particular reality adaptation, hopefully to be replaced by new ones or prostheses. On the other hand, dreams of having one's teeth shattered, or losing them without a chance of repair, might cast a rather doubtful outlook upon the client's recuperative capacity in respect to the functions represented by teeth.

Eyes, nose, and ears serve as means of most elementary orientation and self preservation, on the animal level. We say 'I see' or 'I hear you' when we wish to indicate a perception that has been 'taken in,' that is more than mere intellectual understanding. When we 'smell' trouble, we indicate an intuitive and/or instinctive body awareness of something that rationally is not explainable, yet it provides orientation. Visual motifs tend, on the other hand, to refer to the capacity of relatively conscious and objective 'taking in' across 'lighted' space, or to difficulties in such processing. What comes to or through the ears carries implications of instinctive feeling perception and the subtleties and difficulties of receiving such messages from outer and inner reality.[6]

Metabolic symbolism — eating, digesting, assimilating — is common in dreams and allegorizes the processes and the reality and psychological issues to be metabolized. One woman dreamed that she was eating her own shit in the form of a communion wafer. The dream crudely and emphatically awakened her to a need to metabolize a piece of her shadow negativity, as if it was sacred communion with the transpersonal.

Excretory images refer not only to waste matter. They convey 'negative numinosity.'[7] For what is excreted is also the product of body — hence incarnated soul — activity on an early ego or pre-egoic level. Dreams frequently point to a problem regarding its appropriate containment, when the dream figure urinates or defecates in the living room, or the toilet is overflowing, for instance. Waste or dirt is matter in what is felt to be the wrong place. Hence, excretory material refers to potentially creative or transformative activity or urges, that either still have to find or are in the process of finding their proper channels. Stopped up toilets would refer to a situaton in which the appropriate forms for self-expressive urges and the discharge of needs are clogged, unavailable. The plumber's activity may, then, relate to the therapy process.

Defecation is an activity of usually deliberate, assertive 'expression.' It images an instinctual preliminary stage of conscious and deliberate willing. In constipation one is unable or unwilling to 'bring out' the stuff, in diarrhea it 'runs out' of control. Therefore anal symbolism also includes Freud's notion of the desire to dominate or to withhold. (In German nursery language the chamber pottie or toilet seat is still referred to as the 'throne.')

Urination, as image, depicts self-expression by virtue of yielding to or allowing the flow of what needs to come through one. It is *Self*-expression. It is more feeling-toned than deliberately willed. (Reins, the kidneys, like the heart, are traditionally — hence archetypally —

associated to feeling.) Urinary symbolism has to do, then, with the letting go and allowing of emotion, or of its inhibition, when, for example, one dreams of urgently having to go and holding it back. Very likely, the image of enuresis (or the allegoric meaning of its actual occurrence) may have to do with the self-expression, controlled or over-controlled on the day/conscious level, that breaks through inhibitions during the night.

The dynamic of toilet training, then, would refer to the ways in which raw, instinctual, affect expression is being or has been brought under conscious control — adequately, prematurely, too radically, or insufficiently, according to dream context.

Some examples:

I went to the toilet but found it already filled with feces. I tried to flush it but the only effect was that the water came up and overflowed into the living room.

Here the disposal channels are evidently clogged up. There is no receptacle available for self-expression. In fact, residual stuff, other people's expressions (feces) clog the situation. The available energy (water) cannot overcome the impasse, which fouls up the living space.

The dreamer was stuck in the limitations of his narrowly biased habits and opinionated prejudices (other people's expressions). No space was available for the expression of his individual style, or imagination and feeling. The more he tried by sheer force of will to overcome what he felt to be his shyness, the more he 'fouled up the living space,' for he tried to overcome his inhibitions by, unwittingly, emphasizing the expression of his very biased and opinionated stuff.

Another dream:

I found out that I had stored my dried up feces in mother's jewel box. I was disgusted with the smell and dumped the whole thing into the toilet. But then I realised that I had also thrown out mother's real and precious jewels.

The feces, here, also represent expressions that have been stored away and dried up: unlived assertive or creative possibilities. They are misplaced among mother's 'jewels.' The dreamer recalled, in association, that mother used to call him her 'precious jewel,' and that accordingly he always endeavoured to be worthy of that accolade. In thus confining himself to the over-refined and snobbishly narrow confines of her jewelry box he had to avoid any authentic behavior or self-expression that would not merit her approval. Now the realization of his past self-limitation evoked a backlash overreaction of rebellion. He wanted to discard everything of his mother's values and cultural standards. He had let himself go completely into drugs and self-indulgent acting-out. Thereby, as the dream warns him, he discards genuine self or individuation values (the jewels) along with the waste. The rather 'earthy' language of this dream may be accounted as a compensation for the dreamer's unconsciously, persisting, overrefined snobbishness that still seeks his ivory tower by means of 'spacing out' with drugs.

We have been able to deal only cursorily with the vast and important subject of body symbolism. Our statements, we repeat, should not be taken as a system of fixed interpretations but rather as guidelines for the further exploration of the possible allegorical and symbolic significances.

Chapter Twelve

DREAMS OF THERAPY AND THE FIGURE OF THE THERAPIST

This chapter will touch upon some of the central elements of the therapy process as they are represented in dreams depicting the figure of therapist and metaphors of the therapy process itself. The discussion seeks to illuminate the ways dreams can reveal the complex therapeutic field, one in which many vectors interweave. Thus, it may strike the reader as complicated, requiring intuitive as well as rational understanding. This is no different from the nature of the therapeutic interaction itself, however. Yet, in its attempt to separate some of the strands of the rich matrix, the discussion may also appear too simple, too abstract, and lacking the multidimensional life that every dream evokes — especially such dreams of the therapeutic field itself. We do not seek to simplify or reify the aspects involved in the whole field. Rather we would hope to provide focus on and circumambulate some of the issues and problems that are likely to arise when such dreams are brought. The field of the therapy, as well as the relativity of the observing analyst within it, are brought up for comment by the Guiding Self of the dreamer/analysand and sometimes by the therapist's dreams as well.

Since every dream reveals information about the dreamer's psychological and physical dynamics and spiritual process, every dream also touches upon issues of relationship projected from the past, problematic in the present, and/or newly emerging. Since, further, the exploration of dynamics inevitably involves their projection (and sometimes inducement) into intimate relationships, every dream may reveal transference/countertransference issues, as they are currently constellated, or as they may develop.[1] Thus, dreams facilitate the working through of old patterns which impede relationships — whether it be to the therapist, to others, to life's work and need gratification, to the unconscious, and/or to the Self.

At its best, dream work can serve to build the capacity for open, trusting, and viable relatedness in all of these areas. It can help to build and maintain the therapeutic alliance and the possibility of fruitful dialogue between conscious ego positions and unconscious processes. At worst, focus on dream images can be used to avoid adequate working through of transference and countertransference issues, and even to impede personal relationships.

As Freud once put it, the 'transference is always present,' although it 'may not beckon.'[2] This is equally true in working with dreams. Not every dream is to be approached in terms of the 'beckoning' transference issues, even if the dream also discloses information about the therapy process. The problems it raises may be more general than the therapy; analysis of the transference may not be appropriate for the dreamer now; there may be no currently acute countertransference problem. But more importantly, the dream setting will always present issues from the particular perspective that provides the most fruitful avenue of approach for their assimilation by the dreamer in each given situation. The times and locations presented in the dream setting show where the complex is constellated and projected for optimal working through. It is thus recommended that the interpreter follow the dream's placement of the issues, remembering that they may have already, or will at some point, also occur in the therapeutic transference.[3] The dream setting orients to the best order of approach. If the setting refers to the dreamer's work or home, etc., the dream locates that metaphor as the one through which the problem can best be opened. Even though the analyst may be fully aware of transference implications, these usually need to be held silently by the therapist until the dream's metaphor is explored first. On the other hand, in dreams which pose the problem in a setting that represents the therapist or the therapy process, the reverse order of working through is indicated: transference implications need to be explored first.

In some cases dreams about the figure of the therapist or therapy are best used silently by the therapist for their countertransferential messages. They provide images around which to orient him or her in establishing and maintaining an adequate-enough therapeutic environment for the work to proceed (see below).

When the figure of the therapist appears in a dream, it may represent:

1. The actual therapist and qualities realistically associated to him or her on the object level.
2. A personal transference projection onto the therapist, which refers

to the dreamer's past experience of interpersonal dynamics.
3. The Inner Therapist/Healer/Self.
4. The therapist's countertransference.
5. The therapeutic process.
6. Qualities projected onto the therapist which refer to the dreamer's subject level dynamics — i.e. a shadow issue.
7. The nature of an archetypal projection onto the therapy or figure of the therapist.

Most often there is a complex combination of some or all of the above, and careful sorting is required to find the nature of the interweavings as the multifaceted image of therapist serves to illuminate the therapeutic field. No dream of the therapist can be placed *a priori* into any one particular category. It has to be assessed within the wide range of possibilities within the mutually constellated field. It is only in working through the dream drama in the context of associations, explanations, and amplifications that such dreams of the figure of the therapist can be adequately placed in the transference-countertransference continuum. Until the dream is worked through, hypotheses may come readily to the therapist's mind, but they must be held. Nowhere else are intuition and feeling — and particularly countertransferential defensive blindness — as dangerous as when they foster premature conclusions.

THE ACTUAL REALITY OF THE THERAPIST

Dreams of the figure of the therapist may refer to *the actual reality of the therapist on the object level.*

An example of such a dream was presented at the first session of therapy.

My therapist confronts me about my problem. I am then on the street running.

Since at the time of the dream the dreamer was not yet consciously aware of the analyst's personality, this dream is to be taken as an object level compensation for the dreamer's consciously held idealization of the new therapy. While its image of the therapist undoubtedly picks up a subliminal reaction to the brief telephone contact establishing the time of the session, and while important information for the therapist about subject level transference and countertransference issues can be deduced from it, it is a message about objective reality for the dreamer. It

151

conveys an image of the therapist's confrontative mode and its effects on the dream-ego. Such a confrontative style causes fear and flight in the dream-ego, perhaps because it threatens her own habit of evasive diffuseness, perhaps because it triggers a parental complex and/or a fear of actual harm. These hypotheses can be explored at some point with the dreamer. In this case the therapist recognized the description as an objective description of his style, and could readily admit the reality factor, which the dream image conveyed. His disclosure of the reality of the dream's description, in this instance, conveyed to the dreamer a stance of self-confrontation, which served as a model for her and mitigated her fear. This circumvented the dreamer's withdrawal, and fostered a reality-based alliance in which the work could proceed.

Dreams of the actual therapist may also refer to the dreamer's reactions to the therapist during a previous session which need to become conscious. An example is the dream of the woman (see above, p. 36) who was made aware of her abandonment fears in response to the therapist's vacation plans. Her dream showed the figure of the therapist sitting on her bed as she woke. As stated previously, her association was to her own visit to her dying aunt when she was younger. By implication she identified with the dying aunt and felt she was dying. The dream led to recognition of the reality of the therapist's departure. It opened the possibility of exploring her infantile abandonment depression, one that had felt like death to her. This reaction had been denied when the matter of separation was discussed at the previous session because she had merged with what she assumed were the therapist's feelings, and overempathized with the therapist's vacation needs. Such fusion is now, the dream puts it, comparable to death, for it is a threat to the dreamer's individual life. Thus the dream raises the reality issue around which those separation fears are to be dealt with.

A dream of the therapist's actual reality may compensate a projection. An example is a young man's dream:

I bring my therapist a book.

The associations to the dream brought out an issue which the dreamer had been reluctant to bring into analysis. The book turned out to associate to the catalog of a school in which he was uncertain about enrollment. He both wanted to bring the quandary into therapy and felt inhibited. In working on the dream the nature of the inhibiting complex emerged. He had withheld the information, fearing his father's spoiling envy of his intellectual capacities. This, he discovered, he had projected onto his therapist.

TRANSFERENCE REACTIONS

As in this instance, dreams of the therapist also may refer to personal, subject-level *transference reactions*. Sometimes there is an interaction from a previous session or an aspect of the therapeutic setting that needs to be explored as the specific trigger of the transference projection. The dreamer with the dying aunt had her abandonment transference activated by the therapist's vacation plans. The dreamer with the enrollment problem hung his projection of anti-intellectual envy on the fact that there were few books in the therapist's office. In another example a woman's mother complex was constellated as a transference factor already before the first session. The fact that the therapist was female was enough to bring it forth. She presented the following dream at her first session.

I go to therapy. The woman is busy with the furniture, cleaning and dusting. She pays no attention to me.

The behavior she associated to her mother. In this case the dream, and the dreamer's behavior in telling it, alerted the therapist to the dreamer's sensitivity to rejection. Since the dreamer's attention-holding behaviors began to induce in the therapist an impatient, sadistic reaction, akin to that of the dreamer's harassed mother, the analyst could monitor her own projective identification reactions with the help of the dream's metaphoric transference description (see below, Countertransference dynamics). The dream image also refers to the 'inner therapist,' the way her obsessive busy-ness ignores her own reality. At the time of the dream, this message was still to be held by the therapist, however, since this was the first session and the dreamer's capacity for subject-level assimilation had not been ascertained.

THE INNER THERAPIST

Dreams about the figure of the therapist may also refer to the *Inner Therapist, Healer, or Guiding Self of the dreamer*, and to the dreamer's relationship to and projection upon that center of perception and authority. This Inner Therapist constitutes the way the dreamer treats him or herself therapeutically — the subjective therapeutic attitude to one's own problems — as well as the expectations of treatment in the therapy process. Such dreams may thus point to dynamics, potential or actual, projected into the therapeutic field and to possible countertransference issues, but they need exploration on the subject level as well.

I am with a tour guide at an ongoing working excavation of
Indian ruins. He is casually showing me around. He looks like
my therapist.

The setting is a working archaeological dig, a place to 'dig' up buried
issues. Given the fact that it is a working excavation (explanation), a
tour guide is inappropriately trespassing. Here an attitude of casual touring, rather than digging into the 'Indian' levels of the dreamer's
psychology, intrudes itself upon depth work. To the dreamer the Indians
represented 'people who were passionate, but they were defeated and
almost disappeared . . . who were here first.' Metaphorically, they refer
to primal levels of once-defeated affect that are being systematically
opened for conscious review. Symbolically, they suggest — among other
things — a world view of reverence and spiritual attunement with nature.
Yet the inner therapist 'tours' what is being brought up, rather than
getting into the earth to experience its rediscovery.

When asked where the dreamer felt that there had been a 'touring'
attitude to her feelings, she replied, 'You were overly interested in my
dream image last week, not in my feelings. Usually I try to get you away
from my feelings, and you won't budge; you just tell me what I'm trying
to do.' With the help of the 'touring' dream, and in projection, she could
begin to see and separate from her own tendency to 'tour' by labelling
her problems in order to control them intellectually. The therapist could
further use the projection upon himself as a means of eliciting the very
('passionate') anger and depression that was in need of further excavation in the dreamer.

In the above example it is possible to tell something about the ongoing
quality of the therapy from the fact that the context setting is an
archaeological dig into which the tour-guide therapist's view intrudes.
The countertransference needs to be considered, however.

Whenever the figure of the therapist appears in a dream, the therapist
needs carefully to assess his or her own probable countertransference. In
this dream the message coincided with the dreamer's conscious reaction;
it did not compensate. Thus it needed to be interpreted for the dreamer
primarily on the subject level as her 'therapeutic' attitude to herself (inner
therapist), which here, as it usually does, has become a transference projection. Dreams repeating consciously held attitudes are to be interpreted as
subject-level phenomena (see above, Chapter 6: Compensation and complementation, p. 59). This does not exclude a possible countertransference
hook, however. This therapist needed to reflect on what had induced him

to focus on the dream image to the exclusion of the dreamer in the previous session.

Since the therapeutic field is mutually constellated, at times the fact that the therapist has worked on his/her countertransference may be registered by the dream as helpful in modifying the dreamer's own Inner Healer — one compensatory to consciously held attitudes to suffering and its relief. In one example:

My therapist lies in bed ill and quite relaxed about it. I sit quietly beside him.

There were two associations. The dreamer said, 'You are just lying there, weak and inert.' When asked how she felt this to be the case in her therapy, she said she felt that 'nothing is happening in the work but sitting around while I go on being upset.' On the other hand she was struck by the fact that the therapist figure was not as upset about illness as she herself tended to be. 'There is no sense of panic in you at all in the dream.'

As the dream was being considered, the therapist silently reviewed his own private struggle with the dreamer's panic reactions, with whether or not more intervention might be called for in her case. In dealing with the problem he had had to delve more deeply into memories of his own ill and alarmist mother, and his countertransference tendency to over-react. At that point both dreamer's and therapist's complexes intersected.

The dream confirmed for both dreamer and therapist that, contrary to the dreamer's expectations and the therapist's inner doubt, a patiently waiting attentiveness, which trusted in the transpersonal process of healing, was the best approach in this case and at this time. In the dreamer, to whom precipitous manic action had seemed the only way to relieve suffering and avoid 'weak inertia,' the dream brings about the possibility of a changed attitude, a more accepting and relaxed therapeutic stance to her own life problems.

At other times a dream of the therapist may point to a different kind of intersection of outer and inner therapist. In one instance a man dreamed:

I have to carry my therapist on my back to the hospital.

This dream brings to the dreamer a feeling he had been trying to push away that he did not want to consider as belonging to the actual reality of the person of the therapist. In association to the therapist's illness, the dreamer said he had felt his therapist was not adequately sensitive to him or his problems. Rather than admit this, however, he 'decided it was a projection' and felt he alone was responsible for the impasse in 'the success of the therapy.' He was trying 'to carry' the therapy process all on his own back, as his own problem. Thereby the dream-ego is severely overburdened. He either does not trust the Self's healing process (inner healer) to be able to carry itself and him, and is thus too effortful; and/or he is to be shown that the process with this therapist is, indeed, too ill to be able to sustain itself.

It is probable that the dreamer was taking too much responsibility for 'the success' of the work in that he did not acknowledge or communicate these negative feelings and doubts about his therapy and his therapist until he told this dream years later to a friend. He had felt afraid he would be 'thrown out.' This turned out to be a repetition of his fears due to abandonment threats his mother had made. He had felt a trigger for this fear in an incautious remark that the therapist had made at a previous session revealing some annoyance at the dreamer's passive–aggressive stance.

Such a dream brought into therapy must, however, call for the therapist's attention to assess the adequacy of his/her own work with the dreamer and the nature of his/her 'illness,' which has been impairing the therapeutic dialogue and which is now so serious that it needs to be brought to the 'hospital' to restore the health of the mutually constellated impasse.

COUNTERTRANSFERENCE DYNAMICS

As we have seen, dreams representing the figure of the therapist must also always be investigated as to their *countertransference dynamics*. Such reactions may be projectively induced or they may be reactions belonging to the therapist's actual psychology, of which the therapist needs to become aware at the time of the dream, since they are currently impeding his or her work with the dreamer. A point that can bear repetition is that such awareness of the countertransference issues, while arising from adequate interpretation of the dream, need not be communicated to the dreamer. It requires committed attention from the therapist, not excluding further analytic or supervisory work, but the issues of disclosure within the therapeutic dialogue are best left to clinical judgement in individual cases.[4]

An example of a dream seemingly 'intended' for the therapist was brought to supervision. The analytic candidate's client dreamt:

I go to session and sit down. My therapist leaves me to let in a delivery boy, who brings him a package. The boy somehow steals my bag.

The dramatic structure of the dream, without any associations, shows a serious transference/countertransference tangle. The normal setting of private, therapeutic consultation is interfered with by the analyst's leaving, by the intrusion of a delivery, and by the theft.

The dreamer's associations to the package were 'You seem to like collecting figurines and books. They might be bringing some more or maybe an encyclopedia or more psychology books.' To the delivery boy she associated an acquaintance, whom she felt was 'mean and brutish.' To the figure of the therapist, she associated 'intelligent, supportive, helpful.'

Immediately the interpreter is struck by the compensatory polarity between the idealized therapist-collector of figurines and books and the crude, thieving delivery boy. There is an intimation from the dream content and associations that the therapist is grossly neglectful of his analysand. He leaves her and he allows intrusion and theft. The figure of the therapist is described as a collector of figurines: metaphorically as one who enjoys the possession of non-individual images. Whether these imply a positive relation to archetypal images or a reduction of personal and living reality is not yet sure. There are no associations. He is, however, brought more such stylized images, by a brutish attitude that steals the dreamer's individual feminine identity and libido (her bag, she said, contained her purse with wallet). He leaves the dream-ego's reality to attend to his images. Or perhaps he is brought intellectual, categorized descriptions of the world (encyclopedia). Does he need to learn more about psychology, or does he learn it from books rather than the woman before him? All of these issues, as well as the need to elicit further associations, were raised in supervision.

When later asked for associations as to what figurines meant to her, the dreamer identified them as 'dainty carvings, female figures.' Further, she thought, maybe she had felt 'like a figurine' to her father, whom she idealized as 'cultured and intelligent,' and 'supportive of [her] every wish.' She was unaware of this description as conveying a patronizing, perhaps even sadistic, 'carved,' diminution of herself. And also of the fact that she had used similar adjectives to describe her therapist. Upon further questioning as to how being treated like a figurine might apply to her feelings about therapy, she 'guessed' that she did 'not have to worry about that, because it would be impossible.'

157

There is certainly a strong transference to the therapist of the idealized father, which the dream seems bent on shaking. For it clearly represents the therapist as failing in his attention to her process and as grossly neglectful. The dream contradicts the dreamer's view. Issues which she could not see in relation to her father are being helped by the dream to open into a negative transference where they may be worked through.

Two theoretical points need consideration: Are the delivery boy and the contents of the delivery to be taken as helpful contributions or hindering interferences? Is the dream to be taken on the subject level as referring to the inner therapist, or on the object level as referring to the therapist and his countertransference, or on both levels?

The first question depends on the associations. What is delivered might be a potentially useful contribution unless otherwise stated. The dreamer's associations to 'dainty carved' figurines, encyclopedias, and psychology books make this delivery inappropriate in content as well as in time. The intrusion is one that implies diminution of the dreamer to a dainty image of the female, and a bookishness, which would make the therapist miss the individual relationship that is essential for good therapy. The dream states that this intrusion constitutes a theft of the dreamer's individuality.

The figure of the delivery boy is an archetypal one, the messenger or psychopomp (for example, Hermes). In the dream drama the figure is dramatically central as the antagonist. It is the carrier of an important psychological message for dreamer and therapist alike. It brings consciousness of and interrupts a collusive therapy process. It also brings in qualities of crude aggression (associations to the delivery boy), qualities which are far from the dreamer's ideal ego identity, but which might eventually be discovered as helpful guardians for the seeds of a genuine authenticity, and which may usher in the negative transference as the old 'dainty' and idealizing identity no longer claims the ego's loyalty.

To decide the second theoretical point we need to refer to the principle of compensation. Had the dreamer considered the therapist to be neglectful and bookish, the dream might have had to be taken on the subject level as a revelation of the projection of those qualities, which belong primarily to the dreamer. However, even in such a case the dream should provide food for self-reflection for the therapist. Since, in this case, the dreamer idealizes the therapist, the dream is compensatory already on the object level and implicates the actual therapist. The dream depicts the therapist as unable to pay attention to the dreamer, for his shadow (delivery boy) qualities, namely a brutal attitude, exclude the dreamer, and he is caught up in theoretical ideas (therapy by the book). Caught inductively in the idealized father transference, the therapist may be putting down the dreamer's individuality in a fashion similar to the way she cannot yet see her father did. The dream provides a serious warning to the therapist, apprising him of induced and personal counter-transference issues that need urgent attention.

On the other hand the dream also has clear implications on the subject level for the Inner Therapist of the dreamer as well, pointing towards the dreamer's own self-neglect, false and abstract ego-ideals, and self-diminution. The dream and its associations describe the Inner Therapist conditioned by the father complex. This Inner Therapist tends to an idealization of bookishness and estheticism, which inevitably diminishes the dreamer's self-respect. She can never live up to the ideals of such inner masculine authority. Her own brutish deliverer of ideals (figurines and books) robs her of self-value.

Whenever a projection is induced in the therapist, the therapist's own matching problem will tend to magnify the inductive process. Such meshing problems are common and lead either to disaster or to profound healing, for they can be extremely helpful in supporting an increase of empathy and consciousness as the therapist works through his/her own share of the intersecting problem.

Since the dream of the figure of the therapist points to issues where complexes of dreamer and therapist intersect in their mutually constellated psychic field, such field representations make it possible for the therapist sometimes — and after checking more obvious counter-transference indications — to explore the analysand's dream as if it were the therapist's own, dreamed by an aspect of him/herself. The therapist's own associations to the client's dream may thus shed light on an issue in his/her own dynamics, one which contributes to the mutual field's confusion. Sometimes this can aid in the discovery of the complexes intruding into the field from the analyst's psychology. Needless to add, these associations must be applied to the countertransference only after careful consideration of the dreamer's associations and problems. Perhaps, and cautiously, they may be tested as to their relevance for the dreamer.

Meshing issues are not necessarily negative, as we have seen. They often embroil the therapeutic dyad in deep struggles where both must grow into awareness in order to promote the goal of the client's welfare.

An example of the way the therapist's associations may be added for better understanding of the countertransferential implications of a dream is the following:

> I see my therapist's father looking through the window of the consulting room. He looks very unusual, vaguely mysterious.

His associations were to his own father's 'usual' critical derogations. When the therapist inquired about his sense of being criticized in the previous sessions, he acknowledged that he had feared that his revelations of dependency would bring a disgust reaction from the therapist, even though they did not. As this was worked through as a transference projection and as an issue relating to the analysand's own inner therapist's attitude to dependency, the therapist silently searched herself for feelings of contempt that might have been projectively induced. Finding none, she noted the possibility for future consideration.

The therapist realized that since the dream referred to her father, about whom the analysand overtly knew nothing, she could use her own associations to her father relevant to the issue of dependency to work further and outside of session on the dream. Her father, she realized, encouraged dependency to feed his narcissistic needs and then envied those he infantilized. This association led the analyst to realize that the dreamer's revelation of dependency had, indeed, stimulated her own father complex, not in terms of criticalness, but in terms of encouraging dependency which might lead to spoiling envy toward the dependant. This made the therapist aware that, contrary to her conscious assessment, such envy might become a problem in the countertransference and mesh with transference expectations. It gave her material on which to work to maintain the level of psychic hygiene necessary for the therapeutic process. And it opened a possible avenue of approach to the client/dreamer's fear of criticism.

Beyond the transference/countertransference issue raised by this dream, two additional matters need consideration. The dream father is described as looking 'very unusual and vaguely mysterious.' He is looking on the therapy process in a way that is 'unusual,' unaccustomed to the dreamer because uncritical acceptance of dependency would feel unusual to him. Thus, there is a contrast to his actual father: a new kind of father. This dream father brings the problem of the father complex into therapy. The dreamer can 'see' his personal father problem through the open window of therapy. The issue of the dreamer's criticalness of self and others, introjected from the personal father, is brought into the therapy process to be seen and worked on.

The image of the unusual father, since it is 'mysterious,' needs also to be considered from its otherwordly, or mythic, level. It is an intimation of the archetypal father against which the personal mis-constellation of father can be seen, as if in relief. This father image constellates an archetypal father for the dreamer — the principles of paternal nurturance, authority, order, and objectivity, etc. It presents also an intimation of an archetypal transference (see p. 172).

INDUCTION BY THE THERAPIST

To complicate matters further, there may be an inductive effect upon the analysand of the therapist's outlook. Such a possible bias needs also to be taken into consideration. This is sometimes a factor to consider when judging the direction of interpretation, relative to the likely compensating function of the dream. In the example on p. 157 it took considerable inner work on himself by the therapist to discover in what ways his habitual perspective on and ideals about 'feminine' constituted a distortion of the dreamer's potential individuality and development. Initially he felt comfortable with her 'dainty carved' feminine ideal and could see little amiss with it. His own projection of such an identity for the dreamer continued, thus, to collude with the induced father projection. Until he could discover this by working on the countertransference problem that this dream brought, his bias subtly supported the dreamer's self-diminishment.

To give a few more drastic examples of the analysand's dreams as a call to work on countertransference issues and their inductive effect on the dreamer:

I am being put through a clothes wringer by my therapist.

Or:

My teeth are worked on by an incompetent dentist.

Or:

I cannot see. My therapist pays no attention.

All of these dreamers had *unadmitted* doubts about their therapists. The first felt squeezed into a dogmatic interpretive system by her therapist (she reported that the therapist had interpreted this dream as a defense against the dreamer's having to admit that she had fallen in love with him). The others also felt uneasy about their therapist's competence.

Yet under the suggestive induction effects of the therapist's convictions and self-image, they denied their unease to themselves. They identified with the therapist's position. In such situations the therapist's position, which by induction has become the dreamer's own, has annulled the dreamer's subliminal awareness. The dreams then compensate and challenge what has become a *folie à deux*.

Often, unable or fearing to face the difficulties in working through the material of such dreams with the therapists involved, the dreamers bring such dreams to other analysts. This fosters splitting.

At times such inductive effects are not necessarily negative. Just as a parent tends to hold, mirror, and foster the latent potentials in the child, so sometimes the therapist can see through what is currently problematic to buried potentials in the dreamer/analysand. Working through complexes to uncover these potentials is part of the process. Sometimes only the therapist's intuition that they exist at all can induce hope to carry the client through painful intervals. Such perception of the authentic Self qualities and positive shadow potentials can, negatively, result in the therapist's losing sight of the reality of the impeding complexes. Therefore, such perception and its possible inductive effects need to be held consciously and in balance, lest the actual, inadequate ego structures of the client, as they currently exist, be lost to view. Dreams, as well as the dreamer's reactions, often serve to bring such positive inductions to the therapist's attention when they are problematic.

An example:

My therapist shows me jewels. But they are not mine.

The value is shown as present in the dreamer's psyche, but the dream-ego cannot claim it, for the jewels still 'belong' to an unconscious complex.

The procedure to be followed for the sake of adequately understanding such dreams must include dealing with associations and explanations regarding the images of the dream drama and finding the possible trigger (explanation) in previous sessions for their dream appearance. Second, it is necessary to look for what the dream represents to be problematic or sick in the therapy process, the inner therapist, and/or the counter-transference. Finally, it is important to take account of what the dream might be pointing to in terms of relationship dynamics and of a changed attitude to the dreamer's own life problems. Only by seeing it thus fully in the context of the field which it images can the interpreter begin to fathom its significance.

The only way a therapist can deal with issues involving his own blind-spots — and their effects on the therapeutic field and the psyche of the analysand — lies in taking seriously the fact that all dreams referring to therapist or therapy need to be considered as very likely to have countertransference implications also. This attitude of willingness to explore the countertransference, including its induction effects on the analysand dreamer, is fundamental to therapeutic integrity.

DREAMS OF THE PROCESS OF THERAPY

Dreams of the figure of the therapist may also refer to *the process of therapy itself*. Here any issues regarding any aspects or changes in the analytic field, the very style of therapeutic interaction itself, will be raised for the dreamer's attention.

A woman dreamed that

My therapist is leaving for another city.

Work on the dream brought up fears of abandonment projected onto the therapist's six-month distant vacation. These fears came up, it was discovered, as a self-punitive response to the previous session in which the dreamer had been, as she put it, 'quite obnoxious; I practically ordered you to open the window and told you what I thought when you didn't get up.' When this was worked through to its roots in a crushing mother complex ('I am not supposed ever to be dominating like my mother was'), the therapist asked to where the dream-therapist was moving. Without hesitation the dreamer said, 'to California.' Her associations pointed to California as a place of 'easy freedom and relative self-indulgence.' With the analyst she could then share the dream's humorous metaphor of where her own process was to go as she 'self-indulgently' and with 'easy freedom' spoke up more vociferously to express her needs and feelings.

Dreams referring or associating to the person of the therapist, to the time and place of therapy, or to any changes in these are allegoric comments on the therapy process. Sometimes, as we have seen, they refer to specific experiences of previous sessions or to complexes coming into awareness in the mutual field between dreamer and therapist that intrude negatively or undermine the process. Sometimes, however, they refer to factors and qualities that need to be present and are not yet. This can usually be discovered by exploring associations fully and even by asking the dreamer how the qualities suggested by the image are carried in projection by the intruding figure in a reality situation.

An example:

I arrive early for session, and your son is there. He shows me a safe and good place to park my car.

The dream-ego's early arrival was first explored through associations. It led to the awareness of an eagerness covering impatient control and fears of not being wanted, a dynamic that spoiled his relationships and sexual functioning. It is the problem to which the 'son' — by directing him to a safe spot to 'park' his habitual way of going in order to encounter his own healing therapeutic process — turned out to be the solution.

To the figure of the analyst's son the dreamer associated his fantasies, 'Someone relaxed, direct, open.' Why? 'He feels supported.' When asked further how the son might feel about having to be early, the dreamer said bitterly, 'He wouldn't need to rush; he could trust you'd be there for him.' The fact that he dreamed about such a figure implied the potential was already seeded in him, and discussion made him aware of the moments in which he, indeed, felt such trust. The awareness of such trust and the image of 'the son,' as the child-product and future of the therapy process itself, could then be utilized to begin to alter his habitual identity as a 'bitter' outsider.

Dream images referring to the therapeutic process can range over a wide spectrum. They include medical and dental procedures and other forms of body work and body care: barbering, food acquisition and preparation, gym training; allegories of body care: the care and servicing of the dreamer's car, house, tools, musical instruments, plumbing, electrical fixtures, garden, garbage, animals, clothing, food; shamanic and priestly rituals and teaching; architectural and construction work of all kinds, including excavation and demolition; exploration, journeys; teaching and coaching situations; the taming or training of animals; parent–child interactions; all the way even to performing on a quiz show with a master of ceremonies.

The list is seemingly endless. Each image has its particular tone and important qualitative distinctions as a metaphor for the therapeutic relationship and tasks. Each can reveal the expectations and tone projected upon or objectively present in the dreamer's therapeutic process.

Each may also be considered for countertransference indications, calling for the therapist to examine his or her countertransferential investment in the particular role represented. The dream of the guru's exotic bird is an example (see above, p. 15), calling for the therapist

164

to examine his/her guru-identification needs and to deal with whatever aspects of the power complex this identification serves to gratify at the dreamer's expense.

Details of the behavior of the dream figure in the place of the therapist can express poignantly the dreamer's unconscious reactions and anticipations. A woman brought an initial dream:

> I am sitting in a dentist's chair and refuse to open my mouth for fear of being hurt.

This image pointed to a fear and resistance to the analytic process. Asked to associate to dentists, the dreamer said, 'All dentists are sadists.' It is noteworthy that she could not associate to a particular dentist, showing an incapacity (and/or fear to) differentiate. This incapacity extends to her therapist (as well as to others and herself). She is unable to see him as an individual person rather than as an impersonal member of a sadistic collective. The dream is thus immediately diagnostic about the early and damaged level of her relationships, and the quality of her defense against assumed negative oral intrusion.

A dentist works on the teeth, metaphorically on the processes for getting hold of and beginning to assimilate reality issues and for making nurturance digestible. The dreamer's anticipation, based on former experiences to be explored, projects sadism and impersonality on the therapist and the process and inhibits her own orality and oral aggression.

Another woman dreamed after a few sessions:

> I am getting a new house built. It will take a long time, but I am glad I can move out of mother's little apartment. There is a huge tractor pushing earth around for the foundation. I am terrified it will change the whole landscape. I want it to go away.

The dream is a descriptive metaphor of the way the dreamer was experiencing the analytic process. Her conflict was revealed by the dream-ego's affect — her gladness to leave the maternal space, now too 'little' for her, and her fear of the tractor. The dreamer associated to this image her sense that tractors were 'agents of destruction of the natural land-scape.' The phrasing had a tone of radical political rhetoric, which questioning revealed to have its roots in her mother's socialist dogmas. Because tractors are (explanation) relatively insensitive manifestations of the power to transform, here seen so fearfully, the therapist was alerted to the quality of rather brutal force that the dreamer anticipated and/or experienced as therapy. The analogy could be explored, first as referring to actual experiences in the dreamer's past, then as referring to perceptions from previous therapy sessions, and finally as an expectation projected onto the work, which had its roots in the rather brutal mother complex and memories of 'being shoved around for my own good, uprooted over and over, to go where the Party sent us.'

An initial dream, 'I have boarded an ocean liner. It does not leave the dock,' foretold the outcome of the therapy itself. It would go nowhere. Had the therapist inquired about associations, or encouraged fantasies about what was amiss, the deadlock might have been made conscious, and the 'boat' of therapy might have been able to go to sea. The ship is an archetypal image for crossing the waters of the unknown; hence it is an image of a vehicle of the great journey of transformation, and in this context, as the presenting dream of analysis, would refer to the therapy process.

A seemingly innocent dream brought to a very inexperienced therapist:

> I began a journey, but I stop in Venice. But I get hungry and can't find anywhere to eat except a fast, junk-food hot dog stand.

This dream of a bungled process also uses metaphorical allusions to the analysis. The journey is a frequently occurring allegory. Here the dreamer's associations to Venice, 'a beautiful city of romance that I love,' were in strong contrast to her explanation, 'a decaying, old place, slowly sinking.' The dream puts her in a place of decay with a romanticized, beautiful façade. In this setting the only means of nurturing herself and her journey, that she can find, is 'fast, junk food.' The dream describes a romanticized, 'hot-dog' (phallic–erotic) transference/countertransference tangle which offers 'fast junk' instead of solid, nutritional work. The therapist was overimpressed by the archetypal symbolism (journey, beautiful 'Self' city) and by the dreamer's affect towards the romance, and failed to see the ominous implications of the dream.

VARIATIONS ON THE THEME OF THE THERAPY PROCESS

Some dreams involving the therapist or space of the encounter with the therapist point metaphorically to the issues arising in the therapy process:

> My analyst comes to the house where I lived age 7.

Or:

My mother (or sister, grandfather, etc.) comes to my therapy session . . . .

In the first, the transference aspect comes to the psychological space of the 7-year-old. Therapy has revoked experiences pertaining to age 7, which now require working through. In the second, the issue of the specific relative has intruded itself in order to be dealt with by the working alliance of dreamer and therapist focusing together upon the intrusive factor.

Other dreams point to metaphors showing how the therapy process and the transference and countertransference are coming into focus — whether these may be detrimental repetitions of old dynamics to be made conscious or may even imply potentially corrective (or spoiling) therapeutic interactions. The dream content will specify the nature of the psychological dynamics involved — often through the details of description and the space and time frames of the setting:

I am in the waiting room having my session . . . .

I go to my therapist's house and we meet in the bedroom . . . .

Both of these represent the theme of the therapy process, showing variations from its usual and accepted structure. These variations are to be explored in terms of associations, explanations and — where pertinent — amplifications. To have a session in the waiting room may imply resistance to therapy in hesitation to face the issues, or haste to unburden before entering the appropriate, ritual space. It may imply a lack of privacy and/or fears for confidentiality, or a sibling issue roused by having met another client in the waiting room — or whatever associations occur to 'waiting room' and to the question 'what would it feel like if this were a real situation?'

A session in the therapist's bedroom may imply inappropriate or excessive intimacy experienced, expected, or projected into the therapy. It may point to eroticized transferential/countertransferential dynamics, the presence or need for more intimacy, or even to aspects of infant–parent relationship — all according to associations to bedroom, bedroom arrangements, and the therapy.

Another common variation on the theme of the therapy process involves changes in the usual cast:

I go to therapy. A noisy teenage crowd occupies the space so I can't have my hour.

Because the dream represents the crowd as already present in the therapist's office, rather than as intruding, it presents a possible counter-transferential dynamic — whether induced or as a complex of the therapist's own psychology. The therapist needs to check if such a possibility is valid on the object level. Does he or she have a teenage problem, or is he or she too overly formal, detached, and authoritatively earnest in regard to teenagers? Is he or she failing to see the dreamer as an individual, and instead as typical of, for example, a non-individual collective diagnostic category — a crowd? Such questions need to be allowed to arise in the therapist's mind in contemplating such a dream image. If the teenage crowd were to intrude during an ongoing session, it would more likely suggest an intrusive subject issue, similar to the preceding dream, depending upon associations and compensation factors.

It is important also to probe where such a disturbance may have been felt by the dreamer in previous interactions, specifically in the session before the dream occurred and to explore the dreamer's emotions, attitudes, fantasies, and defenses arising from such perception.

Exploration on the dreamer's subject level is also important. Associations to teenagers and memories of the dreamer's own adolescence need to be elicited and explored. The dreamer's attitude to therapy needs to be checked out. Is it colored by teenage frivolity, rebellion, collectivity, or by an idealizing crush that prevents opening to individual depth work, 'so [he] can't have [his] hour?' The dream may be calling attention to these elements and the need for awareness of their presence as impediments to the therapeutic process.

Had the dream dramatics presented the teenagers and even the noise as a non-interfering addition or even as a helpful compensation to the dreamer's self-concept, it would have implications requiring the search for adolescent attitudes and experience which might be beneficial because they were once shunned, but now are emerging for integration into the process by both therapist and dreamer. The therapist may need to see what prevents him from allowing for these attitudes.

Images of the therapist's involvement with someone besides the dream-ego require exploration of the qualities projected onto the alternative figure.[5] It may be that the dreamer feels the therapist/parent/Self prefers another — thus revealing projected oedipal, sibling, and rejection issues. Or it may be that there are aspects of the dream-ego or dreamer that are, indeed, being missed due to countertransference problems or the therapist's preoccupations which leave little libido for the dreamer's analysis. Such problems may cause the therapist to focus on only certain shadow qualities of the dreamer (these may be positive or negative). Or there may be qualities seen by the outer and/or inner therapist that are not yet valued by the dreamer.

My therapist prefers Agnes.

Associations to Agnes were 'nice,' meaning 'dutiful, she writes her dreams down.' In fact the therapist had never asked for dreams to be written and was not concerned with that chore for this dreamer. The dream may imply the dreamer's assumption that the analyst needs to be pleased by an Agnes-like compliance. Alternatively, it may imply that the dream-ego is too antagonistic and that in her unconscious Agnes aspect there is a capacity to be less obsessively rebellious, which would be 'preferable' for the sake of the therapy process. The interpretation of the dream and whether to take it on a subject level (inner therapist) or object level (outer therapist) will depend on which conscious stance the dream best compensates, on which one best wins that deep confirmatory affirmation from the dreamer's body, Self, and on future dreams correcting and/or commenting on the dreamer's understanding of this one.

IMAGES OF ALTERNATIVE THERAPISTS

Dream figures other than the therapist functioning as therapists, or figures similar in appearance, dress or other detail, or associated to as being the therapist, may be dealt with as aspects of the dreamer's Inner Therapist. They are best approached as the dreamer's attitudes and secondarily applied to transference projections. Dreams of the therapist's family, or therapists of a different sex or another personality than the therapist, generally refer to alternative approaches to the process and to self, called or uncalled for, according to context. Whatever qualities and properties happen to be associated with these figures are indicated as relevant to the process, intrusive, needed, helpful or hindering as the case may be. The images should always be also checked out for hitherto unnoticed countertransferential implications, however.

When, for instance, an alternative therapist conducts the session, perhaps one of the opposite sex from the therapist, the qualities represented by the figure (a more feminine or masculine or whatever the outstanding quality of the alternative happens to be by association and explanation) are either called for or are already present as a hindrance. This can be determined by the structure of the drama, by compensation or complementation, and sometimes also by the dreamer's sense of the encounter if it were a reality situation. For example, a woman dreamt:

I go to session. Your wife is there and does the therapy.

In terms of explanation the wife was not a therapist; hence her appearance as therapist is probably inappropriate. Had she been a therapist, her appearance might compensate a possible countertransference problem as in the dream below.

The dreamer's associations and emotional reactions to the 'wife' were, 'You care more for her than for me; you are always available to her.' What is she like? 'She is warm and attractive.' Working this through helped the dreamer to see that she unrealistically idealized and envied the conjugal relationship as one of almost symbiotic 'availability.' This reminded her of her parents' close relationship, which she felt excluded her. Issues of competition with her own 'warm' and 'attractive' mother were to be looked at, as well as her despair of claiming her own warmth and attractiveness.

In another instance of the same dream, from a different dreamer, the association to wife was, 'She's warmer and more related than you.' In this case these qualities were felt to be absent from the process, and in need of being brought in by therapist and/or dreamer to aid the work. However, conversely, it might be that the dreamer has been trying to elicit such gratifying attention to forestall self-confrontation. The dream would then confront her with the fact that her own Inner Therapist is using the wish for warm empathy as a defense.

It bears repetition that whenever a dream seems to confirm a position that is consciously held by the dreamer, the images are to be understood as relating to the subject level — projections into the therapy of attitudes, emotions, complexes of the dreamer. Since they are represented by the figure of the therapist, they may be best worked on in terms of the transference.

Dreams about specifically erotic or aggressive interaction with the therapist point to attraction/union or destruction/separation tendencies toward the person of the therapist on the object level, to those qualities projected onto the therapist from the subject level, to the process of therapy, or to the inner Healer or Guiding Self of the dreamer.

170

As mentioned above (see Chapter 11: Body imagery), erotic motifs occur when there is repressed sexuality that is awakened in the transference. But they may also occur to make conscious or to compensate inadequate acceptance or awareness (by dreamer and/or therapist) of the therapeutic process and the dreamer's deeply emotional involvement in it. The possible and actual feelings, which such dreams bring to light, need to be worked on first. They are, quite frequently, complementing reactions for inadequate feeling rapport — for example, when therapist and/or dreamer are emotionally distant from their relationship and, thus, from the process itself. They may be compensatory when the dreamer is caught in an entrenched negative transference and/or resists or denies the value of the therapist and therapy.

Sexual motifs can also reveal the presence of an eroticized resistance to the unfolding of preoedipal dependency needs with their inevitably concomitant frustrations. This is particularly true in regressive phases when the projection of ideal care-taker resists challenge.

They may at other times reveal a primitive power dynamic, whereby the dream-ego seeks to enrapture or rape the therapist to gain healing magically or to prevent it.

At other times the archetypal image of sexual intercourse provides an image for the deep communicative and interpenetrating levels of the work. It may emerge in a dream after a particularly painful and negative transferential issue is being worked through to indicate the renewal of a potentially fruitful union between dream-ego and Inner Therapist/Self as well as a revitalized relationship between dreamer and analyst. With the presentation of each dream the specific implications of the psychological rather than only concretistic interaction need to be explored.

An example of an erotic dream:

> At therapy I go to the bathroom to take a shower. I want my
> therapist to come in with me, to undress, and to get into the
> shower with me for sex.

The dreamer associated 'too formal' to the figure of the therapist. He wanted more involvement and personal relatedness. To shower he associated 'warmth, a way to get warm quickly after work outdoors' when he worked in the Arctic. To undress, he said, would mean 'being more personally open.' It was explained as 'the removal of external covers, roles.'

On the object level the dream depicts a 'want' for an inappropriate and counterproductive procedure. It images erotic desires used in the service of immediate gratification. The roots of this need for more 'undressing' and warmth could readily be found in the transference of a cold and rejecting mother complex, experience which the dreamer continually denied.

There are depicted here, however, several archetypal themes of profound significance that we have not yet considered. The image of the shower or bath is cleansing and transforming, a baptismal immersion. Bathing with someone implies being in the same water — being joined in and sharing the same encompassing experience. Sexuality is an archetypal connection process — an instinctual, existential interpenetration. Archetypal themes always point to intrinsically positive and necessary potentials, even when they are constellated in a negative or destructive fashion. Consequently, such a dream cannot be considered to be interpreted adequately until such positive implications can also be found. These lie only on the subject level. The undressing theme refers to the dreamer's need to let down his defensive protection. He also needs to become more closely and warmly involved with his Inner Therapist, more self-accepting. His remote and distant attitude to himself (Inner Therapist), derived from the mother complex, is too cold and formal. This cold impersonalness is projected onto the actual therapist. The dream, then, compensates a negative transference and points to its possible resolution.

The therapist, in this case, also needed to examine a possibly too formal stance, for the dreamer's impetuous sexual demands had, indeed, evoked a defensive distancing in her. She had to deal with the induced countertransference of the cold mother.

THE ARCHETYPAL TRANSFERENCE IN DREAMS

As in the above example, dreams about the therapist refer not only to personal transference and countertransference issues, they can also point to the archetypal aspects of therapy and transference. The process of therapy is, indeed, archetypal: namely, closely allied to the individuation process, of fundamental, transpersonal transformation and integration, independent of personal volition, and potentially enabling the dreamer/analysand to become what he or she 'is meant to be.' We speak of archetypal transference when transpersonal energies and images are symbolically experienced through the person of the therapist or appear as representations of the therapy process.

Generally in the beginning of therapy and often at other times as well, the personal and archetypal levels of the transference are mixed together. Dream images help to sort these levels by calling attention to the particular personal and/or archetypal issues which are to be confronted, according to the timing of the unfolding process. The transference dynamics and the dreams may, at such times, point to the transcendent dimension as the source of corrective and/or destructive/spoiling experiences, above and beyond the purely personal interaction.

A dream revealing, expressing, and constellating such corrective experience in the therapy relationship was brought:

> I dream that there is a figure that has your (the therapist's) face, but she is not you. She wears widely spread skirts and her breasts are bare. I feel I need to crawl under her skirts to be safe.

The dreamer's association was 'it would be arousing. I have been telling you that I have been trying to get that all the time.' An apparently sexual transference is brought up by the dream. But in this case that is bringing out nothing new. Thus, on this level, the dream is not adequately understood.

The description of the dream figure indicates that it resembles many examples of sculpture of the fertile goddess of earth, plants, and animal life. Crawling under the skirt is an aspect of some traditional adoption ceremonies. Crawling between the spread legs of the 'mothers' of the tribe is part of initiation rituals of the second birth into manhood as an initiated tribesman.[6] The dream points to the themes of being adopted by the transpersonal mother, and of achieving full manhood among men by becoming a child of the goddess. What appears to the dreamer as a purely personal and sexual image is shown to contain the hidden need to be reborn as a child of the Great World Mother. If he can assimilate and relate to the numinosity of the images in the dream, the dreamer can be led beyond the mis-constellations of the personal mother–child ruptured bonding, which he suffered, and also beyond his defensive and futile Don Juan attempts to punish the bad mother and regain the good through the seductive overpowering of many women.

When transpersonal transference occurs, the therapist may appear as though she or he were the deliberate director (goddess, priestess, magician, shaman, conductor, alchemist, captain, etc.) — seemingly personally responsible for the process. In such cases the Self is projected onto the therapist, who acquires a potent numinosity, even as the central focus in the dreamer's life.

173

The phenomenology of the archetypal transference can also help in the understanding of grossly unrealistic and split love/hate responses to the therapist who appears as the carrier of the mother or father archetype. Parent–child archetypal constellations activate pre-personal instinctual expectations for mothering, fathering, etc. that are projected into the therapy field where they can be made conscious. Hence, those projected elements in the archetypal transference can, when worked through, ultimately connect the dreamer on the subject level with powerful transpersonal forces of support, nurturance, direction, and energy.

When such profound energies have not been adequately mediated by personal mother and father, they will appear in archetypally exaggerated, often polarized forms. Inadequate mothering will arouse images of destructive and withholding witch, evil queen, closed ice box, cancerous breasts, etc. It will also arouse images of all-nurturant sources: flowing breast, cornucopia or warm cave (often in modernized forms), protective and holding fairy godmother or goddess, etc. The father archetype will appear negatively in dreams as dictator, Mafia chief, evil magician, rapist; or positively as guiding, wise and benign authority, as phallic procreative image, or as any of the traditional father-gods, etc. When worked through personally, these images and their effects in the transpersonal transference constellate and mediate corrective emotional experiences to repair inadequate parenting, by reconnecting the dreamer to the transpersonal source itself.[7]

In regard to the dream on p. 160 in which the 'unusual' father of the therapist is looking through the window, personal transference and countertransference implications were discussed above. As a representation of the potential for corrective experience of the archetypal father pattern, the dream raises the issues of order, support, protection, guiding authority, objective wisdom, and positive relations to collective reality, work and limits — some of the symbolic implications of the father image.

Another example of the archetypal transference is Jung's patient's dream of the grain god.[8] It depicts her analyst as a giant figure striding over the fields, carrying the dream-ego, as if she were a child. It shows an image of the analyst as deity — a confusion of dimensions by virtue of the projections of a transpersonal energy onto his person. Analyzing the projection made it possible to sort out the spiritual dimension from the personal, and to separate what could be integrated with personal responsibility from what could only be seen, accepted, and then suffered and served.

When the images are positive, they are bound to represent some form of idealization. This can serve as a defensive screen, protecting the dreamer from opening him/herself and personally relating to the therapist, and keeping both therapist and process at a distance from himself. Since such idealization often goes with fear and compensates contempt, the dream is likely to be compensatory. It may bring up the therapist's personal shadow, or it may represent the archetypal quality in a negative or humorous fashion. Such dream images serve to revalue the qualities idealized.

'My therapist is the Empress of China' presents a dream image that takes the idealization and hidden envy to its absurd limits, and may also call for the therapist to work on her countertransferential illusions of grandeur.

An idealization involves the projection of transpersonal energies. The projection is a first step towards consciousness. Thus while the idealizing dream may poke fun at the transference projection, it also serves to assist such assimilation.

I am at a dinner table. My therapist is there at the head. I feel honored and shy. He hands me some grapes. Then he turns into a monkey and jumps up and down on his chair.

The image of the therapist turning into a ridiculous monkey compensates the dreamer's idealization of her therapist as an all-wise, serious authority. She felt 'shy and very honored to have been received as a patient' of such 'a great man.' She worked very hard at her therapy, and brought a carefully worked out amplification of the image of grapes to the session, associating them to Dionysus and Christ. When asked for personal associations, she guiltily remembered stealing seedless grapes as a child from her aunt only because she liked their sweetness, and that she was afraid of monkeys because her mother had once been bitten by a friend's pet monkey. She wanted to be able to discuss Hanuman, the monkey god of the Ramayana, but she had not read enough. Her idealizations of the therapist and therapy process are presented by the dream as ridiculous. They are in need of re-evaluation. To this end the ideal therapist turns into a monkey.

The positive potential in the monkey archetype, indeed, needs to be considered. The monkey is certainly not the dreamer's ideal, but its image points to the kernel of an archetypal energy pattern of which she needs to become conscious. The monkey is a symbol for the ever-present, spontaneous, pre-human, hedonistic qualities, that often strike us as funny. Such qualities the dreamer's therapy process could use.

Dream images of the negative archetypal transference usually depict fearsome, destructive powers. They serve to make conscious the forces spoiling the possibilities of therapy by attacking and preventing relationship.

A young woman dreamt:

I am going to analysis. There is a woman doctor who has snakes in her hair. I am terrified.

The dream shows that the archetype of the paralyzing Medusa had been constellated in the therapy. Medusa is a mythological figure. It is inclusive of, but cannot be reduced to, mere personal maternal dynamics. The image implies a need for the dreamer to look at her fear of the therapist, who has become the carrier of frightening reality as such. An extraordinary degree of the general human fear of life and living, and of the unconscious itself, becomes focused in the dreamer's fear of the therapist. She is to look at this fear, the mythologem tells us, through the mirror of Athena's shield — through experiential understanding rather than identifying with the affect. She is to 'behead' the fear-giver with the 'sword' of discrimination, and then to hold its powerful emotions within the transpersonal vessel of the therapy process itself. This image and the mythology behind it present the particular approach called for by this client's need at this stage — one stressing heroic confrontation. Exploring the dreamer's terror of the person of the therapist in terms of the specific experiences of previous sessions revealed her fear of the therapist's sharpness, which in turn reminded her of her envious mother. This the therapist decided to admit as one of the shortcomings with which she struggled, and which she tried to overcome, but which might provide an opportunity for the dreamer to risk 'heroic' confrontation. In disclosing the reality factor and bonding with the dreamer to confront it, the therapist sought to begin to mediate and humanize an archetypal fear-giver, which was also a fear of life. In so doing, she moved toward the comrade-to-hero position of Athena in the myth of Medusa.

When the sick, shadow side of the therapist is shown, it is often a negative experience for the idealizing client unless the archetypal character of this fact can be realized. With some acceptance such a revelation can serve to build an empathic connection between dreamer and therapist and bridge the gap between consciousness and the wounded aspects of the dreamer:

My therapist lies in bed ill and quite relaxed about it. I sit quietly beside him.

This dream has been discussed above. Here it will be explored from the archetypal perspective. Often, as stated before, archetypal and personal motifs appear together in the same dream, and/or an archetypal image occurs with a more personal and modern disguise.

Here the would-be healer is shown as sick himself. The motif of the wounded or suffering healer is a universal one: Jesus, Odin, Chiron, are some examples.[9] As the Delphic oracle put it, 'the wounder shall heal.' For only by his own suffering, consciously borne, can the healer know adequately the nature of illness and be helpful. Moreover, by realizing that the therapist himself has suffered and is patiently working his way through his own life problems, the dreamer can better accept the shortcomings of the therapist's humanity, and thereby his own — can accept with an attitude of empathy rather than flee with defensiveness and rejection.

DREAMS OF THERAPY FOR THE THERAPIST ONLY

There is a large class of dreams of the therapist and the process which present images of the therapy process and transference and counter-transference interaction. They are dreamed, it would seem, for the therapist only, or primarily in order that he or she may adjust him/herself to the mutual field. Such dreams occur when the therapy process is limited to the working through of regressive transferential relationships. For such dreamers, work on an image, or especially an amplification, is experienced as a detraction from the management of overwhelming affects or even as an injury to the fragile therapeutic bond. Yet the client continues to dream and present dreams, and sometimes works attentively on one, or sometimes takes pleasure in destroying any possibility of interpretation, or tantalizes by withholding associations.

Nevertheless the dreams are invaluable for the therapist. They provide clues to what is happening in the archetypal field of early parent–child relationship that is constellated in the therapeutic transference and countertransference. In the face of an absence of verbal associations, the behavior concurrent with the dream takes their place, as though it were an association. To the dreamer this is what is usually to be interpreted rather than the dream itself. To the therapist, however, these behavioral associations often furnish means to understand the dream as well as the changes in the therapy process to which the dream points. And even while there are no verbal associations forthcoming when the dream is told, sometimes the therapist can piece out a deeper understanding of the dream images by remembering communications from other sessions that provide relevant material.

One example was dreamt by a woman who came to therapy only because the court required it and who 'destroyed' every attempt to discuss her dreams; although she presented them from time to time:

> I visit your house [the therapist's]. I am hungry, but I wouldn't say. You give me a meat sandwich. I eat it, and it's okay.

The facts that the setting is not the office, and that the dreamer is given meat the therapist knew to be problematic from material mentioned at other sessions. There was strong envy connected to an earlier fantasy about the therapist's 'rich house.' And the dreamer was a vegetarian.

Nonetheless, the dream is a metaphoric statement that the therapy process may be having strong effects on the dreamer, rousing hungers that were being met, even though the dream-ego and dreamer 'wouldn't say.' Regardless of resistances and fear, change may be occurring. This is stated in the last sentence of the dream: the dreamer is receiving nourishment that the dream-ego finds 'okay.' The message is contrary to and compensates her overt behavior. Knowing this nourished the therapist's patience with the difficult client.

The therapist had to consider a number of questions as she privately considered that dream:

> Is the therapist's house still a place of envy? Who is envious, the dream-ego or the one who fed her? Does envy make the dreamer hungry? Is she no longer so envious that she can 'visit' the 'richer' psychological space? If she can't 'say,' is that fear, resistance, or preverbal regressive dynamics? What happened to her hungers that made it impossible to 'say' them? What kind of spoiling lies under the silence? Is she meant to speak her needs, to 'say'? Why is her vegetarian diet not available? Is she willing to change her diet; or even if it's 'okay' is meat no longer a taboo nor too strong for her? etc.

All of the questions can lead to hypotheses to be held in the therapist's mind for future consideration. At this point, and in view of the absence of the dreamer's current associations, no conclusions can be drawn.

THERAPIST'S DREAMS ABOUT THE CLIENT

Dreams of the therapist about the client always imply countertransference problems; hence the need for work by the therapist to see what complex or archetypal problem of his or hers is being projected onto that client.[10] Most commonly the projection involves a shadow problem, an affect that cannot be metabolized, or a merging of the client into the therapist's family. But there can also be archetypal countertransferences. The figure of the client may appear as a Self figure, a child figure, as a lover or enemy, an ideal to be envied or a spoiling devil. The projection, whether personal or archetypal, implies that the therapeutic relationship is in difficulty and that the therapist has become overly identified with the client or is 'using' him or her as carrier of some part of his or her own psychology. Working on the dream is usually essential and extremely helpful in untangling a transference–countertransference muddle.

In some cases the therapist's dream compensates an incorrect perception of the client. Jung's dream of the client on whom he 'looked down' appeared in his dream at the top of a tower.[11] The fact that she aroused dismissal in the sessions, as much as the fact that she appeared in the dream, points to the countertransference problem. The dream brought his countertransference to Jung's attention, however.

Chapter Thirteen

CONCLUSION

> The dream is a little hidden door in the innermost and most
> secret recesses of the soul, opening into that cosmic night which
> was psyche long before there was any ego-consciousness, and
> which will remain psyche no matter how far our ego-
> consciousness extends.

(*CW*, 10, para. 304)

Dreams are a portal to the source of life.

They show the dreamer's situation as it is. In this they may at times
be experienced as being ruthless and even threatening or destructive,
and called 'bad' dreams, for they confront the dreamer with seemingly
harsh psychological and spiritual facts regarding his/her current reality.
Yet, this ruthlessness is as objective and unsentimental as any other piece
of natural process. In that respect, there are no good or bad dreams.
When the dreamer can assimilate the dream's intention and adapt to
the perspective of the Guiding Self, such adaptation to the individual's
existential ground results in feeling 'good' or 'in Tao.' Hence the source
or Self feels helpful and 'good.' When such adaptation is not possible
the threatening sense of a 'bad' dream may, indeed, remain.

In working with dreams one may encounter a feeling of profound
numinosity and of wonder at the objectivity and creativity of the unknown
entity we call, for lack of a better name, the Guiding Self. These feelings grow out of the experience of receiving successions of precisely relevant dream image messages and of the concomitant sense of personal
growth.

On the other hand, even after years of therapeutic work, one may
sometimes have to mourn the fact of a dreamer's incapacity to open
himself to the Guiding Self's offerings — the dreamer's alienation from
his or her own potential, wholeness, and reality. Such an alienation from

individual life-meaning can, at times, be so profound that it blocks or spoils perception of change and development.

Many therapists, working with people with borderline or psychotic conditions, have found that the dreams of their patients cannot be adequately worked with and understood by the dreamer. They may wonder what clinical purpose such dreams may serve except to further the therapist's understanding of transference/countertransference and the therapy process. The therapist, in such cases, may have to lend him/herself as a surrogate for the dreamer's terrorized consciousness, modeling an attitude of reverential attention toward the messages from the dreamer's Guiding Self. With patience and persistence, the therapist may bring about the dreamer's first limited, then increasingly full, participation. And even if this is not possible, the therapist may be left with a sense of wonder that the dreams do not stop, that the Guiding Self does not withdraw the supportive flow of its expression, no matter who is or is not listening.

For dreamers who have — often with the help of therapeutic dream work — developed a more coherent ego position, the processes described in this guidebook may help to unlock as much of a fruitful, multileveled dialogue with the unconscious as is possible. As we have seen, the same message can come from various modes of approach. Careful work to elicit associations, explanation, and amplifications to ground the symbolic and metaphoric images of the dream enactment, guided or active imagination; and/or work to explore the transferential implications of the dream on both personal and archetypal levels — optimally all will intersect to give the dreamer and therapist essentially similar basic messages about the dreamer's development and process.

On the other hand, the living with and working on dreams need not be limited to pathology and therapy. Hopefully the therapist no less than the analysand/dreamer will have learned the immeasurable value of dialogue with the ever-fertile unconscious, and have acquired a reverence for these expressions of the Guiding Self to be continued with suitably experienced partners.

According to legend,[1] before birth the angel sets a light above the soul, 'whereby the soul can see from one end of the world to the other . . . , where she will live and where she will die . . . , and he takes her through the whole world and points out the just and the sinners and all things.' But upon birth, the angel 'extinguishes the light and the child forgets all his soul has seen and learned, and he comes into the world crying, for he loses a place of shelter and security and rest.' Yet, once

CONCLUSION

having entered life on earth 'the soul escapes from the body every night, rises up to heaven, and fetches new life thence' . . .

Perhaps, in dreaming we attempt to recall what our soul has always known.

NOTES

1. INTRODUCTION TO CLINICAL DREAM INTERPRETATION

1. For an excellent book raising and discussing these issues see W.D. O'Flaherty (1984) *Dreams, Illusions, and other Realities*, Chicago and London: University of Chicago Press.
2. For such comparative material see *Dream Interpretation: a comparative study* (1978) ed. by James L. Fosshage and Clemens A. Loew, New York and London: Spectrum Publications.
3. For bibliography see *Dreams in New Perspective: the royal road revisited* (1987) ed. by Myron L. Glucksman and Silas L. Warner, NY: Human Sciences Press. Cf. J. Allan Hobson and Robert W. McCarley, 'The brain as a dream state generator: an activation-synthesis hypothesis of the dream process,' *American Journal of Psychiatry*, 134, no. 12 (Dec. 1977), 1335–48.
4. See Thomas B. Kirsch, 'The relationship of REM state to analytical psychology,' *American Journal of Psychiatry*, 124, no. 10 (April 1968), 1459–63.
5. See, however, J. Hall (1977) *Clinical Uses of Dreams: Jungian interpretations and Enactments*, Grune and Stratton, NY; J. Hillman (1979) *The Dream and the Underworld*, Harper and Row, NY; M. Mattoon (1978) *Applied Dream Analysis: a Jungian approach*, Winston, Washington; M.-L. von Franz (1986) *On Dreams and Death*, Shambala, Boston and London; E.C. Whitmont (1978) 'Jungian approach,' in *Dream Interpretation: a comparative study*, ed. by J.L. Fosshage and C.A. Loew, Spectrum Publications, NY and London, pp. 53–77.
6. C.G. Jung (1963) *Memories, Dreams, Reflections*, Pantheon, N.Y., 161–2.
7. Although it is remembered and often felt to be in the past, the telling of a dream in therapy is best done in the present tense. This brings it closer to the dreamer and enhances the vividness of re-experiencing its images and story.
8. We are not dealing here with the phenomena of lucid dreams, nor

with the various therapies that encourage the dreamer to activate the
dream-ego within the dream to carry out conscious purposes.
9. Ramon Greenberg (1987) discussing research with the dreams of
aphasic patients, in *Dreams in New Perspective: the royal road revisited.*
Human Sciences Press, NY p. 134.
10. W.D. O'Flaherty (1984) *Dreams, Illusions and other Realities*, University
of Chicago Press, Chicago and London, p. 3.
11. Kekule's famous dream of whirling snakes, one of which bit its own
tail, gave him the idea for the formula of the benzene ring. See this
and other dreams in Raymond de Becker (1968) *The Understanding of
Dreams and their Influence on the History of Man.* New York, Hawthorn
Books Inc., p. 84; cf. *Dreams in New Perspective*, pp. 9–21.
12. James L. Fosshage (1983) 'The psychological function of dreams: a
revised psychoanalytic perspective,' *Psychoanalysis and Contemporary
Thought*, vol. 6, no. 4, p. 657.
13. Jean Gebser (1985) *The Ever-Present Origin*, translation by N. Barstad
and A. Mickunas, Athens, Ohio, London, Ohio University Press,
Chapter 3.
14. *CW*, 8, para. 527.

2. WORKING WITH THE DREAM IN CLINICAL PRACTICE

1. For a brief discussion of the main points of divergence between the
Freudian and Jungian positions, see A. Samuels, *Jung and the Post-
Jungians* (1985) Routledge and Kegan Paul, London.
2. See, for example: R. Stolorow and G. Atwood (1982) 'The
psychoanalytic phenomenology of the dream,' in *Annual of
Psychoanalysis*, 10, pp. 205–20. J.L. Fosshage (1987) 'A revised
psychoanalytic approach,' in *Dream Interpretation: a comparative study.*
Revised Edition. Fosshage and Loew, eds. PMA Publishing Corp.,
New York. *Dreams in New Perspective: the royal road revisited* (1987) M.
Glucksman and S. Warner, eds. NY, Human Sciences Press.
3. Dreams referring to material that is psychologically most distant from
consciousness will often not be remembered, or they may present
images remote in time or form. What can most readily be assimilated
may have clues, such as being clearly lit, vivid to perception, or seem
to have some personal relationship to the dreamer.
4. An example would be Jung's patient's dream of him as a deity. *CW*,
7, paras 214–16. See also Chapter 12: Dreams of therapy and the
figure of the therapist — The archetypal transference in dreams.
5. This phrase was brought to our attention by Edward Edinger.
6. In group process it is generally most helpful to elicit the dreamer's
responses and then to encourage dreamer and group to interact with
questions, reactions, associations, and tentative interpretations. The
different personalities and perceptions of various group members tend
to evoke and pick up a wide spectrum of nuances and responses, even
though, due to relative lack of clinical experience, they may not be

able to utilize these responses fully for interpretation. A summing up of the dream's message becomes the task of the group leader.

7. Jung encouraged such activity in relation to dreams: 'I always took good care to let the interpretation of each image tail off into a question whose answer was left to the free fantasy-activity of the patient.' (*CW*, 8, para. 400, p. 203.); see J. Hall (1977) pp. 331–47 for references to specific modes of imaginative activity.

8. M.L. von Franz, *Dreams of Themistocles and Hannibal*, London Guild of Pastoral Psychology, August 1960, lecture 111, p. 16.

9. M. Masud R. Khan (1972) 'The use and abuse of dream in psychic experience,' in *The Privacy of the Self: papers on psychoanalytic theory and technique*, International Universities Press, NY, pp. 306–15.

10. The writer's debt to D.W. Winnicott is not adequately paid by simply footnoting his terms.

11. In the case of psychotic patients, this may not be the case, W.R. Bion (1967, *Second Thoughts: selected papers on psycho-analysis*, Heinemann, London, p.98) refers to lack of dreaming in schizophrenic patients with whom he worked, their 'invisible–visible hallucinations,' and their later experience of the images in dreams as 'solid' objects like feces, in contrast to 'the contents of dreams which were a continuum of minute, invisible fragments' analogous to urine. Taking these products symbolically, rather than only as reductions to preoedipal stage dynamics, points to their profound value. (See Chapter 11: Body imagery. By contrast, J.W. Perry (1976, *Roots of Renewal in Myth and Madness*, Jossey-Bass, San Francisco) reports the dreams of his young schizophrenics as the source of images guiding them through a process of dismemberment, death, and rebirth.

12. Jung, C.G. (1984) *Dream Analysis: notes of the seminar given in 1928–1930*, Princeton University Press, Princeton NJ, p. 475.

13. *CW*, 8, para. 568.

14. Freud made this point in 1909, *The Interpretation of Dreams*, Random House, NY, p. 10.

15. Jung, C.G. (1966) *CW*, 16, para. 316.

16. Neumann, Erich (1976) 'On the psychological meaning of ritual,' *Quadrant* 9/2, p. 11.

3. THE SITUATION AS IT IS

1. *CW*, 7, para. 210, 'The relation between the ego and the unconscious' 1928.

2. *CW*, 16, para. 304. *The Practice of Psychotherapy*, 'The practical use of dream-analysis.'

3. *CW*, 8, para. 482.

4. It is, of course, important for the conscious ego to decide how to manifest these in daily life, if at all. To dream of being a killer, or of being chased by one, implies the need to recognize and confront

murderous affect as it already exists in one's life. Dreams do not tell what to do. That is left to the responsibility of the dreamer's conscience. But they do point out what is 'just-so' in the dreamer's existential situation — on both object and subject levels.

5. *CW*, 11, para. 391. 1958, *Psychology and Religion.*
6. 'Our models are adequate but not true, for in order that a description be capable of being true, it must be capable of being compared directly with actual facts. That is usually not the case with our models [of the atom].' Schrodinger, E. (1961) *Science and Humanism.* Cambridge University Press, p. 22.
7. In contradistinction to the early use of the term individuation, which limited it to a process of introversion during the second half of life, it would appear that 'becoming what one is' destined to be is an ongoing process throughout the whole of life and includes extraverted relating as well as introverted centering.
8. See Chapter 6: Compensation and complementation.
9. See in Chapter 6, Object and subject levels in dreams.
10. *Shadow* is Jung's term for the unconscious part of the personality characterized by traits and attitudes — either negative or positive — which the conscious ego tends to ignore or reject.
11. Bion, W.R. (1967) *Second Thoughts: selected papers on psycho-analysis.* New York, Jason Aronson, p. 265.
12. The therapist took this as both an objective statement of the quality and danger of discriminating order in the patient's life, from which her diffusion was a mode of defensive survival, and as a transference dream. As a statement about the previous session's work, it suggested that the therapeutic attempt to evoke orderly consciousness, by questioning even about the dream images, was to the analysand sharp and like ordering an impersonal card file of meaningless discriminations that were wounding to her capacity to get her fingers into the work. (See Chapter 12, Transference reactions.) The dream images permitted the therapist to shift the style of therapy — excluding even asking about dreams — in order more empathically to companion the diffusion and build trust in the therapeutic relationship.
13. Bion (1967), p. 165.
14. *CW*, 10, para. 304.
15. *The Oxford Book of Dreams*, chosen by Stephen Brook, 1987, Oxford University Press, pp. 143-4.
16. *CW*, 8, para. 542.

4. THE LANGUAGE OF DREAMS

1. Freud's description of primary process is relevant; although we would not see it from the perspective of repression and wish-fulfillment. He states 'so far as we know, a psychic apparatus possessing only the primary process does not exist . . . [yet] the essence of our being . . . remains something which cannot be grasped or inhibited by the

preconscious . . . [These] processes . . . [are] the modes of operation of the psychic apparatus when freed from inhibition.' Cf. *The Interpretation of Dreams* (1909) Modern Library (1950) (transl. Dr A.A. Brill), pp. 455–6.

2. *CW*, 8, para. 402.
3. See Susan K. Deri, *Symbolization and Creativity*, New York, International Universities Press (1984), esp. Part II.
4. *CW*, 11, para. 307.
5. Therapists often discover their clients bringing dreams containing images from material they are currently studying. This is a poignant example of the potency of the psychic field which envelops both partners in the therapeutic relationship, and provides evidence for the fruitfulness of the therapist's continuing to work on his or her own process and development.
6. *CW*, 12, para. 403; Rycroft, C. (1979) *The Innocence of Dreams*. New York, Pantheon, p. 71.
7. *CW*, 6, *Psychological Types*, para. 814.
8. *CW*, 11, *Psychology and Religion*, para. 307.
9. *CW*, 8, para. 644.
10. *CW*, 11, para. 222.
11. *CW*, 6, para. 401.

5. ASSOCIATION, EXPLANATION, AMPLIFICATION: THE DREAM FIELD

1. *CW*, 8, para. 471.
2. Perera, Sylvia Brinton (1989) 'Dream Design: some operations underlying clinical dream appreciation,' *Dreams in Analysis*, Chiron Clinical Series, Wilmette, IL.
3. Haft-Pomrock, Yael. 'Number and myth: the archetypes in our hands,' *Quadrant*, Fall 1981, pp. 63–84.
4. *CW*, 8, paras 816–986. Cf. Jung's account of the scarab beetle, *CW*, 18, para. 202–3.
5. For active imagination see J. Hall (1977), pp. 339–48; Barbara Hannah. For guided imagination see Assagioli (1965); Desoille (1966); Epstein (1978); Happich (1932); Leuner (1955).
6. See Hans Dieckmann (1980) 'On the methodology of dream interpretation,' in *Methods of Treatment in Analytical Psychology*, ed. I. Baker, Bonz, Fellbach; and James Hall (1977) *Clinical Uses of Dreams: Jungian interpretations and enactments* NY, Grune and Stratton, pp. 331–48.

6. COMPENSATION AND COMPLEMENTATION: OBJECT AND SUBJECT LEVELS

1. *CW*, 8, para. 493.
2. Jung, 1938–9. *Psychologische Interpretation von Kinderträume und Älterer Literatur über Träume*, seminar notes, Zurich, Eidgerossische Technische Hochschule, pp. 5–6.

NOTES

3. *CW*, 12, 1944, para. 48.
4. Jung's term. These are common in patients with preoedipal pathology, those with a primarily positive shadow and a severely wounded or fragmented and split conscious identity.
5. Very likely this applies equally to post-traumatic stress dreams, which repeat the fearful incidents of war, incest, catastrophe, etc. These may be a call to face, endure, and work through the suffering consciously; but they may point to inner or subject level complex dynamics as well.
6. Jung's dream of his patient on the top of a tower, *CW*, 7, para. 189-90.

7. THE DRAMATIC STRUCTURE OF THE DREAM

1. *CW*, 8, para. 565.
2. For further discussion of this dream see S.B. Perera (1986) *The Scapegoat Complex: toward a mythology of shadow and guilt*, Inner City Books, Toronto, p. 90.
3. Jung first called attention to the usefulness of these categories, *CW*, 8, para. 561-5.
4. E.C. Whitmont (1989) 'On dreams and dreaming,' in *Dreams in Therapy*, Chiron Publications, Willmette.
5. For examples, see S.B. Perera (1989) 'Dream design: some operations underlying clinical dream appreciation,' ibid.

8. MYTHOLOGICAL MOTIFS

1. *CW*, 8, para. 644.
2. Complexes are affect-toned, personal and partial modes of perceiving, thinking, feeling, behaving and living out these underlying patterns. See E.C. Whitmont (1969), *The Symbolic Quest*, Chapter 4; and J. Jacobi, 1959, *Complex/Archetype/Symbol in the Psychology of C.G. Jung*. Princeton University Press, pp. 6-30.
3. *CW*, 9i, para. 271.
4. *CW*, 8, para. 404; cf. A. Stevens, 1982, *Archetypes: a natural history of the self*, New York, Wm. Morrow and Co, pp. 48-61.
5. Letter to Joyce from Jung.
6. These are imaged in alchemy as the mortification, putrefaction, dismemberment, or nigredo processes. See *CW*, 12, para. 433; *CW*, 14, para. 168, no. 164; cf. E. Edinger (1985) *Anatomy of the Psyche: alchemical symbolism in psychotherapy*. Open Court, La Salle, Illinois, pp. 146-80.
7. J. Gebser (1985) *The Ever-Present Origin*, pp. 36-73. G. Ujhely (1980) 'Thoughts concerning the *causa finalis* of the cognitive mode inherent in pre-oedipal psychopathology,' Diploma thesis, C.G. Jung Institute of New York. E.C. Whitmont (1969) *The Symbolic Quest*, Barrie and Rockliff, London and Princeton University Press, pp. 271-6.
8. See above, Chapter 5, Association, Explanation, p. 50.

NOTES

9. See below.
10. C. Kerenyi (1976) *Dionysos: archetypal image of indestructible life*, translated from the German by R. Manheim, Princeton University Press, pp. 239–40.
11. E.C. Whitmont (1987) 'Archetypal and personal interaction in the clinical process' in *Archetypal Processes in Psychotherapy*. Chiron Publications, Wilmette, IL, pp. 1–25.
12. For details of active and/or guided imagination, the reader is referred to the extant literature.
13. *The Mabinogion* translated with an introduction by G. Jones and T. Jones, Everyman's Library, Dent, London, 1906, p. 11.
14. In guided imagination it is enough to suggest a stage setting or general approach, and to intervene with suggestions only when the enactment gets stuck or out of hand. This ensures that the analysand's initiative will structure the autonomous responses of the figures in the fantasy.
15. Sophocles: *Iphigenia at Aulis*.
16. Stanislas Grof: (1975) *Realms of the Human Unconscious*, Viking, NY; and (1985) *Beyond the Brain*, State University of NY.
17. Jung, 1940, 'The psychology of the child archetype,' in *CW*, 9/1, Princeton University Press (1977), paras 259–305.

9. TECHNICAL POINTS

1. The dream journal is a responsibility that may support development in therapy; however, some analysands need the therapist to remember their dreams for them until they are ready to undertake such a task on their own.
2. 'General aspects of dream psychology,' *CW*, vol 8, para. 493.
3. *CW*, 12, para. 34.

10. PROGNOSIS FROM DREAMS

1. Jung (1961) *Memories, Dreams, Reflections*, New York, Random House, pp. 136–7.
2. Marie-Louise von Franz (1986) *On Dreams and Death*, Shambala Publications.
3. Quoted in Whitmont, *The Symbolic Quest*, p. 53.
4. J.W.T. Redfearn (1989) 'Atomic dreams in analysands.' *Dreams in Therapy*. Chiron Publications, Willmette, Illinois.

11. BODY IMAGERY

1. *CW*, 13, para. 304–482.
2. This dream is published in Whitmont, *The Symbolic Quest*, pp. 286–7.
3. Erich Neumann (1955) *The Great Mother: an analysis of the archetype*, Princeton University Press.

NOTES

4. Jung, 1938–39, *Psychologische Interpretation von Kinderträume und Älterer Literatur über Träume,* winter semester, Zurich, Eidgenossische Technische Hochschule, p. 19.
5. E. Neumann (1954) *The Origins and History of Consciousness,* translated by R.F.C. Hull, New York, Harper and Brothers, p. 19.
6. According to legend, the immaculate conception of Jesus occurred by virtue of the Holy Spirit's entering Mary through her ear.
7. E. Edinger's term.

12. DREAMS OF THERAPY AND THE FIGURE OF THE THERAPIST

1. We have seen that most dreams brought into analysis also have transference, and sometimes countertransference, implications, cf. above, pp. 94–5, 106, 114, 119, 122.
2. S. Freud, 1912. 'Dynamics of transference,' in *Standard Edition.* 12:97–108, 1958.
3. Cf. pp. 95, 109 above.
4. See Michael Gorkin (1987) *The Uses of Countertransference.* Jason Aronson Inc., Northvale, NJ, esp. 'The disclosure of counter-transference,' pp. 81–104.
5. Cf. also the dream of the delivery boy above, p. 157.
6. M. Eliade (1958) *Rites and Symbols of Initiation: the mysteries of birth and rebirth,* translated by Willard Trask, Harper and Row, New York, pp. 50–60.
7. Jung, 'The dual mother,' *Symbols of Transformation, CW,* 5, para. 508.
8. *CW,* 7, paras 214–16.
9. See C. Groesbeck (1975) 'The archetypal image of the wounded healer,' *Journal of Analytical Psychology,* 20:2, pp. 122–45.
10. Cf. Gorkin (1987), p. 42.
11. *CW,* 7, paras. 189–90.

13. CONCLUSION

1. Louis Ginzberg (1961) *The Legends of the Jews,* Simon & Schuster, New York, pp. 29–31.

BIBLIOGRAPHY

Assagioli, R. (1965) *Psychosynthesis*, New York: Viking Press.

Bion, W.R. (1967) *Second Thoughts: selected papers on psycho-analysis*, London: Heinemann, New York: Jason Aronson.

de Becker, R. (1968) *The Understanding of Dreams and their Influence on the History of Man*, New York: Hawthorn Books Inc., p. 84.

Deri, S.K. (1984) *Symbolization and Creativity*, New York: International Universities Press.

Desoille, R. (1966) *The Directed Daydream*, New York: Psychosynthesis Research Foundation.

Dieckmann, H. (1980) 'On the methodology of dream interpretation,' in I. Baker (ed.), *Methods of Treatment in Analytical Psychology*, Bonz: Fellbach.

Edinger, E. (1985) *Anatomy of the Psyche: alchemical symbolism in psychotherapy*, La Salle, Illinois: Open Court.

Eliade, M. (1958) *Rites and Symbols of Initiation: the mysteries of birth and rebirth* (transl. Willard Trask), New York: Harper and Row.

Epstein, G.N. (1978) 'The experience of waking dream in psychotherapy,' in J.L. Fosshage and P. Olsen (eds) *Healing: Implications for Therapy*, New York: Human Sciences Press, pp. 137–84.

Fosshage, J.L. (1983) 'The psychological function of dreams: a revised psychoanalytic perspective,' *Psychoanalysis and Contemporary Thought* 6, (4) 641–69.

Fosshage, J.L. (1987) 'A revised psychoanalytic approach,' in J.L. Fosshage and C.A. Loew (eds) *Dream Interpretation: a comparative study* (rev. edn), New York: PMA Publishing Corp.

Fosshage, J.L. and Loew, C.A. (eds) (1978) *Dream Interpretation: a comparative study*, New York and London: Spectrum Publications.

Freud, S. (1909) *The Interpretation of Dreams* (transl. Dr A.A. Brill), New York: Modern Library, Random House (1950 edn).

Freud, S. (1912) 'Dynamics of transference,' in *Standard Edition*. 12:97–108, 1958.

Gebser, J. (1985) *The Ever-Present Origin* (transl. N. Barstad and A. Mickunas), Athens, Ohio, London: Ohio University Press.

Ginzberg, L. (1961) *The Legends of the Jews*. New York: Simon & Schuster.

Glucksman, M.L. and Warner, S.L. (eds) (1987) *Dreams in New Perspective: the royal road revisited.* New York: Human Sciences Press.

Gorkin, M. (1987) *The Uses of Countertransference*, Northvale, N.J.: Jason Aronson Inc.

Groesbeck, C. (1975) 'The archetypal image of the wounded healer,' *Journal of Analytical Psychology* 20 (2): 122–45.

Grof, S. (1975) *Realms of the Human Unconscious*, New York: Viking.

Grof, S. (1985) *Beyond the Brain*, New York State University.

Haft-Pomrock, Y. (1981) 'Number and myth: the archetypes in our hands,' *Quadrant* 14 (2): 63–84.

Hall, J. (1977) *Clinical Uses of Dreams: Jungian interpretations and enactments*, New York: Grune and Stratton.

Happich, Carl (1932) '*Bildbewusstsein als Ansatzstelle psychischer Behandlung,*' *Zentralblatt für Psychotherapie* 5: 633–77.

Hillman, J. (1979) *The Dream and the Underworld*, New York: Harper and Row.

Hobson, J.A. and McCarley, R.W., (1977) 'The brain as a dream state generator: an activation–synthesis hypothesis of the dream process,' *American Journal of Psychiatry* 134 (12): 1335–48.

Jacobi, J. (1959) *Complex/Archetype/Symbol in the Psychology of C.G. Jung*, Princeton, N.J.: Princeton University Press.

Jung, C.J. References are to the *Collected Works (CW)* and by volume and paragraph number, except as below. Bollingen Series, Princeton University Press.

Jung, C.J. (1938–39) '*Psychologische Interpretation von Kinderträume und Älterer Literatur über Träume,*' seminar notes, winter semester, Zurich, Eidgenossische Technische Hochschule.

Jung, C.J. (1961) *Memories, Dreams, Reflections*, New York: Random House. (Also published in 1963 by Pantheon, New York.)

Jung, C.J. (1984) Dream Analysis: Notes of the seminar given in 1928–1930, Princeton University Press, Princeton, N.J.

Kerenyi, C. (1976) *Dionysos: archetypal image of indestructible life* (transl. from the German by R. Manheim), Princeton University Press.

Khan, M.M.R. (1972) *The Privacy of the Self: papers on psychoanalytic theory and technique*, New York: International Universities Press.

Kirsch, T.B. (1968) 'The relationship of REM state to analytical psychology,' *American Journal of Psychiatry* 124 (10) (April):1459–63.

Leuner, H. (1955) 'Exper. Katathymes Bilderleben als ein klinisches Verfahren cl. Psychother', *Z. Psychother und med. Psychol*, 5: 185–202, 233–60.

Mabinogion, The (transl. with an introduction by G. Jones and T. Jones) Everyman's Library, Dent, London, 1906.

Mattoon, M. (1978) *Applied Dream Analysis: a Jungian approach*, Winston: Washington.

Neumann, E. (1954) *The Origins and History of Consciousness* (transl. R.F.C. Hull), New York: Harper and Brothers.

Neumann, E. (1955) *The Great Mother: an analysis of the archetype*, Princeton University Press.

Neumann, E. (1976) 'On the psychological meaning of ritual,' *Quadrant* 9/2: 5–34.

O'Flaherty, W.D. (1984) *Dreams, Illusions, and other Realities*, Chicago and London: University of Chicago Press.

Oxford Book of Dreams, The (1987), chosen by Stephen Brook, Oxford University Press.

Perera, S.B. (1986) *The Scapegoat Complex: toward a mythology of shadow and guilt*, Toronto: Inner City Books.

Perera, S.B. (1989) 'Dream design: some operations underlying clinical dream appreciation,' *Dreams in Analysis*, Willmette, Illinois: Chiron Publications.

Perry, J.W. (1976) *Roots of Renewal in Myth and Madness*, San Francisco: Jossey-Bass.

Redfearn, J.W.T. (1989) 'Atomic dreams in analysands,' *Dreams in Therapy*, Willmette, Illinois: Chiron Publications.

Rossi, E.L. (1985) *Dreams and the Growth of Personality: expanding awareness in psychotherapy*, New York: Brunner Mazel.

Rycroft, C. (1979) *The Innocence of Dreams*, New York: Pantheon.

Samuels, A. (1985) *Jung and the Post-Jungians*, London: Routledge & Kegan Paul.

Schrodinger, E. (1961) *Science and Humanism,* Cambridge University Press.

Stevens, A. (1982) *Archetypes: a natural history of the self*, New York: Wm. Morrow and Co.

Stolorow, R. and Atwood, G. (1982) 'The psychoanalytic phenomenology of the dream,' in *Annual of Psychoanalysis* 10:205–20.

Ujhely, G. (1980) 'Thoughts concerning the *causa finalis* of the cognitive mode inherent in pre-oedipal psychopathology,' Diploma thesis, C.G. Jung Institute of New York.

von Franz, M.-L. (1960) *Dreams of Themistocles and Hannibal*, London Guild of Pastoral Psychology, August, lecture 111.

von Franz, M.-L. (1986) *On Dreams and Death: a Jungian interpretation* (transl. E.X. Kennedy and V. Brooks), Boston and London: Shambala Publications.

Whitmont, E.C. (1969) *The Symbolic Quest*, London: Barrie and Rockliff, London and Princeton University Press.

Whitmont, E.C. (1978) 'Jungian approach', in J.L. Fosshage and C.A. Loew (eds) *Dream Interpretation: a comparative study*, New York and London: Spectrum Publications, pp. 53–77.

Whitmont, E.C. (1987) 'Archetypal and personal interaction in the clinical process,' in *Archetypal Processes in Psychotherapy*, Wilmette, Illinois: Chiron Publications.

Whitmont, E.C. (1989) 'On dreams and dreaming,' in *Dreams in Therapy*, Willmette, Illinois: Chiron Publications.

Winnicott, D.W. (1971) *Playing and Reality*, New York: Basic Books, Inc.

DREAMS

Note: These entries are listed in the order of their appearance in the text and not alphabetically.

Hannibal's dream of making war on Rome 9
locked in room with prostitutes 13
exotic guru and peacock 15, 164
carpenter brings boat 18
rescuing hurt child 19
princess in swimming pool 19
lying on the shore 21
standing at fire 21
dirty cockroach 21
dream ego in pieces 21
Lincoln's dream of dead president 22
shakes hands with beggar and has heart attack 24
Jung's patient's fiancée as prostitute 25
finding a muddy penny 28
sitting at desk finding pill with deer image imprinted on it 31-3, 42, 52, 55, 63
therapist sits on dreamer's bed 36, 152, 153
carrying old bags to son's room 37
trying to turn raft 39
upon receiving jewels as a gift; dream ego feels guilty and anxious 40, 43
powdering feet with cleaning powder 41
index finger injured 43
flying 44, 47
condemned for smuggling 44
dream ego as leader of adolescent dance 46
tomato thrown away 48
picnicking on volcano edge 50, 83
car dangling over edge of cliff 51

strangers in therapy group 51
hand in wolf's jaws 53
neighbor intends to give son a puppy 53
Indian woman walking 58
threatening friend 59
cutting into traffic recklessly 60
dead grandfather 61
beggar at door 61
toll-booth operator 61
colliding stars 61
wife as shrew 62
dream ego scolded by mother 64
female thief scratches at dream ego's eyes 65
dismemberment 65
dream ego lies in bed between husband and dog 68
caged black goat 68
in sports clothes at formal party 71
counting poem's grammatical parts 71
in grocery store in China 72-3
dream ego tells woman friend about typewriter 72
in shack with sister 74-8
accosted by man in cellar 84-7
business partner left his family 87, 91
family cat rampages 87-90
hoodlum robs dream ego 92-6
in Spanish dungeon 97
men kill deer; dream ego turns into a boy 99
repetitive movie with Richard Burton in granary 100

therapist offers body position as treatment 102–4
baby in crib 105
child wrecks jewelry box 106
tidal wave 107
fox stares at dream ego 108
wine from fallen glass keeps pouring out 110
dream ego refuses man's help on trail 111
dream ego and husband are poor and dying 112
Time magazine takes over 113
terrorist 114
nephew comes out of a different house from that expected by dream ego 115
warning against homosexual haters 115
dream ego as pacifist soldier 116
intruder as Chassidic student 117
in dental office 118
medical examination repeats day residue 119
tornado 121
killer loose in cellar 121
man grabs dream ego 122
in childhood room 123
sun to cook fish 124
eating fruit salad 124
dreamer's wife to provide help 124
living in ghost-ridden, decrepit house 127
animal face in corner of room framed as picture 127
walking in deserted city as blackness falls 128
Jung's patient in medieval city finds idiot child 129
floating like Ophelia through own house 129
computers down and programs mixed 130
lion eating dream ego's hand and arm 130
finding a new garden 130
dream ego saves cat 131
piranha fish under oriental rug 131
dream ego throws teddy bear 131
barges at seashore 132–3, 135

man on horseback rides down minstrel 133
city building falling 134
house pierced by falling tree branch 138
grandmother says it is five minutes to four 138
woman and man arousing dream ego in car 140
in bed with brutal rapist 143
toilet filled with feces 147
storing feces in mother's jewelry box 147
therapist confronts dream ego who runs off 151
dream ego brings book to therapist 152
therapist is busy cleaning, ignores dream ego 153
At Indian ruins with tour guide 154
therapist ill 155, 176
dream ego carries sick therapist 155
therapist leaves dream ego to receive delivery 157–9, 161
therapist's father at consulting room window 160
therapist puts dream ego through clothes' wringer 161
therapist ignores patient's blindness 161
therapist shows jewels 162
therapist is leaving city 163
therapist's son helps park dreamer's car 164
refusing to open mouth at dentist's 165
new house being built by dream ego who fears tractor 165
on ship that does not sail 166
in Venice finding junk food 166
therapist visits dream ego at childhood home 166
intruders in therapy session 167
dream ego in waiting room 167
session in therapist's bedroom 167
teenage crowd in consulting room 168
therapist prefers Agnes 169
therapist's wife provides treatment 170
dream ego showers in session 171

wanting to crawl under therapist's skirt 173

Jung's patient dreams of him as a giant god 174

therapist as Empress of China 175

therapist as Medusa 176

therapist ill 176

eating meat sandwich at therapist's house 178

Jung dreams he is looking up at his client 179

INDEX

affect: and association 14, 35-7, 39,
42-5; avoidance 53; and feeling
quality 49-52, 72, 121;
unmanageable 64
allegory: 7-8, 27, 28-9, 30, 62, 88, 93,
95, 118; of therapeutic process 163,
164, 166
amplifications: 28, 34, 43, 51-2, 72,
83-4, 122, 181; and mythological
motifs 52-4, 88-90, 92-5, 98, 101,
108, 109-10, 116-17
animals: and body imagery 137-8; as
mythological motif 88-90, 107-9,
127-8, 131, 133, 175
animus figure 86, 143
archetypes see motifs; mythological;
transference, archetypal
assent, of dreamer 13-15, 19, 63
assimilation of dream image 23-4
associations: 12-14, 20, 34, 58, 69-70,
72, 122, 124, 164, 181; and
archetypes 84, 86, 88-91, 93-4, 103,
108; and body imagery 135;
elicitation 35-6, 45-6; as essential
10; evaluation 31, 33; and
explanations 38-42; grounding
of 35-8; of therapist 43-5,
54-5, 159-60; see also affect;
transference

bathing imagery 171-2
Behaviourism, and dream 6
Bion, W.R. 185n
birth, as basic theme 102-4, 120
blind spots 7-9, 28, 45, 57, 63, 118,
163
block 38

body reactions 42-5

causality, in dreams 31, 68, 111-12
child, inner 19, 104, 110, 129
children, as basic theme 104-7
coherence, lack, and psychotic levels
20, 81-2
communication, primary 26-7
compensation: 33, 51, 56-9, 62-3, 68,
103, 112-13, 118, 129, 142, 148,
169, 171; and fragmented identity
63-6
complementation: 56-62, 68-9, 118,
129, 171; and fragmented identity
63-6
complexes 79
consciousness: dualistic 2, 3; integrative
3-4
context 14-15, 20, 34, 43, 71, 89-90, 113
countertransference: 10, 12, 45, 64,
103, 106-7, 109, 114, 149;
archetypal 179; avoidance 150; and
dreams of therapy 150-1, 154-5, 163,
164-5, 170, 178-9; dynamics of 14, 54,
156-61, 168-9; monitoring 54-5
crisis 69, 70, 73, 77, 141

day residue 60-1, 117-19
death: 22, 83, 132-6; and birth 102;
and transformation 112, 135, 139
defecation imagery 146-8
dependency: needs 24, 106, 111, 145,
160, 171; on therapist 106-7
destruction, themes and transition
phases 82
development, psychological: role of
archetypes 81, 107; role of dream in

197

2-3, 7-8, 11, 22-5, 54, 57-8, 65, 127
dialogue, with dream figure 9, 19, 48-9, 93-4
diffusion 20-1
dismemberment imagery 21-2, 65, 125
dissociation 20, 82
drama: dream as 6, 7, 14-16, 39, 67-78, 99, 135; overview 67-9; structure 69-78, 170
dramatization 61-3
dream: oracular 56, 60, 107, 134; parallel 56, 58-9; prospective 56-7, 78, 120
dream-ego: 9, 18-22, 49, 64, 68, 85, 99, 121-2; patient's relation to 9
dreams, historic examples 9-10

Edinger, E. 190n
ego: deficit 130; strength 7, 130-1; see also dream-ego
ego-ideal 19-20
Emerson, R.W. 8
enactment 9, 19, 43, 45, 48-9, 93, 95, 103, 181
excretion imagery 146
experience 102-4
explanations: 70, 72, 91, 93, 108, 154, 181; objective-collective 31, 34, 38-42, 139; subjective-individual 38-42
exposition 69, 70-3, 75-6, 86, 94-5, 112, 116-17, 129, 133, 141

fantasy 45-9, 51, 88, 90, 93, 96-7, 104-5, 140
father figure, archetypal 84, 121-2, 159, 160-1, 174
fetishism, as motif 144
flood, as dream image 135
Fosshage, James L. 2, 184n
Freud, Sigmund: on anal symbolism 146; on horse and rider image 132; on meaning of dream 185n; on primary process 186-7n; on transference 150
Freudian school, on dream images 6, 56

Gestalt techniques 9, 45, 48, 93, 103
Greenberg, Ramon 184n
group, therapeutic 8-9, 48, 184n

healer, as sick 177
healing, dreams in 2-3
homoeroticism 115-16, 142

identity, loss of 15, 77, 92-6, 115-16, 157-8
identity: fragmented 20-3, 49, 56; and compensation/complementation 63-6
illness, dreams of 132-6, 139
images: 26-8; ability to deal with 11, 185n; archetypal 51, 52-3, 65, 67, 77; see also motifs, mythological; body 137-48; body orifices 118-29, 144-8; grouping 68; see also allegory; metaphor; rebus; symbol
imagination, guided 24, 45-6, 47, 51, 88, 90, 93, 95-6, 105 181, 189n
incarnation 64, 137
individuation: 24, 33, 41, 121, 144, 172; role of dream images 11, 114; role of the Guiding Self 8, 18, 142
interpretation: as art 6-8, 67; definition 2; dyadic nature 8-10, 11; learning 6-7
intruder figure 15, 74-7, 113, 117, 142

journal, dream 120
journey, as motif 166
Jung, C.J.: on archetypes 79, 80; on association 34; on body imagery 137; on clinical practice 12; on compensation and complementation 56; on dream as drama 67, 188n; function of dream 1, 6-7, 17, 120, 180; on interpretation 1, 4, 5, 185n; on patients 25, 128-9, 174; on the Self 17-18, 22; on symbol 29-30

Kekule von Stradonitz, August 184n

life force, dream as expression of 2, 31, 132-3
life play, as basic theme 100-2
Lincoln, Abraham 22
logic, of dream images 15-16
lysis 69, 70, 73-4, 77-8, 85, 93, 96, 103, 128

masochism, as motif 40, 103, 142
masturbation 42, 142
meaning: 12, 30, 31-2, 34, 38; and

mythological motifs 109-10
memory, variation from 13, 96-7, 118
metabolism, as symbol 145, 146
metaphor, in dream 7-8, 21, 23, 28-9,
   65, 95, 105, 134, 150, 181
mirroring, therapeutic 8, 11, 104
monster, as basic theme 109, 126
mother, as archetypal figure 49, 125,
   131-2, 138-9, 173-4
motifs, mythological 79-110, 134-5,
   144; and animals 88-90, 107-9, 131,
   133, 138, 175, 176; basic 99-109,
   139; and birth 102-4; and children
   104-7; dealing with 97-9;
   interpretation 109-10; and life play
   100-1; and personal grounding
   83-97, 98-9, 102; recognizing 81-3,
   97-8; see also amplification; images,
   archetypal

nightmares 24, 40, 84, 120, 125-6

object level: 8, 37, 45, 119, 144;
   assimilation of dream image 25; and
   compensation 29, 59-61, 151-2, 158;
   dream as warning 78
observer, dreamer as 20
oppositions 68-9, 78, 123
outcome, of dream 23-4

parallel dreams 56, 58
peripeteia 69, 70, 73, 76-7, 141
Perry, J.W. 185n
personification in dream 60
perversions, as motif 144
plants, and body imagery 137-8
polarizations 68-9, 78, 123, 128-9, 174
potentialities, in dream 20, 104, 135,
   141-4, 162
pre-ego 64
problem solving, dreams in 2, 7, 24-5,
   78
process, primary 26-7, 186-7n
prognosis 7, 24, 127-36
projection: 3, 59-60, 61, 64-5, 106-7,
   118, 122, 151; on to client 179;
   negative 64; on to therapist 94-5,
   119, 152, 153-4
prospective dreams 56
psychoanalysis, and dream as wish-
   fulfillment 6, 62

psychology, individual, as revealed in
   dream 3, 7
psychopathology, borderline 20-2, 65,
   69, 82, 84, 130, 181
psychosis, prognosis of 56, 82, 107,
   127-9, 181
purpose, in dreams 1, 2, 17, 112-17,
   120, 180-3

re-evaluation as function of dream
   112-17, 175
rebus pattern 14, 30-3, 42, 63
REM processes 1, 2
repetition of dream themes 14, 84,
   100-1, 123-5, 126, 136
resistance, to interpretation 10, 15, 171
role play 9, 48, 49

sadism, as motif 131, 142-4, 165
schizophrenics 185n
Schrodinger, E. 186n
Self: alienation from 180-1; assent of
   14; dream as manifestation of 3, 8,
   12, 17-20, 22, 24-5, 50, 124, 180; as
   inner therapist 103, 151, 153-6; as
   projected on to therapist 173-7; and
   psychological development 28, 57,
   65, 95-6, 103, 109, 130, 142, 150
sequentiality, in dreams 111-12
series, dream 61, 66, 119-25
sexuality: 13-14, 42, 139-44, 170-2,
   173; oral 145
shadow: 58, 68, 76-8, 146, 158;
   patient's confrontation of 9, 19-20,
   22, 49; of therapist 175, 176, 179
ship, as archetypal image 166
simultaneity, in dreams 111-12
stress, post-traumatic, dreams 188n
subject level: 25, 37, 45-6, 88, 114,
   118-19, 139, 144; and compensation
   29, 59-61, 62, 64, 159; dream as
   warning 78; ignored 8; transference
   151, 153-6
symbol: 6-8, 12, 27-8, 29-30, 31, 41,
   51, 62, 120, 181; anal 146; body
   144-6; and mythological motif 79,
   80, 88-90, 92, 95-6, 98, 105; sexual
   139-44
synchronicity 45, 46

themes: 6, 7, 14, 70, 72, 120-1; basic

99-109; variations on 68, 122-5
therapist: actual reality 151-3; and
    association 43-5, 54-5; and dream
    images 27-8, 43, 149-51; dreams of
    alternative 169-72; induction by 44,
    54-5, 114, 159, 161-3, 172; inner
    106, 114, 153-6, 158-60, 169-72;
    own dreams 149, 159, 178-9
therapy, in dream imagery 118-19,
    149-50, 163-79
time sequence 111-12, 118, 123
transference: 8, 14-15, 58, 64-5, 94-5,
    103, 106, 109-10, 114, 149, 150,
    167, 181; analysis of 150, 153;
    archetypal 158, 161, 172-7; and
    association 36-7, 157-60; avoidance
    150; negative 171, 172, 176
transpersonal: 51, 52, 80, 95-6, 97-8,
    104, 121, 146; and animal motif

89-90, 107-8; and transference 172-5
triviality 45-6, 59, 123

unconscious: collective 79-80; revealed
    through dream 2, 7, 12, 18, 49, 181
urination imagery 146-7
uses of dream 2, 11-12

vampirism, as motif 144
volcano, as archetypal motif 50-1, 83
voyeurism, as motif 144

war, as metaphor 134
warnings, dreams as 18, 22, 23, 78, 97,
    135, 138
Winnicott, D.W. 185n
wisdom figures 14-15, 83
wish-fulfillment, dream as 6, 56, 62